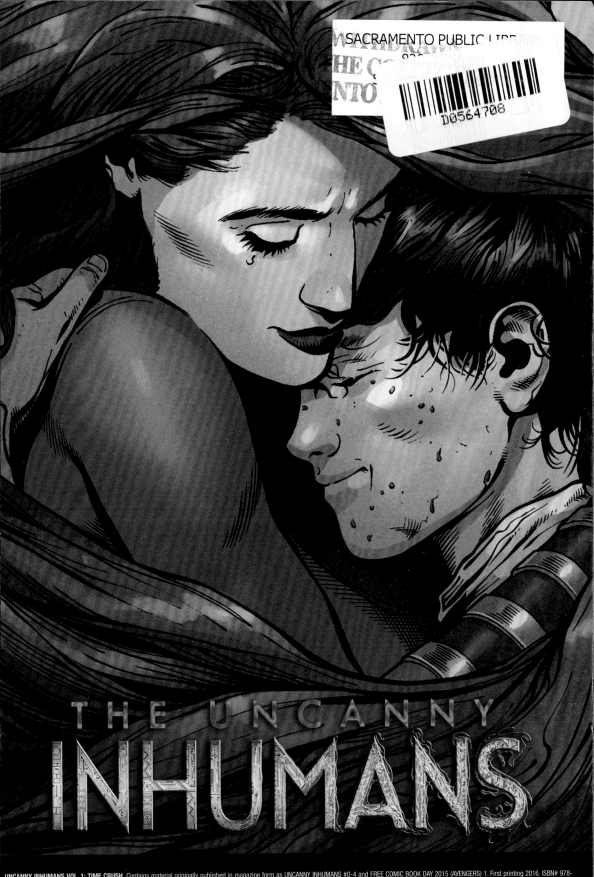

THE UNCANNY INHUMANS

UNCANNY INHUMANS VOL. 1: TIME CRUSH. Contains material originally published in magazine form as UNCANNY INHUMANS #0-4 and FREE COMIC BOOK DAY 2015 (AVENGERS) 1. First printing 2016. ISBN# 978-0-7851-9706-5. Published by MARVEL WORLDWIDE, INC., a subsidiary of MARVEL ENTERTAINMENT, LLC. OFFICE OF PUBLICATION: 135 West 50th Street, New York, NY 10020. Copyright © 2016 MARVEL No similarity between any of the names, characters, persons, and/or institutions in this magazine with those of any living or dead person or institution is intended, and any such similarity which may exist is purely coincidental. **Printed in Canada.** ALAN FINE, President, Marvel Entertainment; DAN BUCKLEY, President, TV, Publishing and Brand Management; JOE QUESADA, Chief Creative Officer; TOM BREVOORT, SVP of Publishing; DAVID BOGART, SVP of Operations & Procurement, Publishing; C.B. CEBULSKI, VP of International Development & Brand Management; DAVID GABRIEL, SVP Print, Sales & Marketing; DAN CARR, Executive Director of Publishing Technology; SUSAN CRESPI, Editorial Operations Manager; ALEX MORALES, Publishing Operations Manager; STAN LEE, Chairman Emeritus. For information regarding advertising in Marvel Comics or on Marvel.com, please contact Vit DeBellis, Integrated Sales Manager, at vdebellis@marvel.com. For Marvel subscription inquiries, please call 800-217-9158. **Manufactured between 2/5/2016 and 3/14/2016 by SOLISCO PRINTERS, SCOTT, QC, CANADA.**

10 9 8 7 6 5 4 3 2 1

THE UNCANNY
INHUMANS

TIME CRUSH

COLLECTION EDITOR: SARAH BRUNSTAD
ASSOCIATE MANAGER, DIGITAL ASSETS: JOE HOCHSTEIN
ASSOCIATE MANAGING EDITOR: ALEX STARBUCK
EDITORS, SPECIAL PROJECTS: JENNIFER GRÜNWALD & MARK D. BEAZLEY
VP, PRODUCTION & SPECIAL PROJECTS: JEFF YOUNGQUIST
BOOK DESIGN: JAY BOWEN

SVP PRINT, SALES & MARKETING: DAVID GABRIEL
EDITOR IN CHIEF: AXEL ALONSO
CHIEF CREATIVE OFFICER: JOE QUESADA
PUBLISHER: DAN BUCKLEY
EXECUTIVE PRODUCER: ALAN FINE

CHARLES SOULE
WRITER

JUSTIN PONSOR (#0) &
SUNNY GHO (#1-4)
WITH JAVA TARTAGLIA (#3)
COLORISTS

STEVE McNIVEN
PENCILER

VC'S CLAYTON COWLES
(#0-2 & #4) &
JOE SABINO (#3)
LETTERERS

JAY LEISTEN
INKER

STEVE MCNIVEN &
JUSTIN PONSOR (#0) AND
STEVE MCNIVEN,
JAY LEISTEN & JUSTIN PONSOR (#1-4)
COVER ART

+

FREE COMIC BOOK DAY 2015

CHARLES SOULE
WRITER

BRANDON PETERSON
ARTIST

JUSTIN PONSOR
COLORIST

VC'S CLAYTON COWLES
LETTERER

NICK BRADSHAW & RICHARD ISANOVE
COVER ART

"EVOLUTION," FROM UNCANNY INHUMANS #0

RYAN STEGMAN
WRITER

RYAN LEE
ARTIST

JAMES CAMPBELL
COLORIST

VC'S CLAYTON COWLES
LETTERER

"THINGS TO COME" SPREAD
BY BRANDON PETERSON

A TASTE OF A MAJOR FUTURE INHUMAN STORY, FROM UNCANNY INHUMANS #1

CHARLES SOULE
WRITER

BRANDON PETERSON
ARTIST

NOLAN WOODARD
COLORIST

VC'S CLAYTON COWLES
LETTERER

CHARLES BEACHAM
ASSISTANT EDITOR

NICK LOWE
EDITOR

INHUMANS CREATED BY STAN LEE & JACK KIRBY

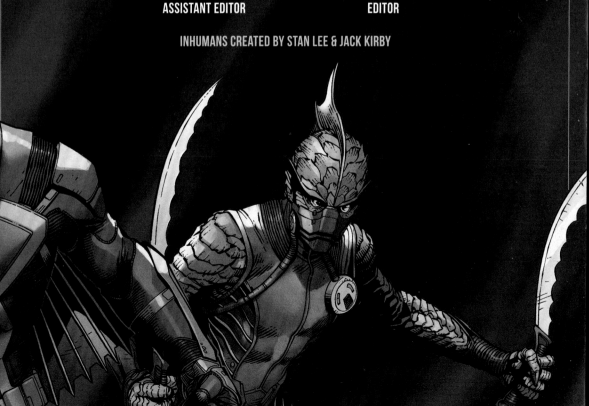

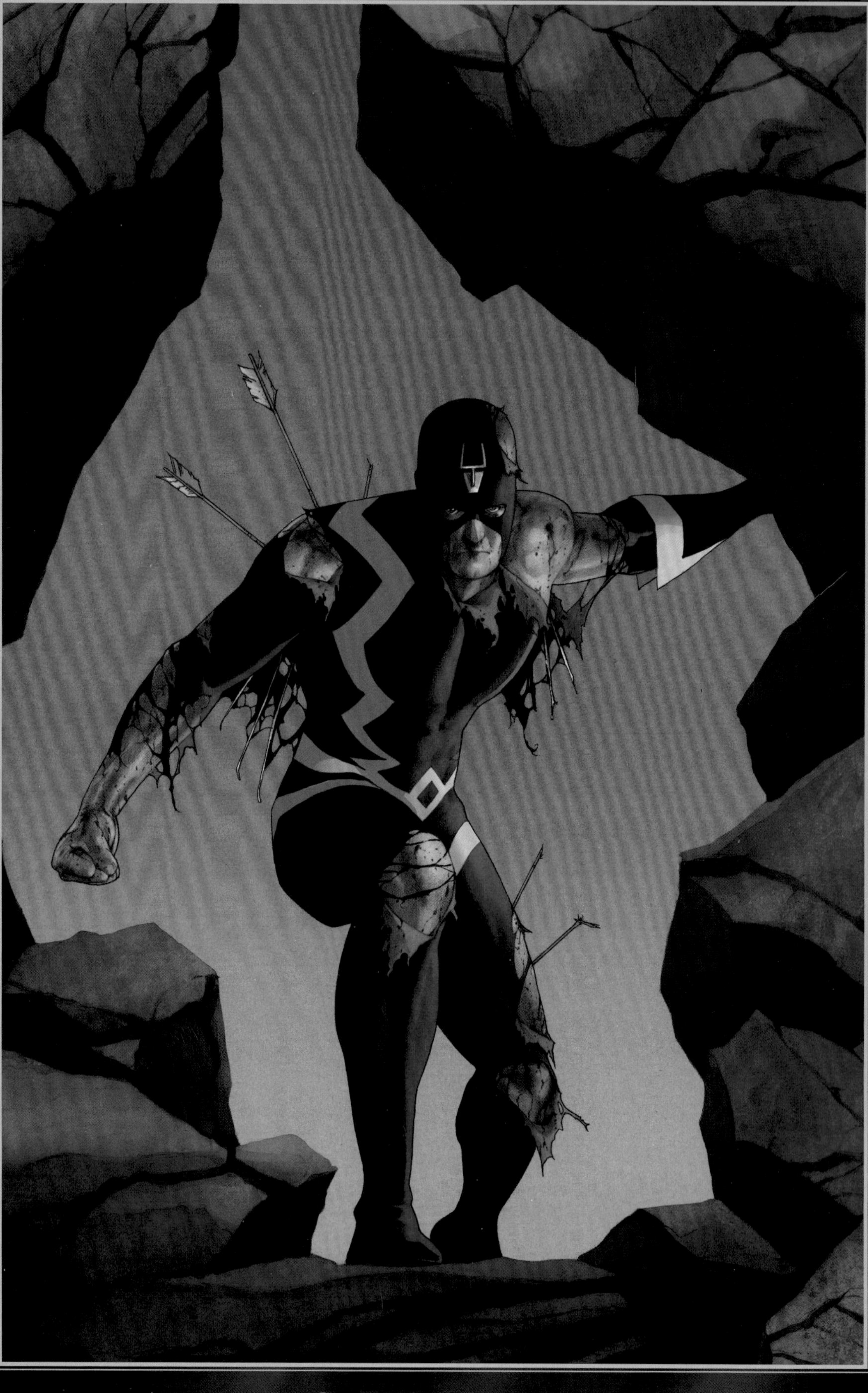

0: END TIMES

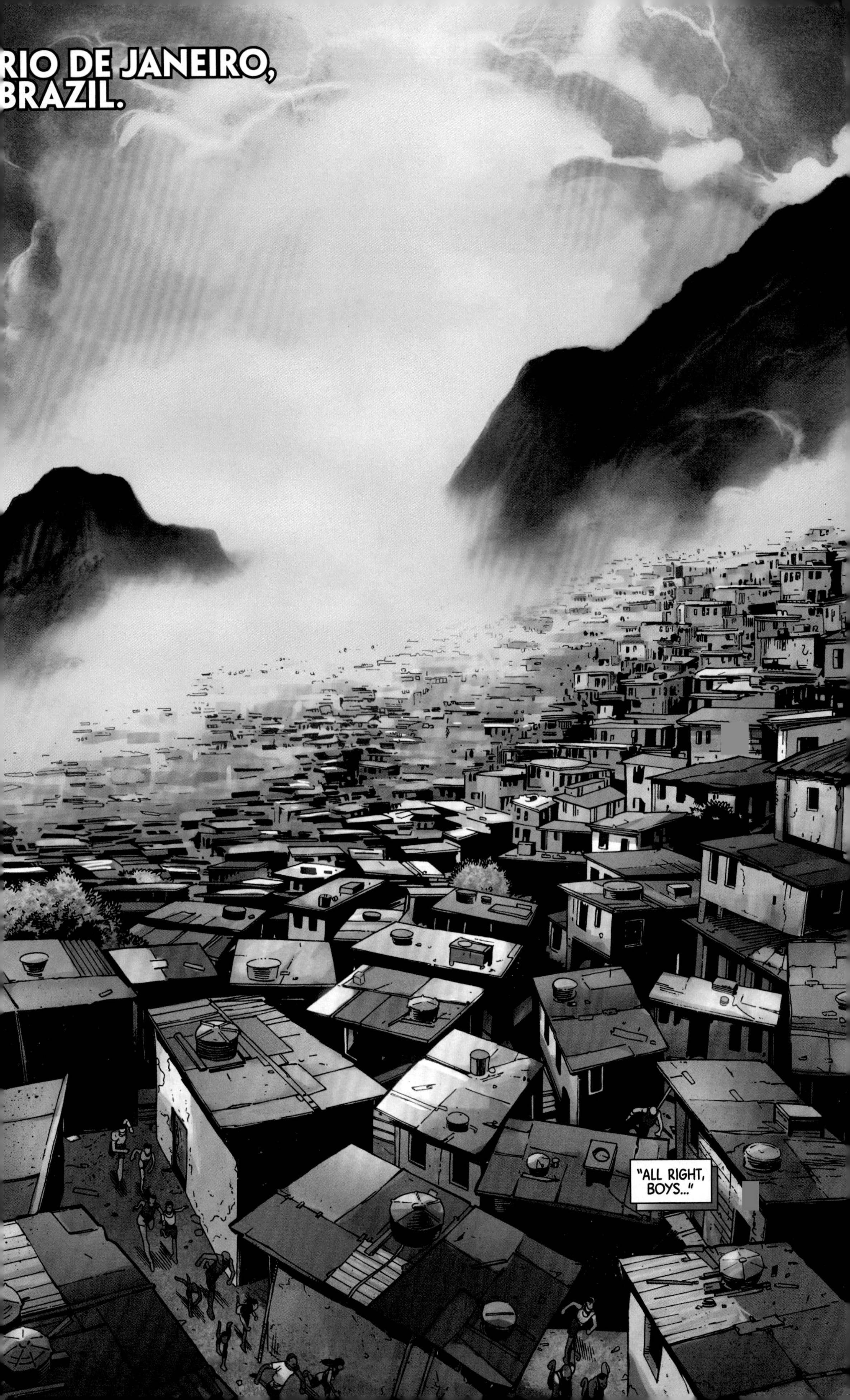
RIO DE JANEIRO,
BRAZIL.
"ALL RIGHT,
BOYS..."

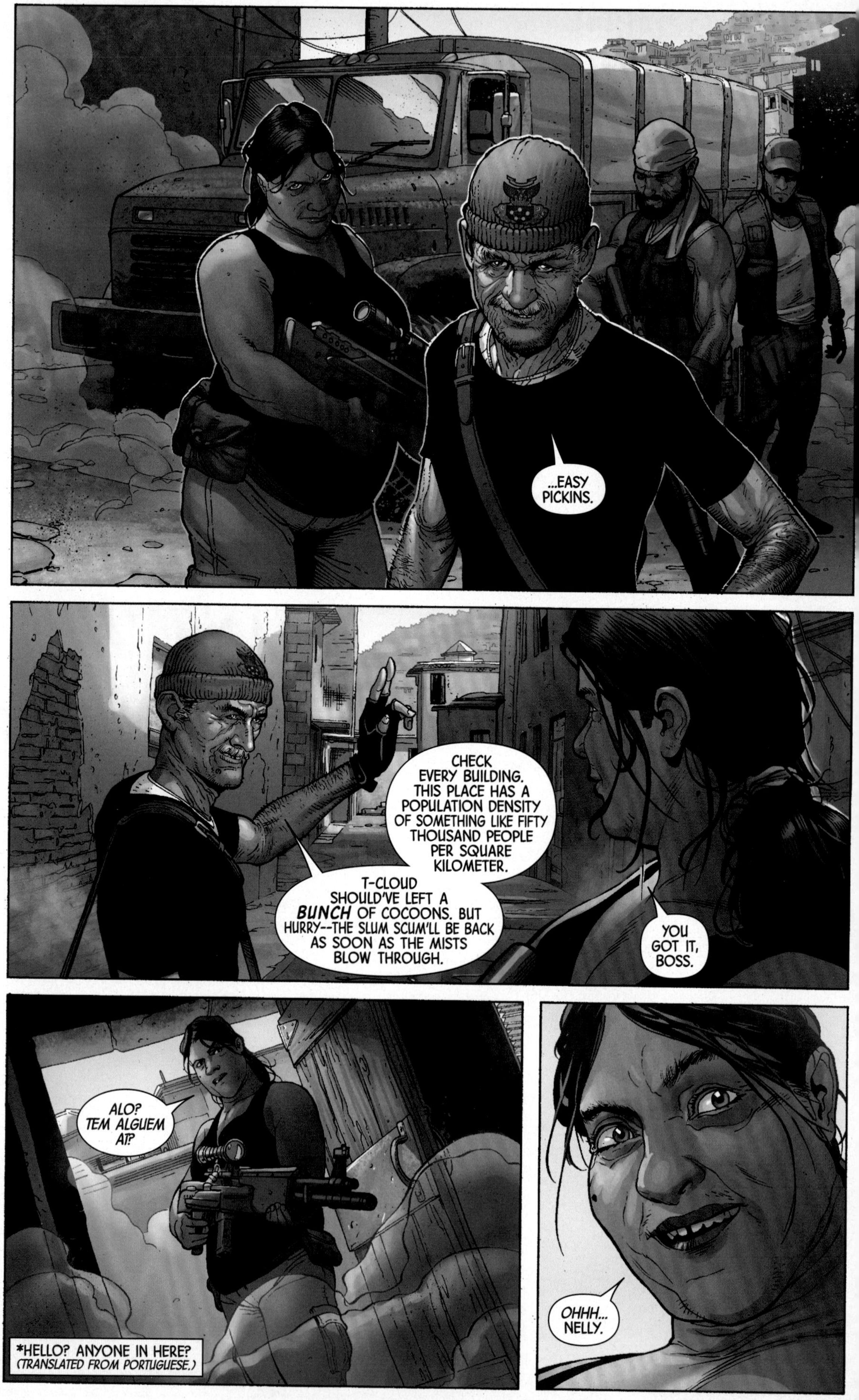
...EASY PICKINS.
CHECK EVERY BUILDING. THIS PLACE HAS A POPULATION DENSITY OF SOMETHING LIKE FIFTY THOUSAND PEOPLE PER SQUARE KILOMETER.
T-CLOUD SHOULD'VE LEFT A BUNCH OF COCOONS. BUT HURRY--THE SLUM SCUM'LL BE BACK AS SOON AS THE MISTS BLOW THROUGH.
YOU GOT IT, BOSS.
ALO? TEM ALGUEM AT?
*HELLO? ANYONE IN HERE? (TRANSLATED FROM PORTUGUESE.)
OHHH... NELLY.

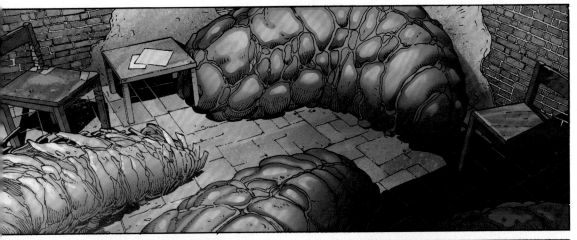

DAMN, I HATE WHEN ONE GOES BAD. LIKE FLUSHING MONEY DOWN THE DRAIN.

WE JUST FOUND A WHOLE *FAMILY*, AND WE'VE BARELY STARTED LOOKING. ENNILUX WILL PAY US *FOUR HUNDRED GRAND* FOR HALF AN HOUR'S WORK. YOU NEED TO COUNT YOUR BLESSINGS, YOU KNOW?

ANYWAY, WE NEED TO HURRY. WE HAVE TO GET THEM IN STASIS BEFORE THEY EMERGE FROM THE COCOONS. GOD KNOWS WHAT WE'LL BE DEALING WITH *THEN*.

KRRAK

YOU KNOW, YOU'RE RIGHT. I SUPPOSE THINGS COULD ALWAYS BE--

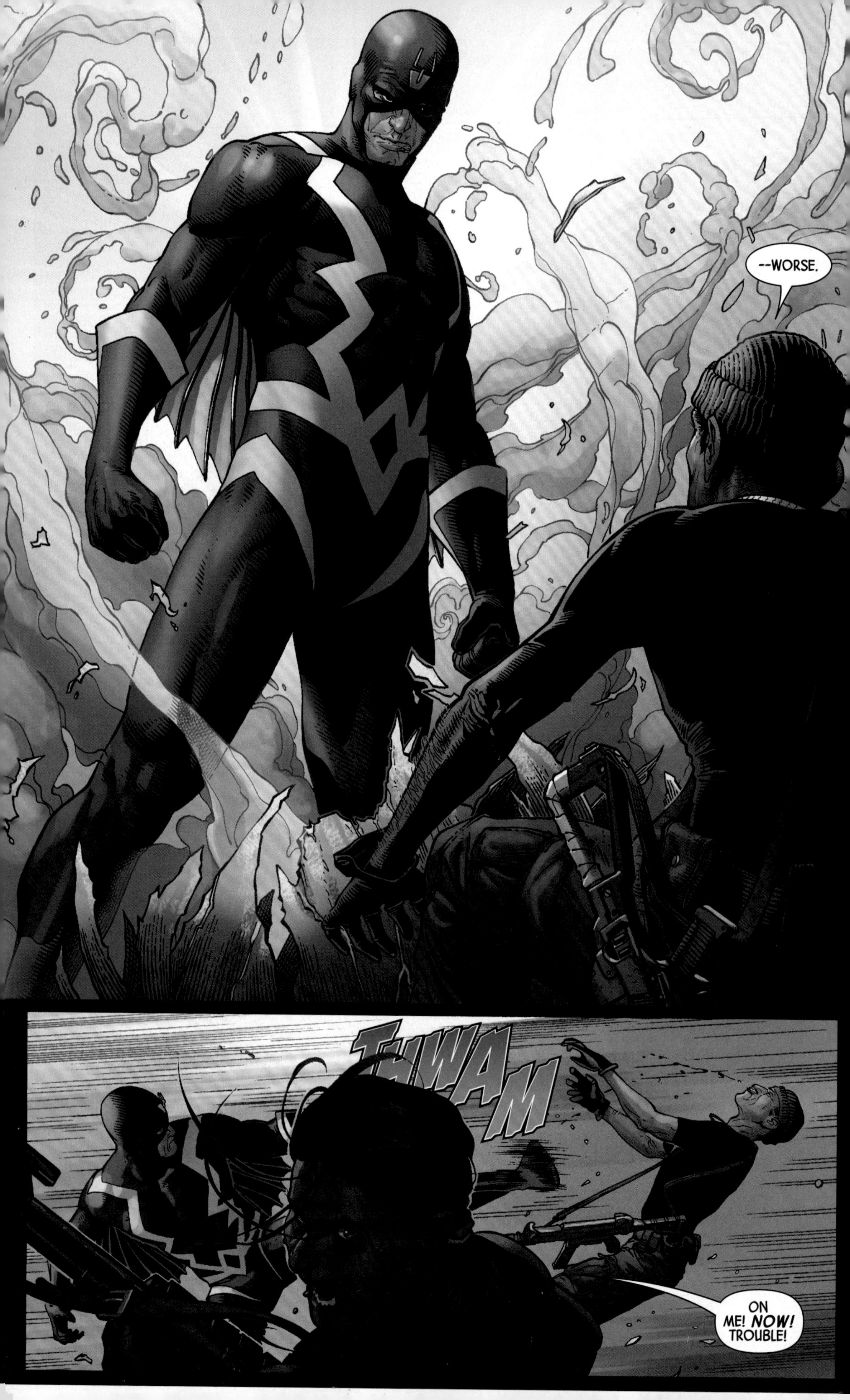
--WORSE.
THWAM
ON ME! NOW! TROUBLE!

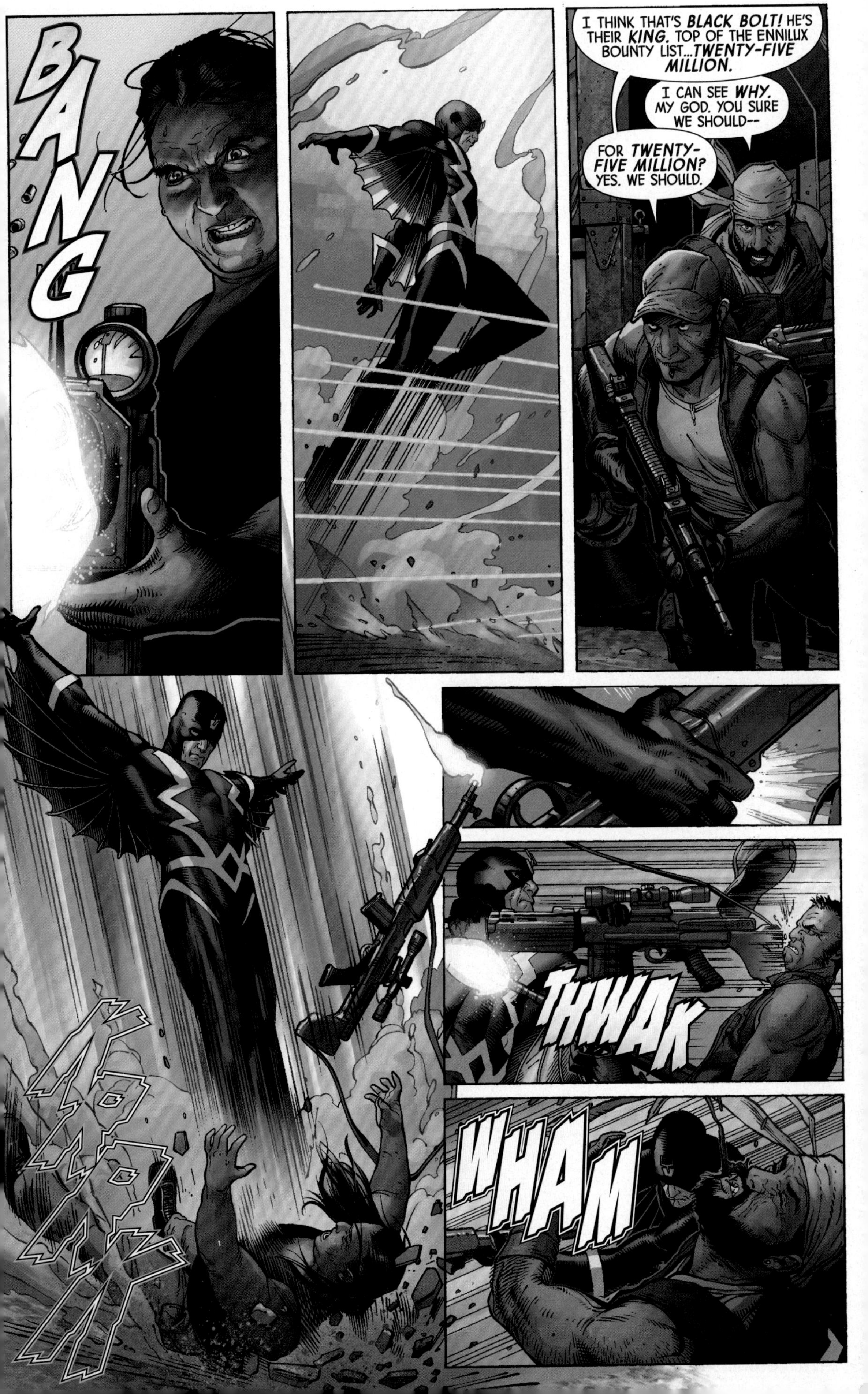
BANG
I THINK THAT'S BLACK BOLT! HE'S THEIR KING. TOP OF THE ENNILUX BOUNTY LIST...TWENTY-FIVE MILLION.
I CAN SEE WHY. MY GOD. YOU SURE WE SHOULD--
FOR TWENTY-FIVE MILLION? YES. WE SHOULD.
THWAK
WHAM

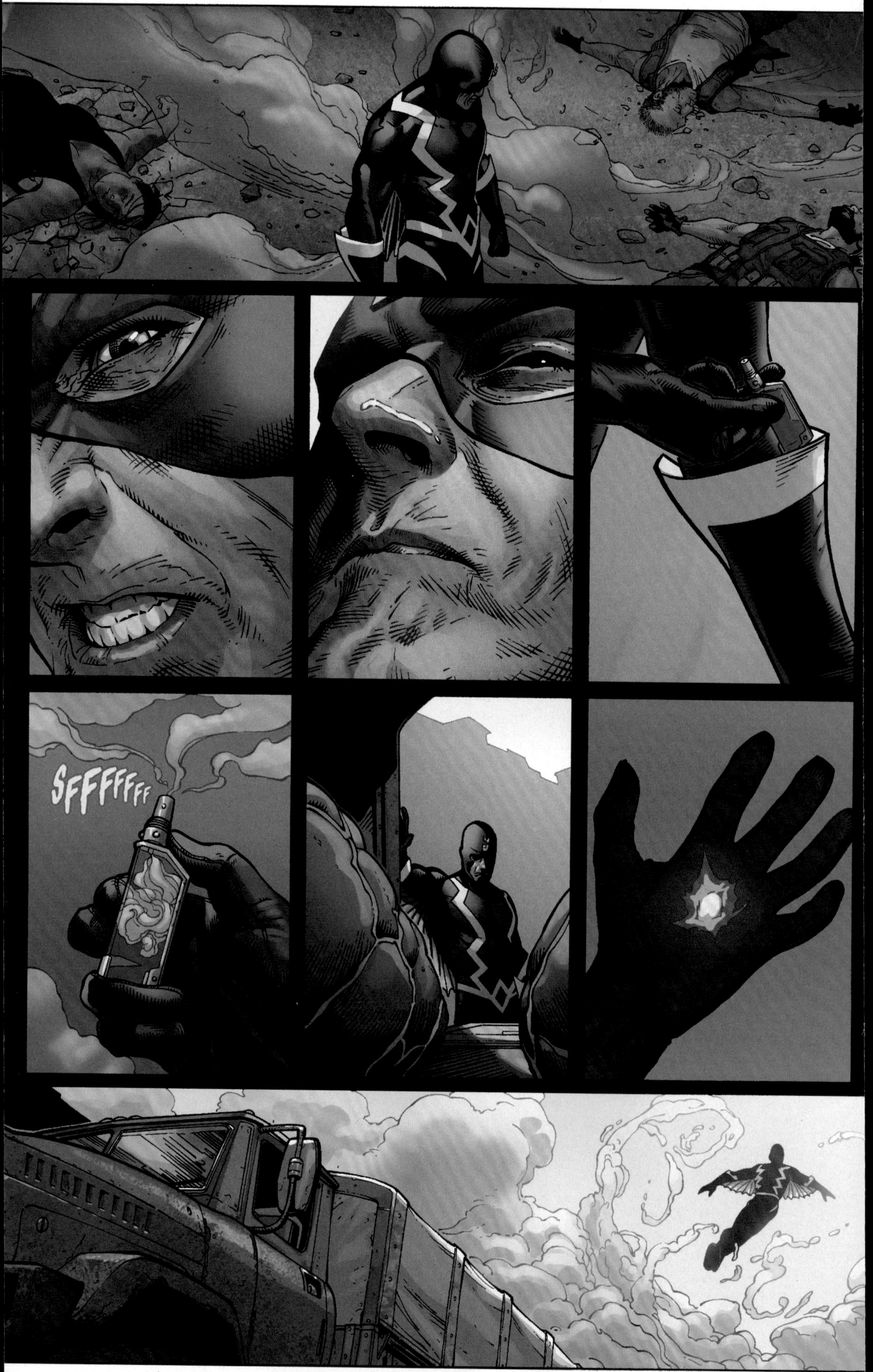
SFFFFFFF

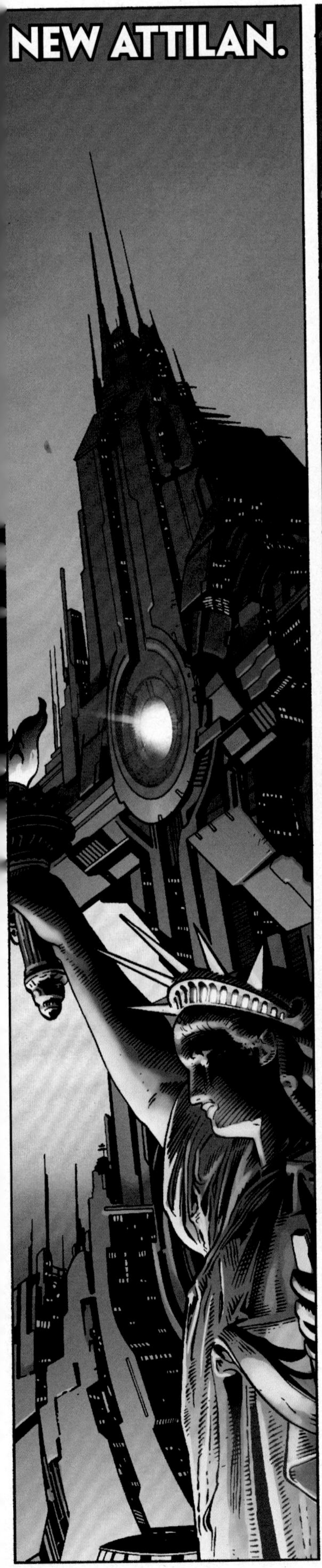
NEW ATTILAN.

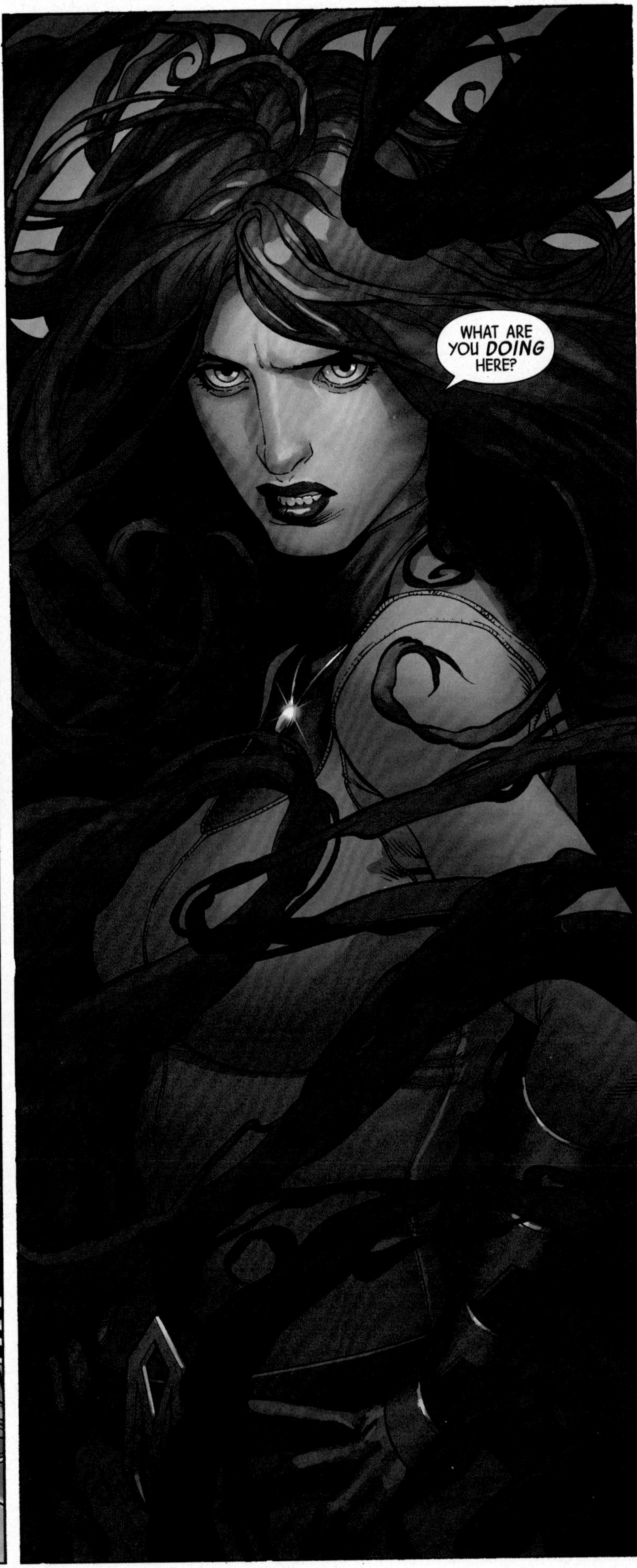
WHAT ARE YOU DOING HERE?

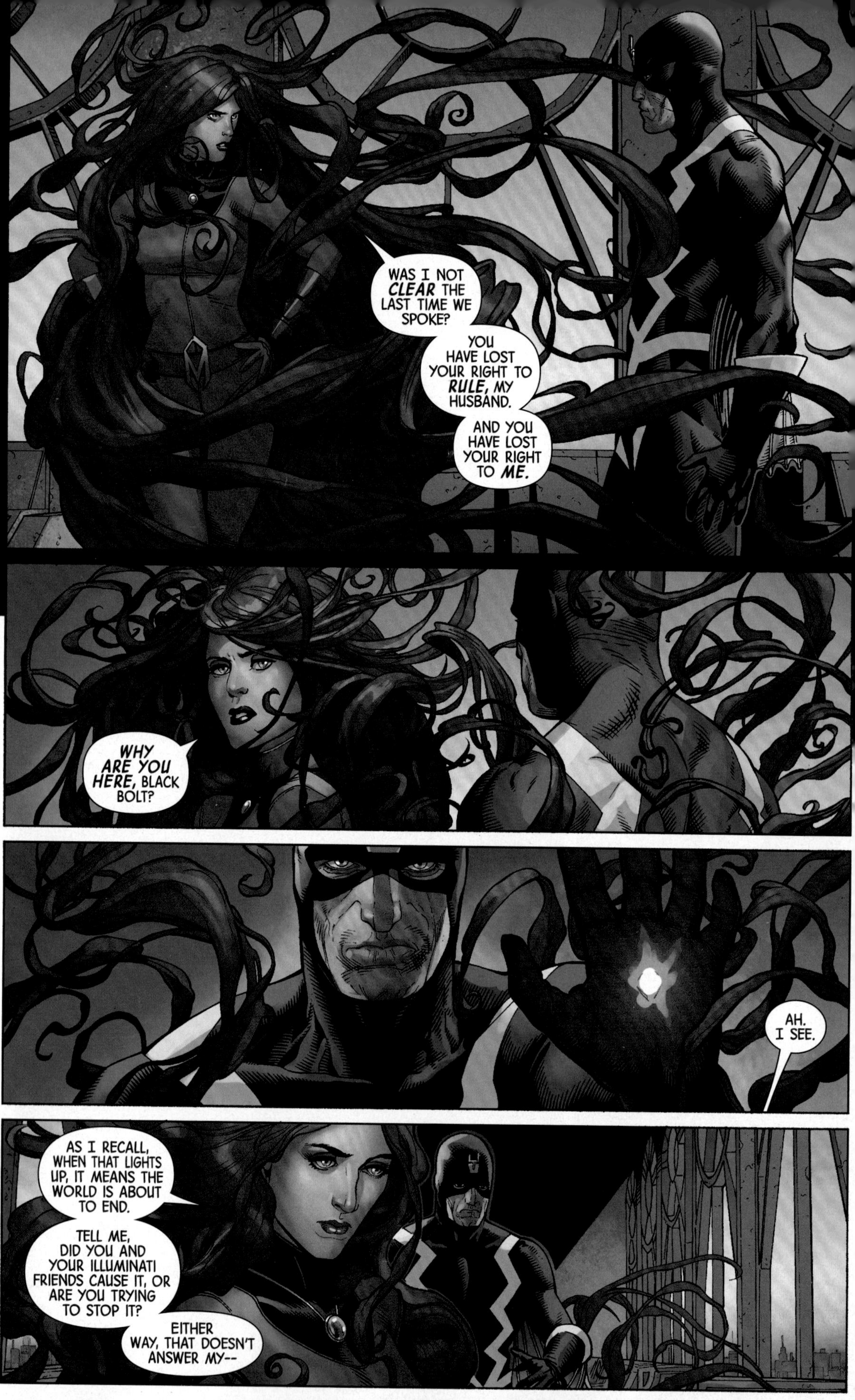
WAS I NOT CLEAR THE LAST TIME WE SPOKE?
YOU HAVE LOST YOUR RIGHT TO RULE, MY HUSBAND.
AND YOU HAVE LOST YOUR RIGHT TO ME.
WHY ARE YOU HERE, BLACK BOLT?
AH. I SEE.
AS I RECALL, WHEN THAT LIGHTS UP, IT MEANS THE WORLD IS ABOUT TO END.
TELL ME, DID YOU AND YOUR ILLUMINATI FRIENDS CAUSE IT, OR ARE YOU TRYING TO STOP IT?
EITHER WAY, THAT DOESN'T ANSWER MY--

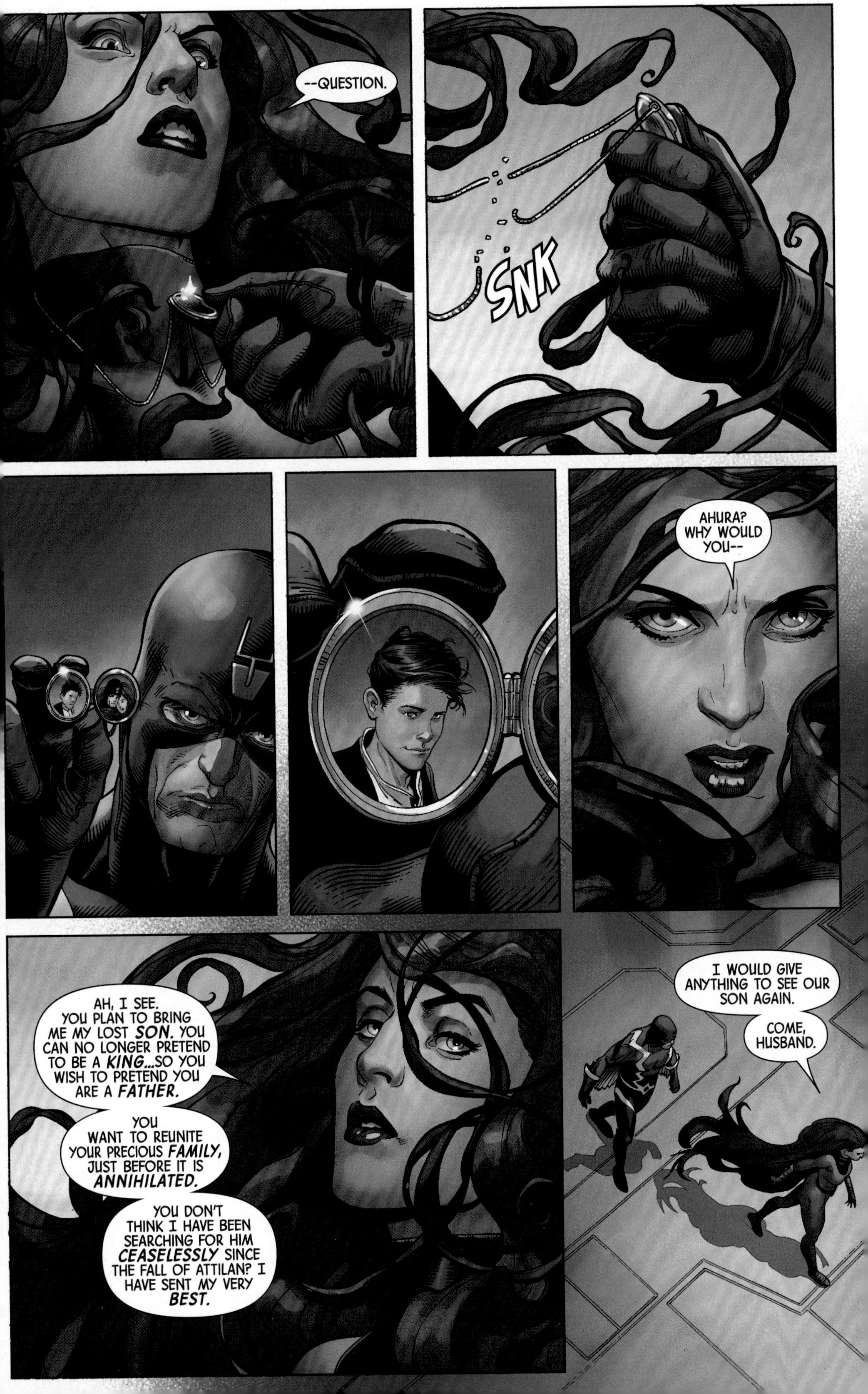
--QUESTION.
SNK
AHURA? WHY WOULD YOU--
AH, I SEE. YOU PLAN TO BRING ME MY LOST SON. YOU CAN NO LONGER PRETEND TO BE A KING...SO YOU WISH TO PRETEND YOU ARE A FATHER.
YOU WANT TO REUNITE YOUR PRECIOUS FAMILY, JUST BEFORE IT IS ANNIHILATED.
YOU DON'T THINK I HAVE BEEN SEARCHING FOR HIM CEASELESSLY SINCE THE FALL OF ATTILAN? I HAVE SENT MY VERY BEST.
I WOULD GIVE ANYTHING TO SEE OUR SON AGAIN.
COME, HUSBAND.

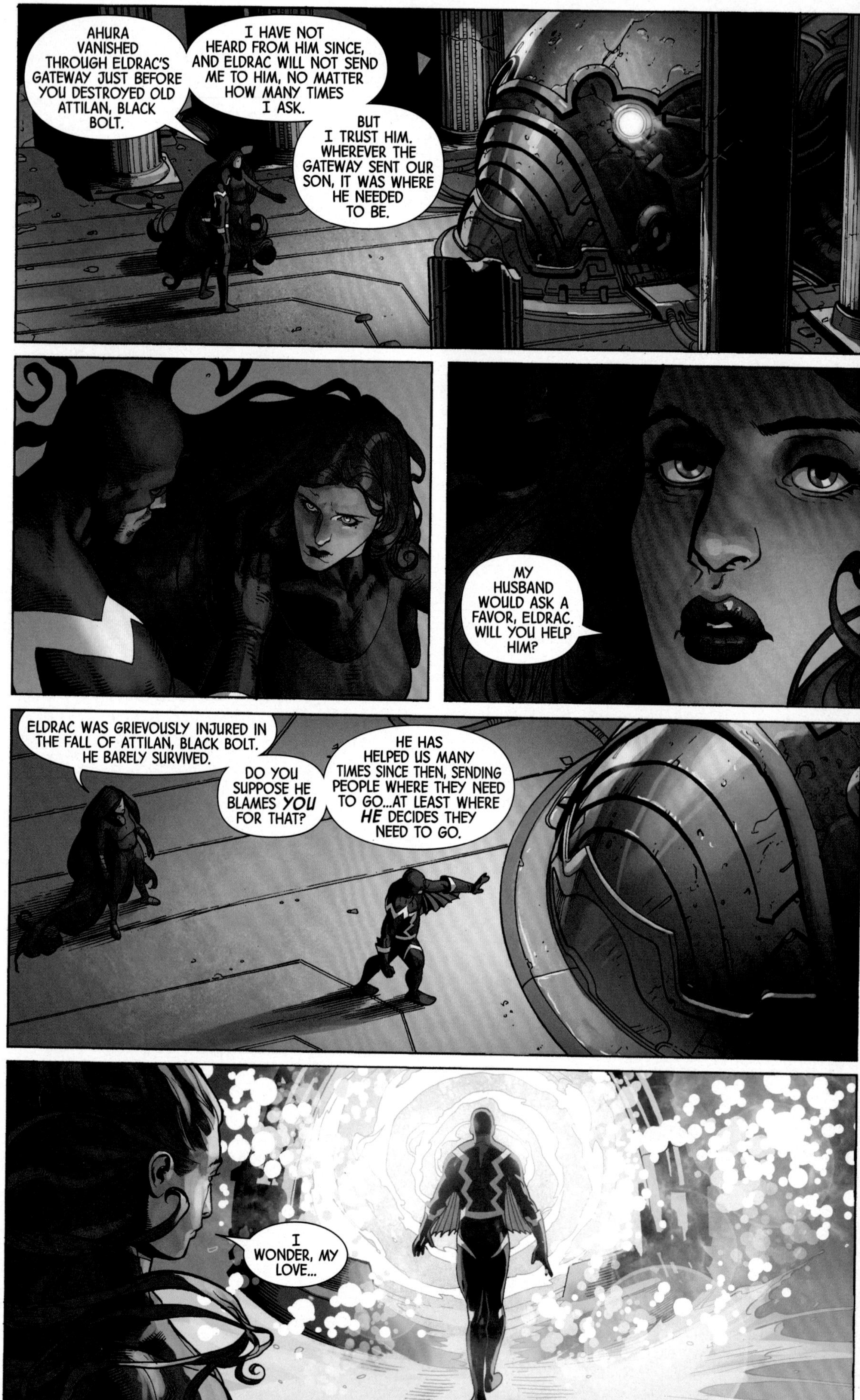
AHURA VANISHED THROUGH ELDRAC'S GATEWAY JUST BEFORE YOU DESTROYED OLD ATTILAN, BLACK BOLT.
I HAVE NOT HEARD FROM HIM SINCE, AND ELDRAC WILL NOT SEND ME TO HIM, NO MATTER HOW MANY TIMES I ASK.
BUT I TRUST HIM. WHEREVER THE GATEWAY SENT OUR SON, IT WAS WHERE HE NEEDED TO BE.
MY HUSBAND WOULD ASK A FAVOR, ELDRAC. WILL YOU HELP HIM?
ELDRAC WAS GRIEVOUSLY INJURED IN THE FALL OF ATTILAN, BLACK BOLT. HE BARELY SURVIVED.
DO YOU SUPPOSE HE BLAMES *YOU* FOR THAT?
HE HAS HELPED US MANY TIMES SINCE THEN, SENDING PEOPLE WHERE THEY NEED TO GO...AT LEAST WHERE *HE* DECIDES THEY NEED TO GO.
I WONDER, MY LOVE...

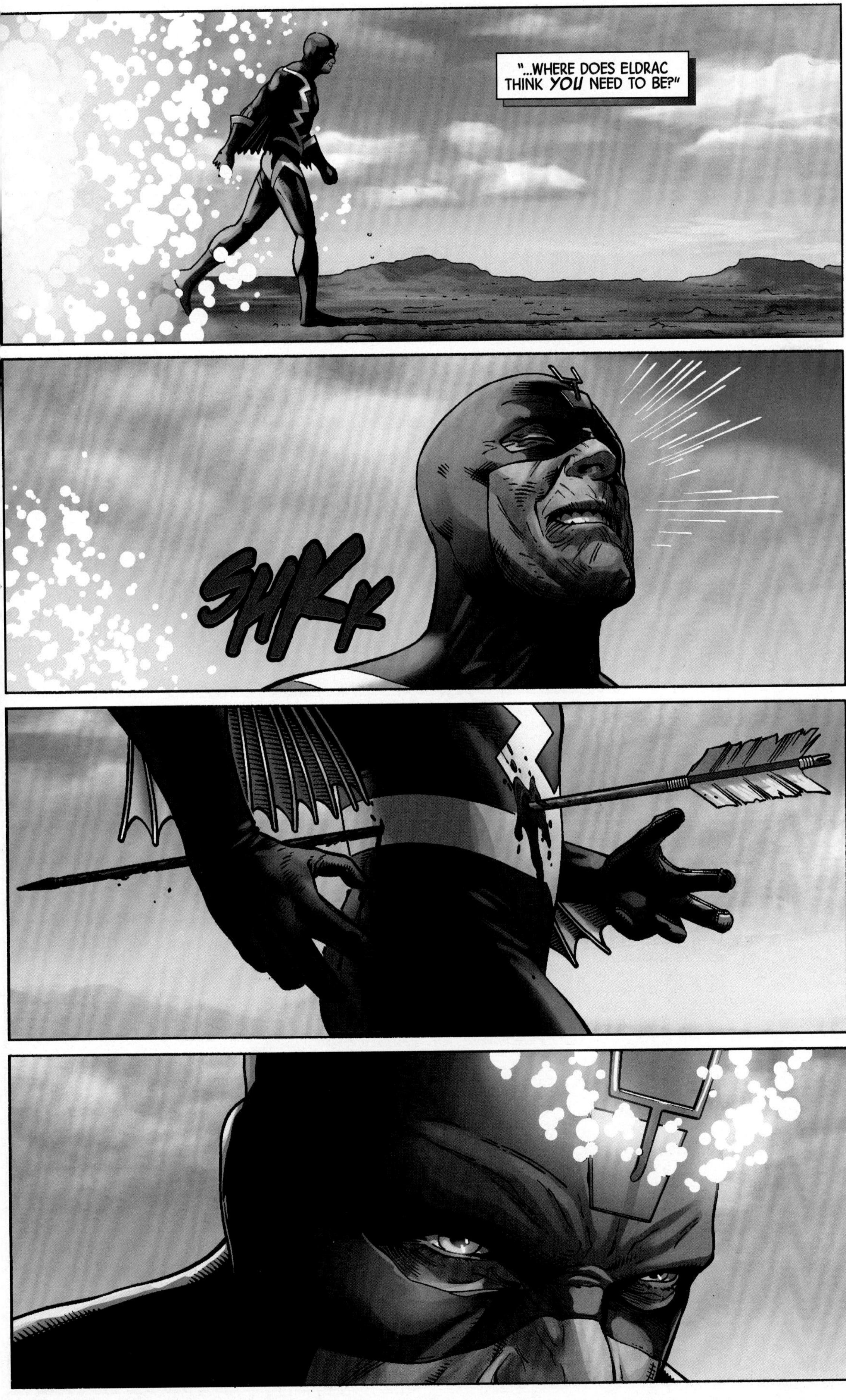
"...WHERE DOES ELDRAC THINK YOU NEED TO BE?"
SHKK

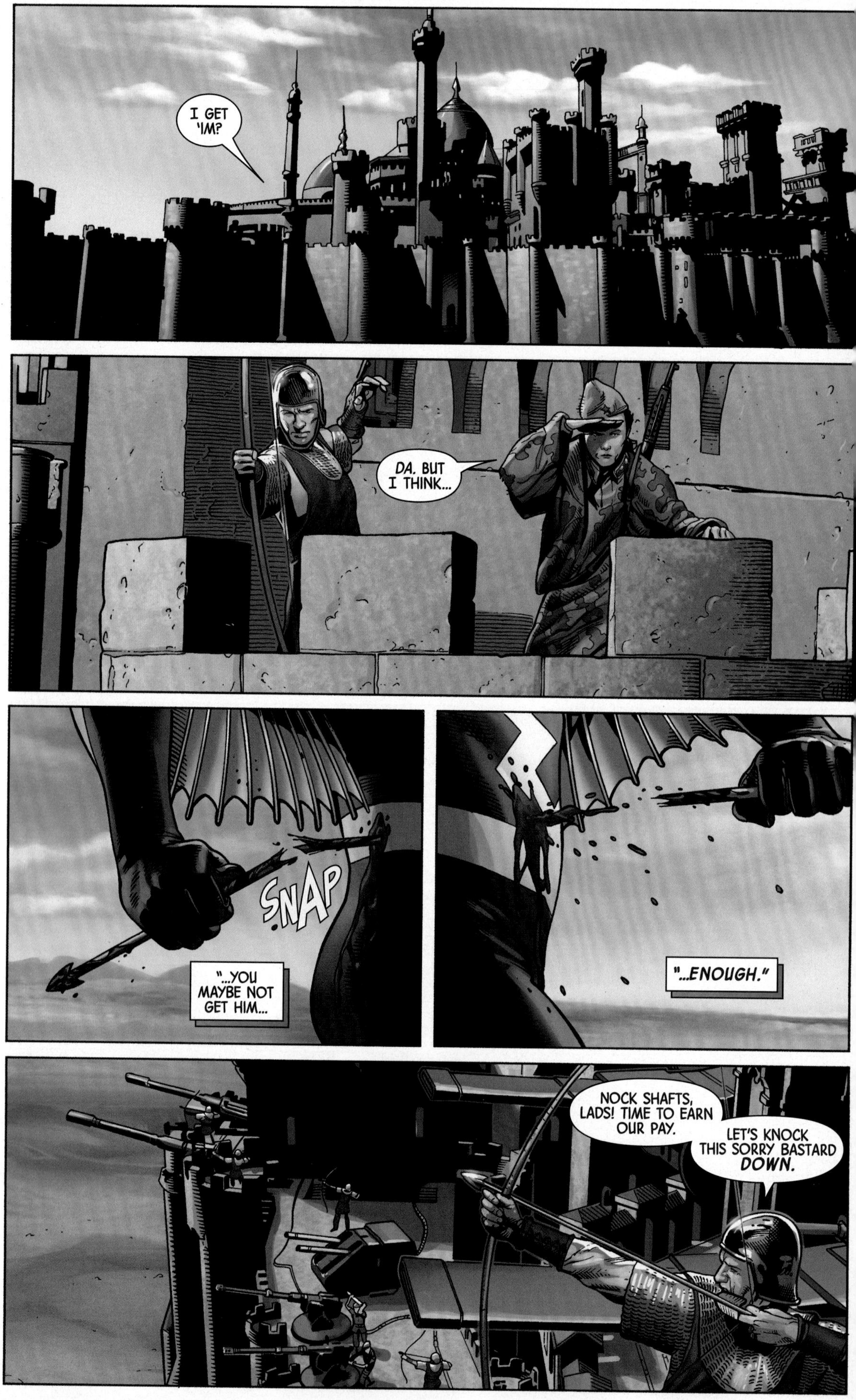
I GET 'IM?
DA. BUT I THINK...
SNAP
"...YOU MAYBE NOT GET HIM...
"...ENOUGH."
NOCK SHAFTS, LADS! TIME TO EARN OUR PAY.
LET'S KNOCK THIS SORRY BASTARD DOWN.

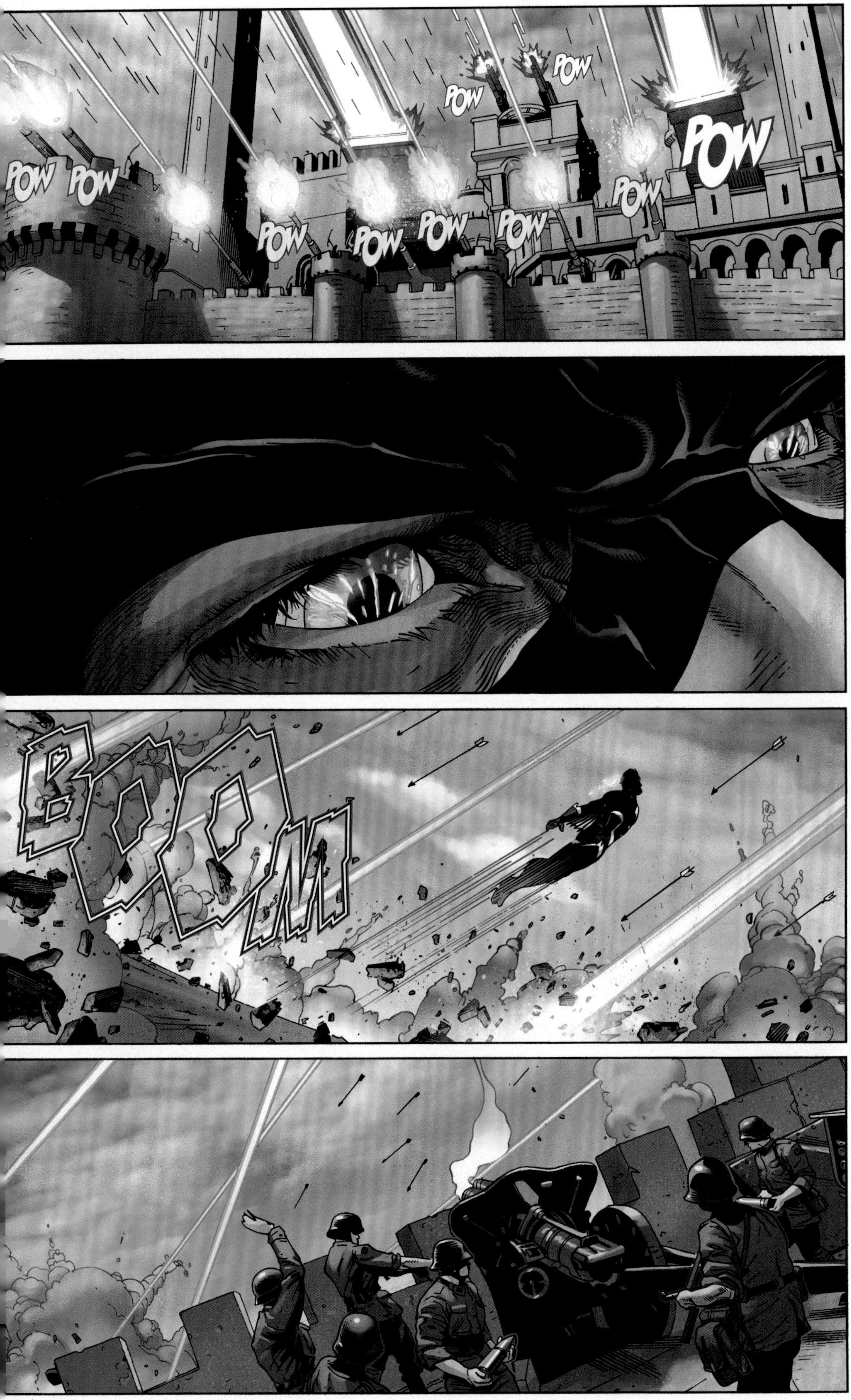
POW
POW
POW
POW
POW
POW
POW
POW
POW
POW
POW
BOOM

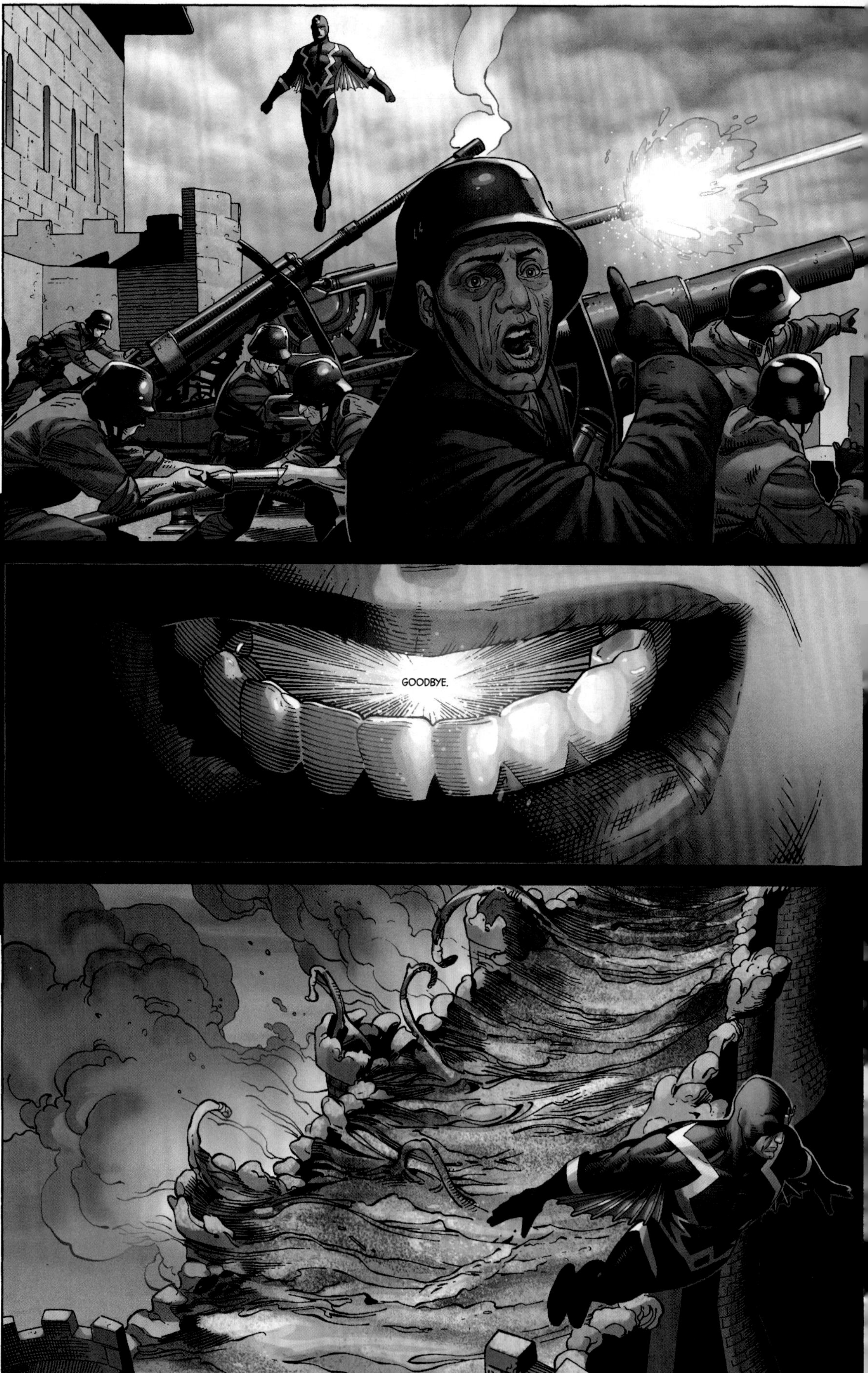
GOODBYE.

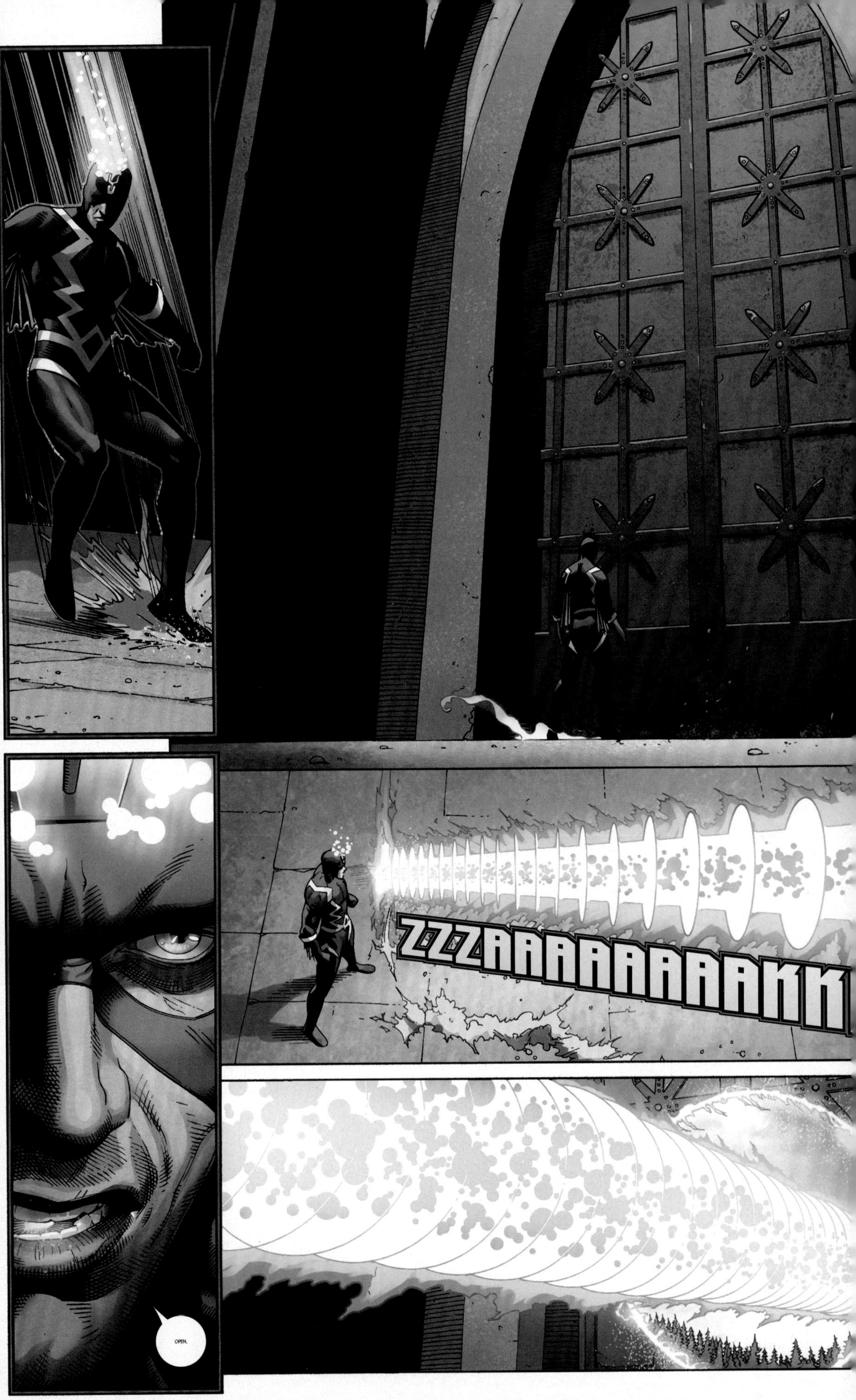
OPEN.
ZZZAAAAAAAAKK

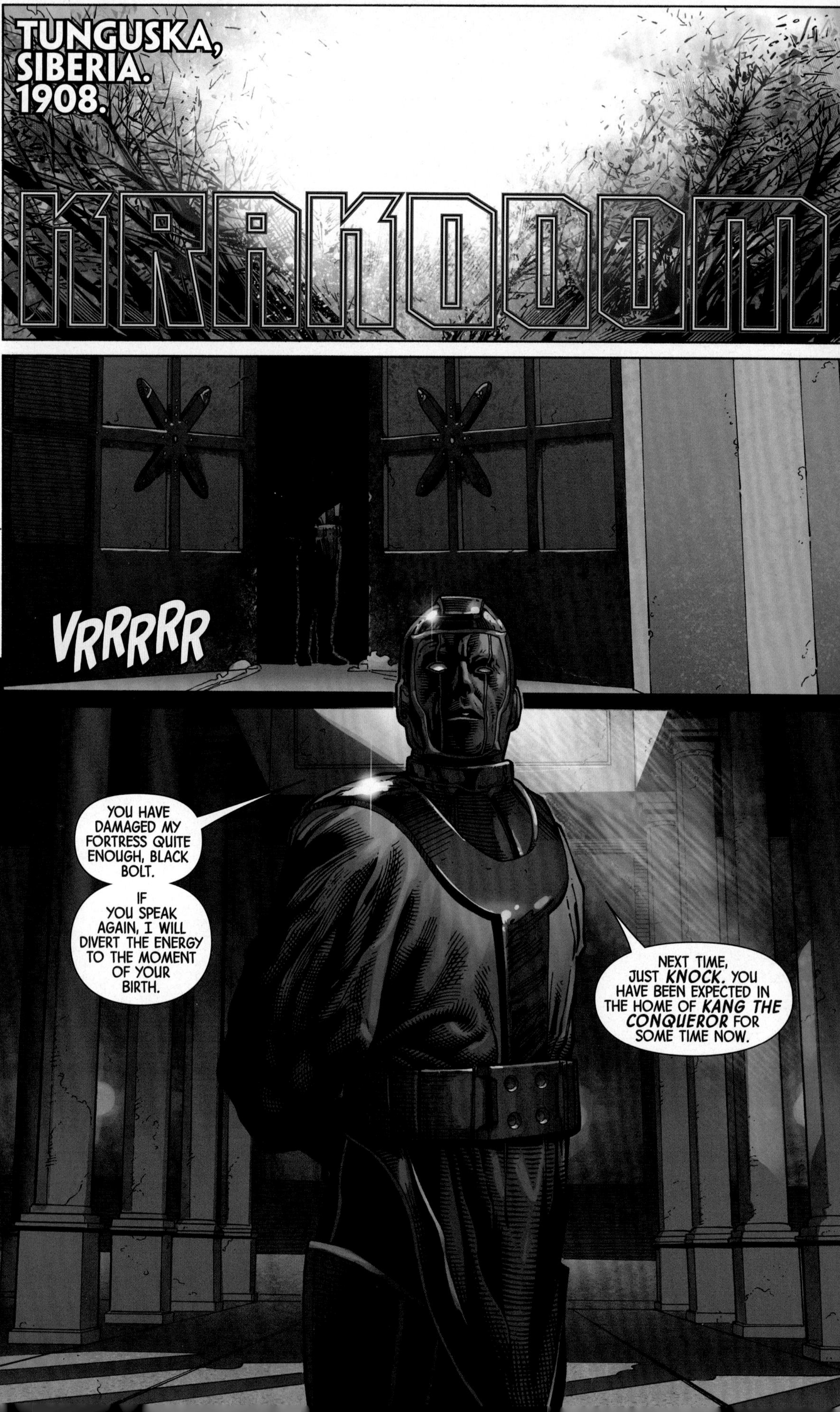

TUNGUSKA, SIBERIA. 1908.
KRAKOOOM
VRRRRR
YOU HAVE DAMAGED MY FORTRESS QUITE ENOUGH, BLACK BOLT.
IF YOU SPEAK AGAIN, I WILL DIVERT THE ENERGY TO THE MOMENT OF YOUR BIRTH.
NEXT TIME, JUST KNOCK. YOU HAVE BEEN EXPECTED IN THE HOME OF KANG THE CONQUEROR FOR SOME TIME NOW.

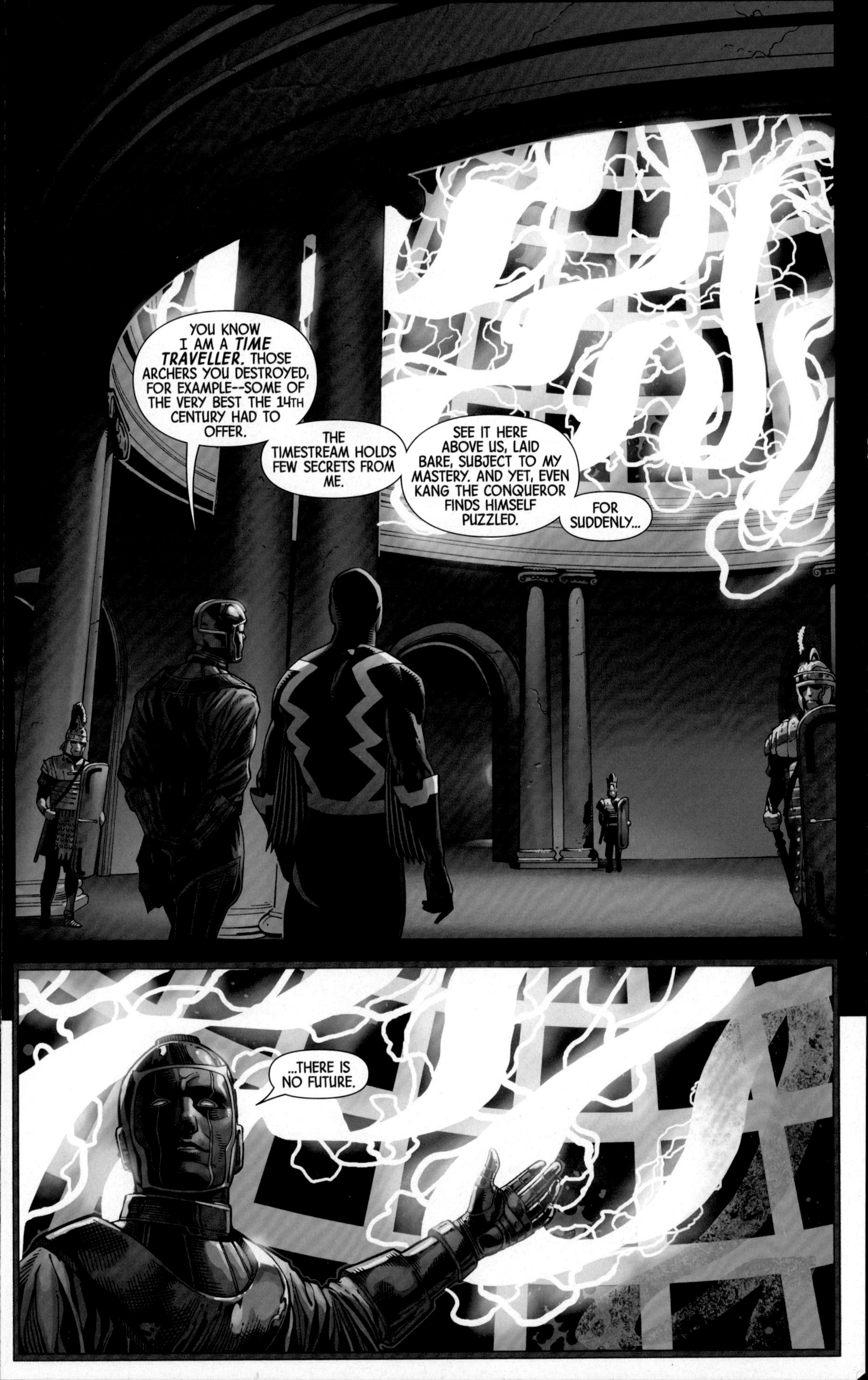
YOU KNOW I AM A TIME TRAVELLER. THOSE ARCHERS YOU DESTROYED, FOR EXAMPLE--SOME OF THE VERY BEST THE 14TH CENTURY HAD TO OFFER.
THE TIMESTREAM HOLDS FEW SECRETS FROM ME.
SEE IT HERE ABOVE US, LAID BARE, SUBJECT TO MY MASTERY. AND YET, EVEN KANG THE CONQUEROR FINDS HIMSELF PUZZLED.
FOR SUDDENLY...
...THERE IS NO FUTURE.

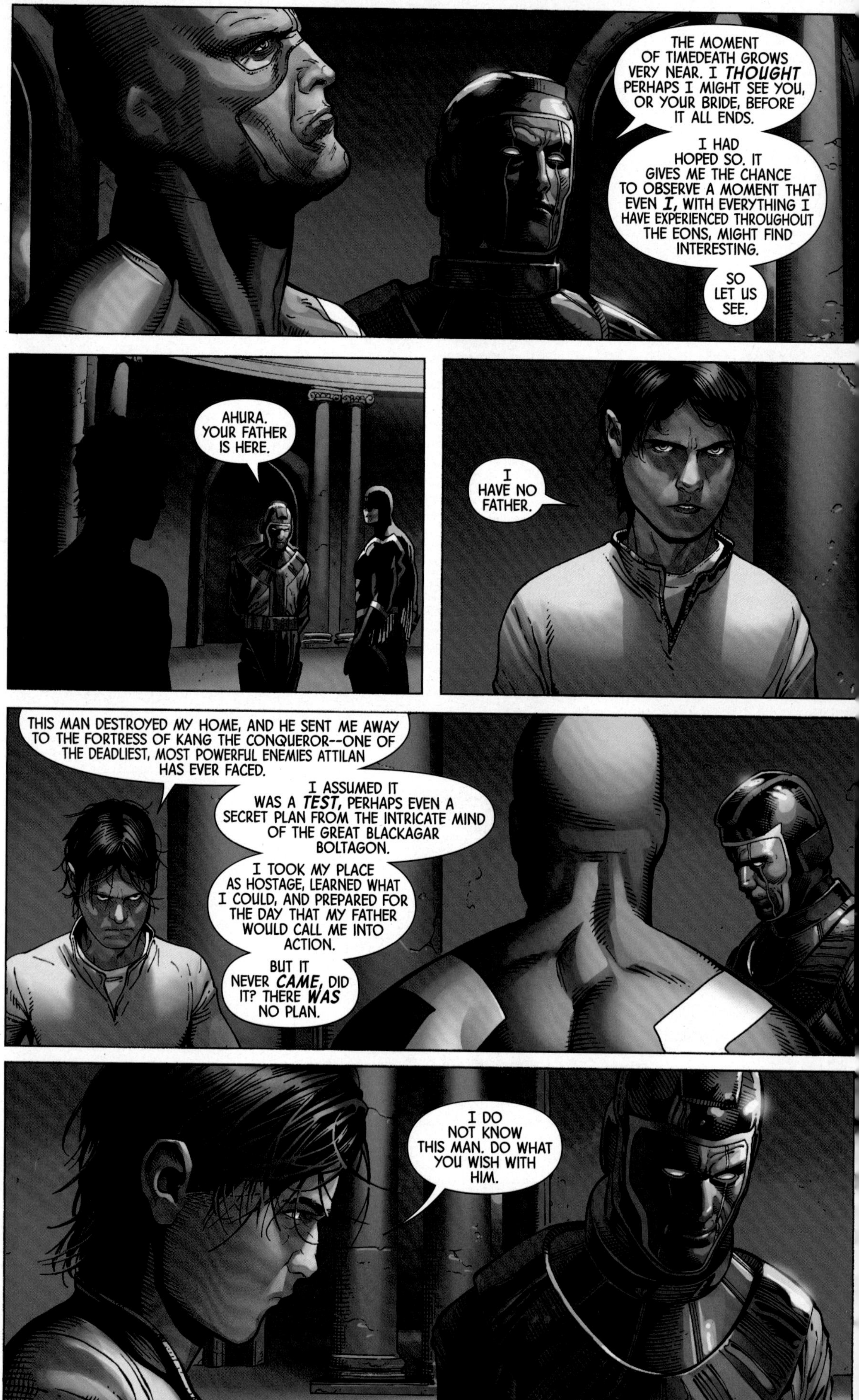
THE MOMENT OF TIMEDEATH GROWS VERY NEAR. I THOUGHT PERHAPS I MIGHT SEE YOU, OR YOUR BRIDE, BEFORE IT ALL ENDS.
I HAD HOPED SO. IT GIVES ME THE CHANCE TO OBSERVE A MOMENT THAT EVEN I, WITH EVERYTHING I HAVE EXPERIENCED THROUGHOUT THE EONS, MIGHT FIND INTERESTING.
SO LET US SEE.
AHURA. YOUR FATHER IS HERE.
I HAVE NO FATHER.
THIS MAN DESTROYED MY HOME, AND HE SENT ME AWAY TO THE FORTRESS OF KANG THE CONQUEROR--ONE OF THE DEADLIEST, MOST POWERFUL ENEMIES ATTILAN HAS EVER FACED.
I ASSUMED IT WAS A TEST, PERHAPS EVEN A SECRET PLAN FROM THE INTRICATE MIND OF THE GREAT BLACKAGAR BOLTAGON.
I TOOK MY PLACE AS HOSTAGE, LEARNED WHAT I COULD, AND PREPARED FOR THE DAY THAT MY FATHER WOULD CALL ME INTO ACTION.
BUT IT NEVER CAME, DID IT? THERE WAS NO PLAN.
I DO NOT KNOW THIS MAN. DO WHAT YOU WISH WITH HIM.

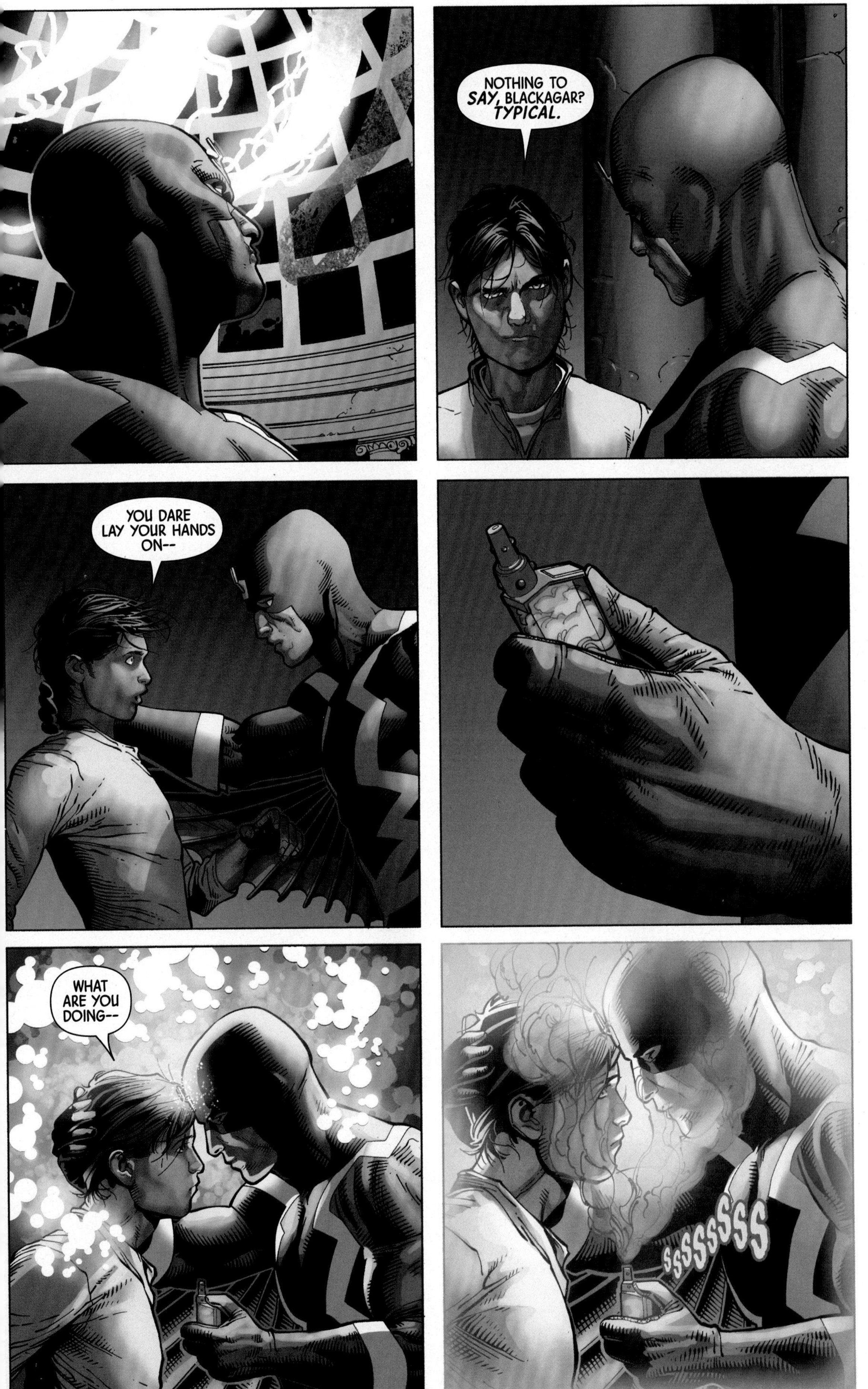
NOTHING TO SAY, BLACKAGAR? TYPICAL.
YOU DARE LAY YOUR HANDS ON--
WHAT ARE YOU DOING--
SSSSSSSS

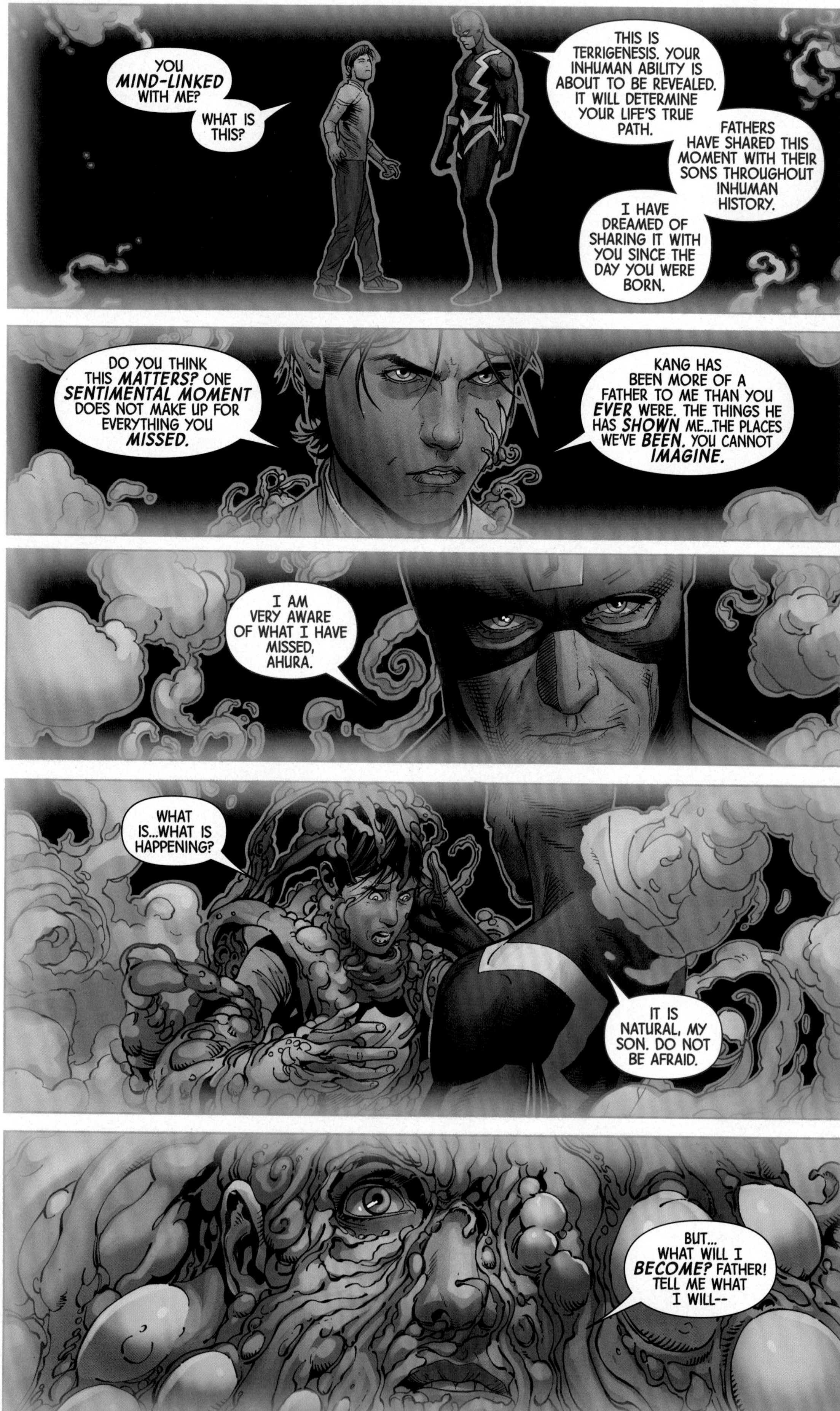
YOU MIND-LINKED WITH ME?
WHAT IS THIS?
THIS IS TERRIGENESIS. YOUR INHUMAN ABILITY IS ABOUT TO BE REVEALED. IT WILL DETERMINE YOUR LIFE'S TRUE PATH.
FATHERS HAVE SHARED THIS MOMENT WITH THEIR SONS THROUGHOUT INHUMAN HISTORY.
I HAVE DREAMED OF SHARING IT WITH YOU SINCE THE DAY YOU WERE BORN.
DO YOU THINK THIS MATTERS? ONE SENTIMENTAL MOMENT DOES NOT MAKE UP FOR EVERYTHING YOU MISSED.
KANG HAS BEEN MORE OF A FATHER TO ME THAN YOU EVER WERE. THE THINGS HE HAS SHOWN ME...THE PLACES WE'VE BEEN. YOU CANNOT IMAGINE.
I AM VERY AWARE OF WHAT I HAVE MISSED, AHURA.
WHAT IS...WHAT IS HAPPENING?
IT IS NATURAL, MY SON. DO NOT BE AFRAID.
BUT... WHAT WILL I BECOME? FATHER! TELL ME WHAT I WILL--

TOUCHING.

WHAT NOW, INHUMAN KING? DO WE DO BATTLE AT THE EDGE OF THE END OF EVERYTHING?

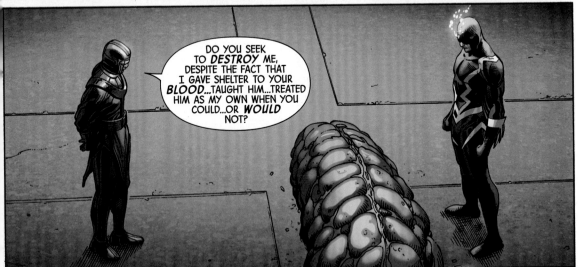

DO YOU SEEK TO DESTROY ME, DESPITE THE FACT THAT I GAVE SHELTER TO YOUR BLOOD...TAUGHT HIM...TREATED HIM AS MY OWN WHEN YOU COULD...OR WOULD NOT?

THAT IS A FIGHT NEITHER ONE OF US WOULD SURVIVE, I SUSPECT.

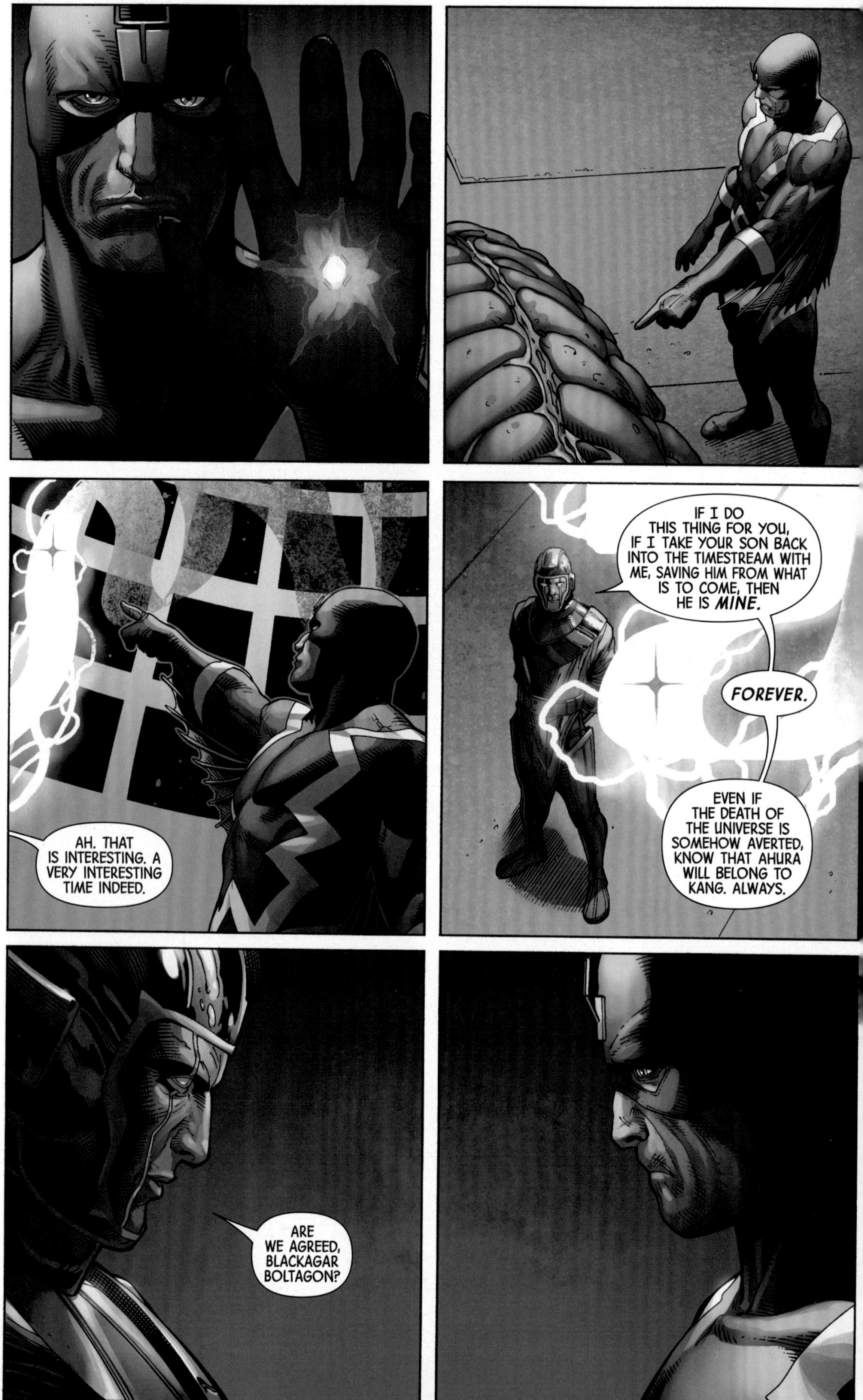
AH. THAT IS INTERESTING. A VERY INTERESTING TIME INDEED.
IF I DO THIS THING FOR YOU, IF I TAKE YOUR SON BACK INTO THE TIMESTREAM WITH ME, SAVING HIM FROM WHAT IS TO COME, THEN HE IS MINE.
FOREVER.
EVEN IF THE DEATH OF THE UNIVERSE IS SOMEHOW AVERTED, KNOW THAT AHURA WILL BELONG TO KANG. ALWAYS.
ARE WE AGREED, BLACKAGAR BOLTAGON?

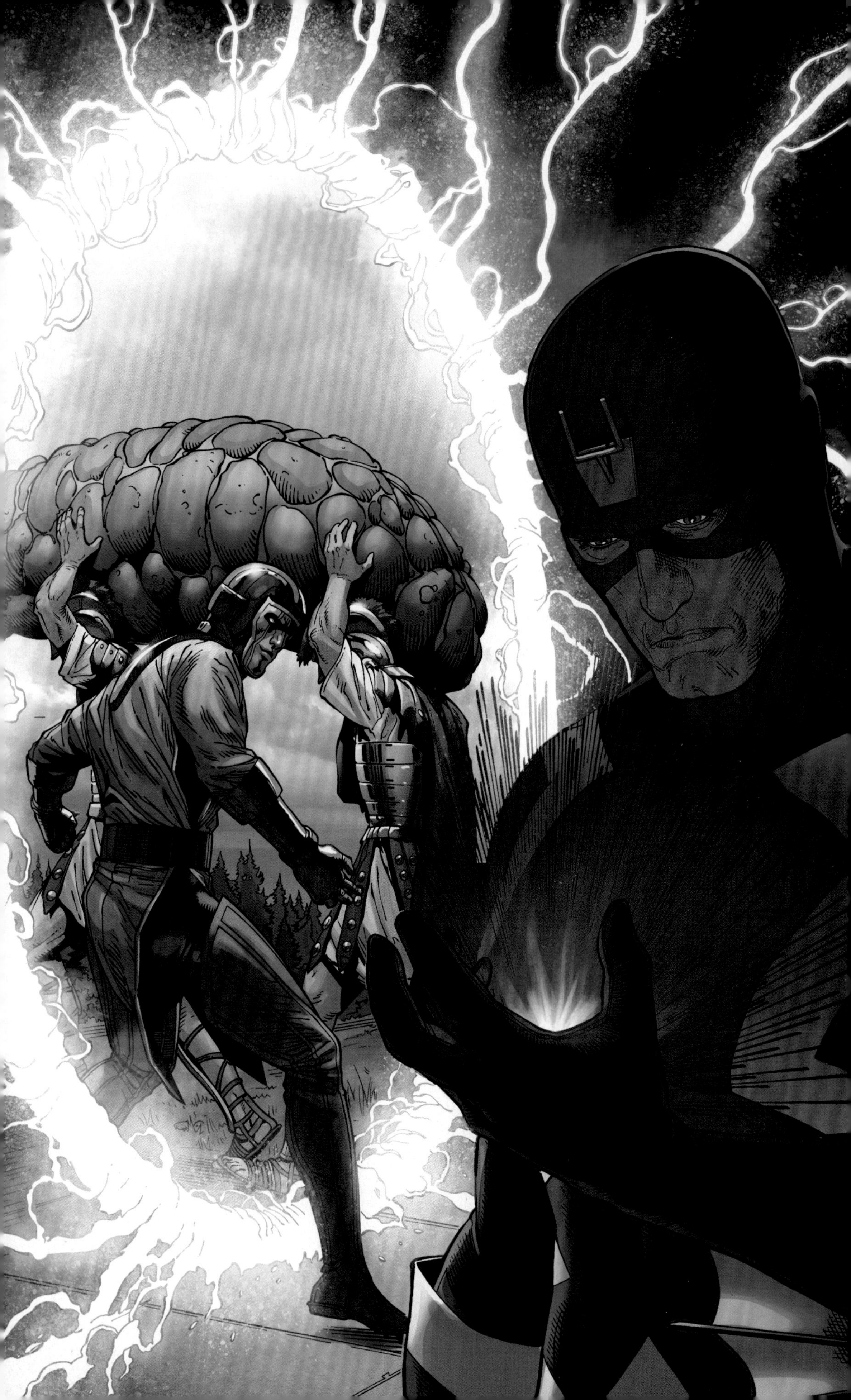

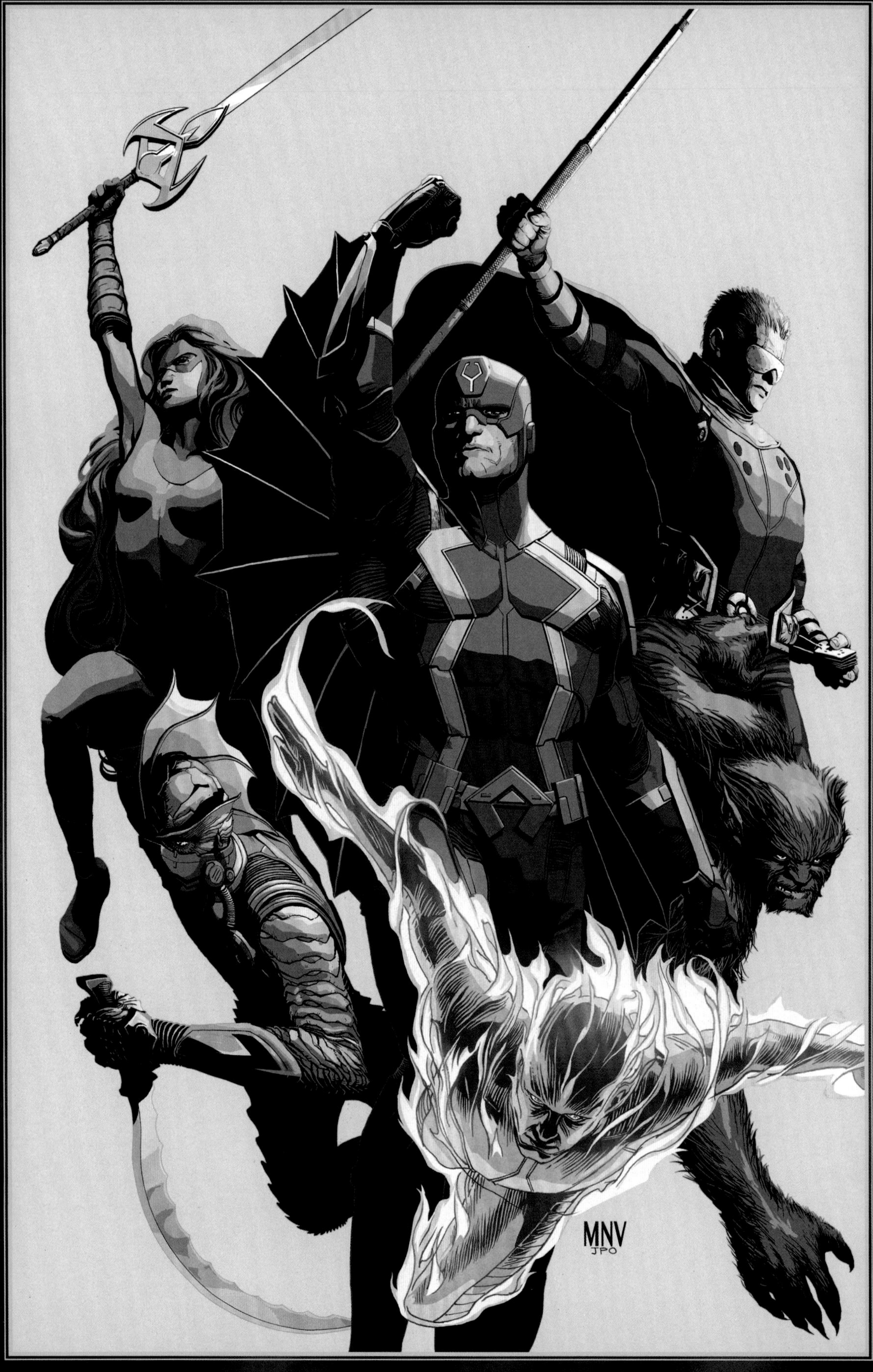
MNV
JPO

1

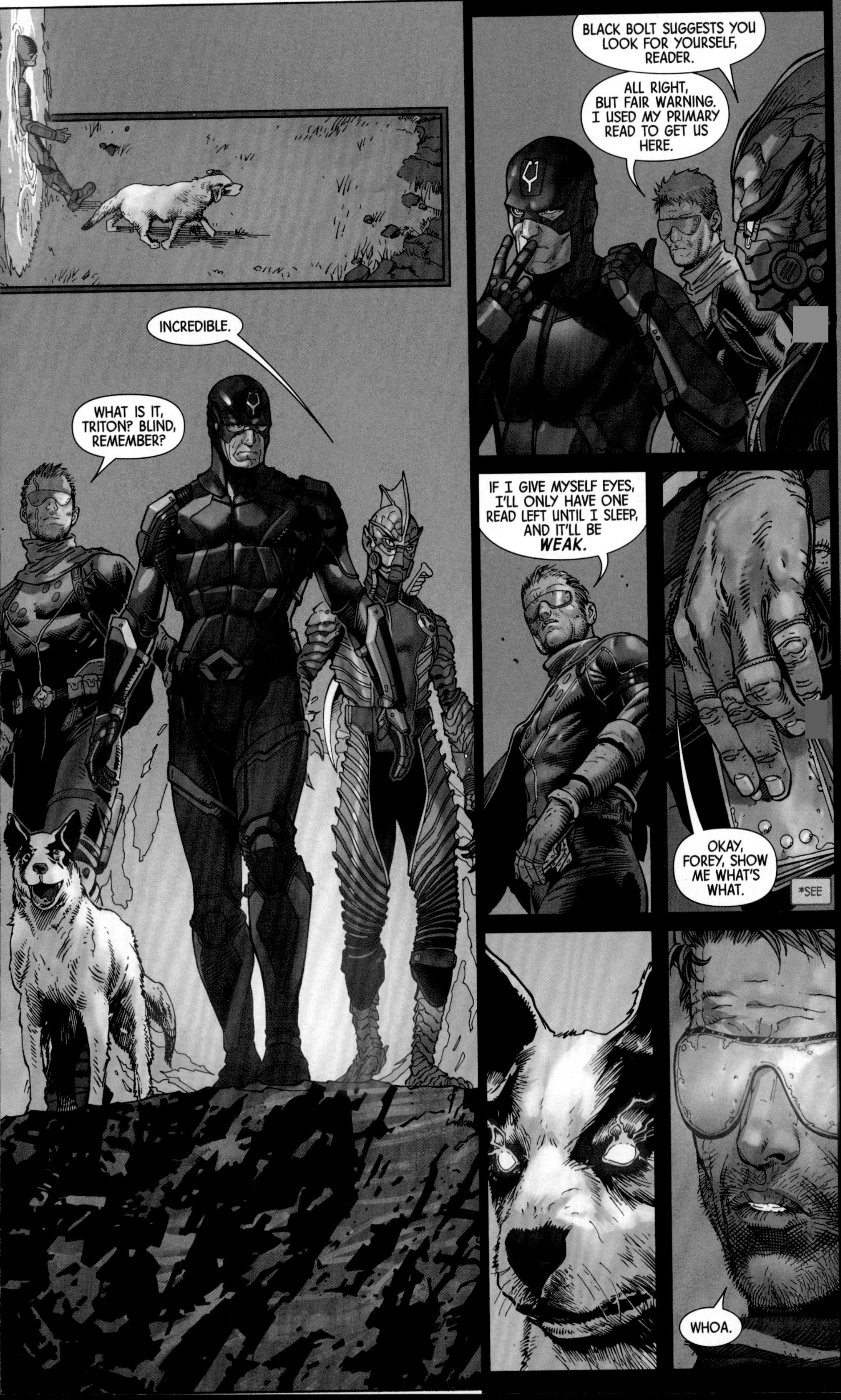
INCREDIBLE.
WHAT IS IT, TRITON? BLIND, REMEMBER?
BLACK BOLT SUGGESTS YOU LOOK FOR YOURSELF, READER.
ALL RIGHT, BUT FAIR WARNING. I USED MY PRIMARY READ TO GET US HERE.
IF I GIVE MYSELF EYES, I'LL ONLY HAVE ONE READ LEFT UNTIL I SLEEP, AND IT'LL BE *WEAK.*
OKAY, FOREY, SHOW ME WHAT'S WHAT.
*SEE
WHOA.

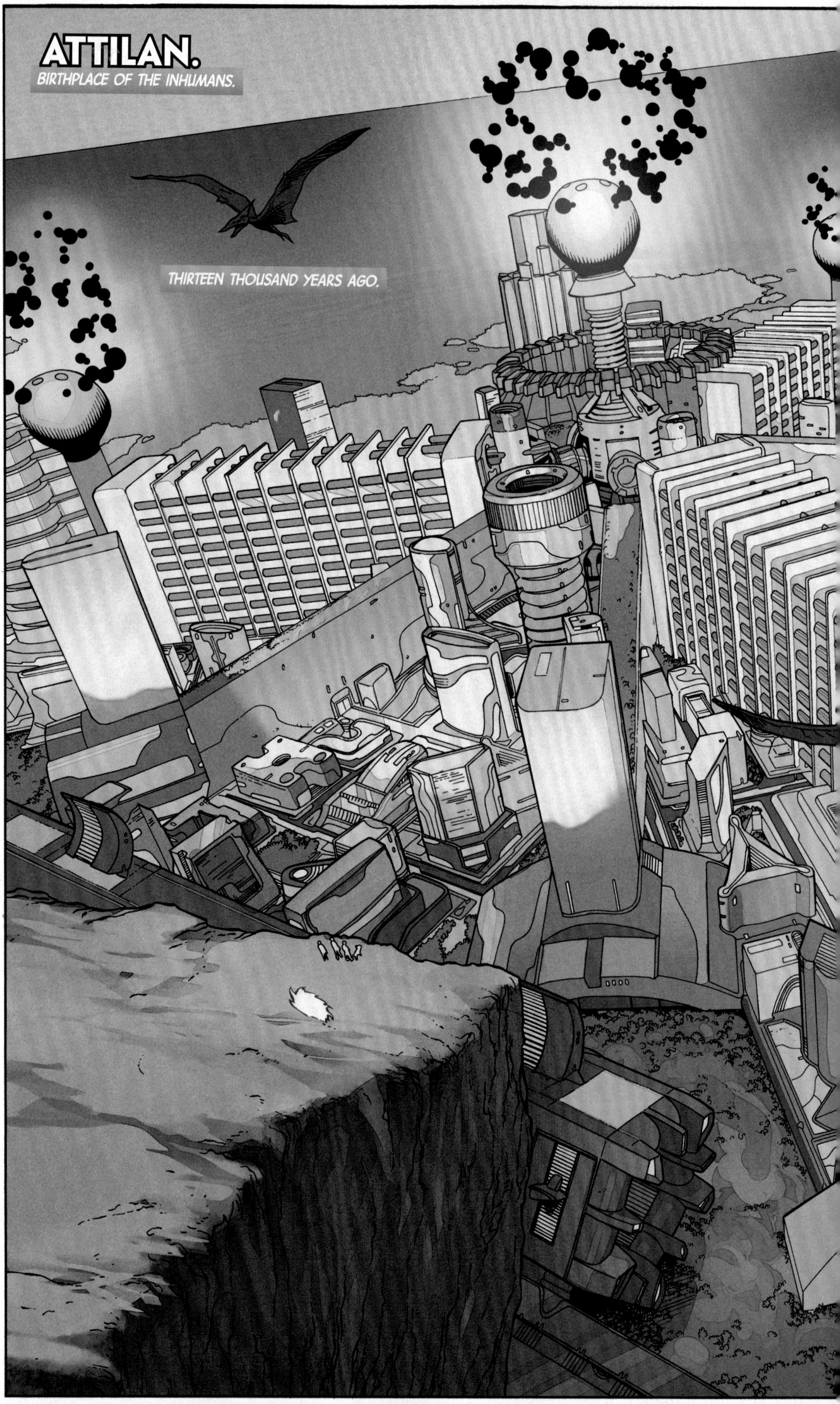
ATTILAN.
BIRTHPLACE OF THE INHUMANS.
THIRTEEN THOUSAND YEARS AGO.

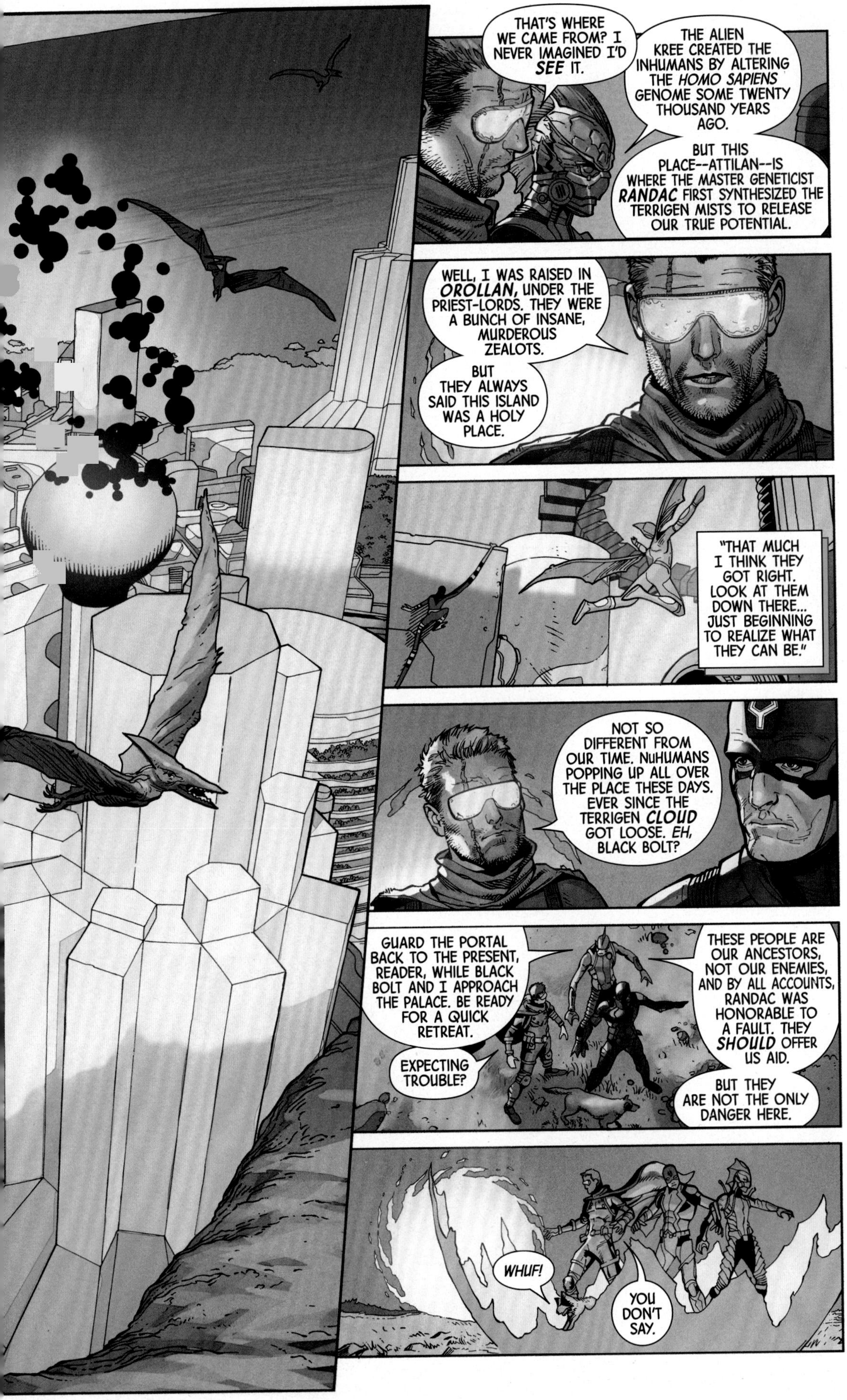
THAT'S WHERE WE CAME FROM? I NEVER IMAGINED I'D SEE IT.
THE ALIEN KREE CREATED THE INHUMANS BY ALTERING THE HOMO SAPIENS GENOME SOME TWENTY THOUSAND YEARS AGO.
BUT THIS PLACE--ATTILAN--IS WHERE THE MASTER GENETICIST RANDAC FIRST SYNTHESIZED THE TERRIGEN MISTS TO RELEASE OUR TRUE POTENTIAL.
WELL, I WAS RAISED IN OROLLAN, UNDER THE PRIEST-LORDS. THEY WERE A BUNCH OF INSANE, MURDEROUS ZEALOTS.
BUT THEY ALWAYS SAID THIS ISLAND WAS A HOLY PLACE.
"THAT MUCH I THINK THEY GOT RIGHT. LOOK AT THEM DOWN THERE... JUST BEGINNING TO REALIZE WHAT THEY CAN BE."
NOT SO DIFFERENT FROM OUR TIME. NUHUMANS POPPING UP ALL OVER THE PLACE THESE DAYS. EVER SINCE THE TERRIGEN CLOUD GOT LOOSE. EH, BLACK BOLT?
GUARD THE PORTAL BACK TO THE PRESENT, READER, WHILE BLACK BOLT AND I APPROACH THE PALACE. BE READY FOR A QUICK RETREAT.
EXPECTING TROUBLE?
THESE PEOPLE ARE OUR ANCESTORS, NOT OUR ENEMIES, AND BY ALL ACCOUNTS, RANDAC WAS HONORABLE TO A FAULT. THEY SHOULD OFFER US AID.
BUT THEY ARE NOT THE ONLY DANGER HERE.
WHUF!
YOU DON'T SAY.

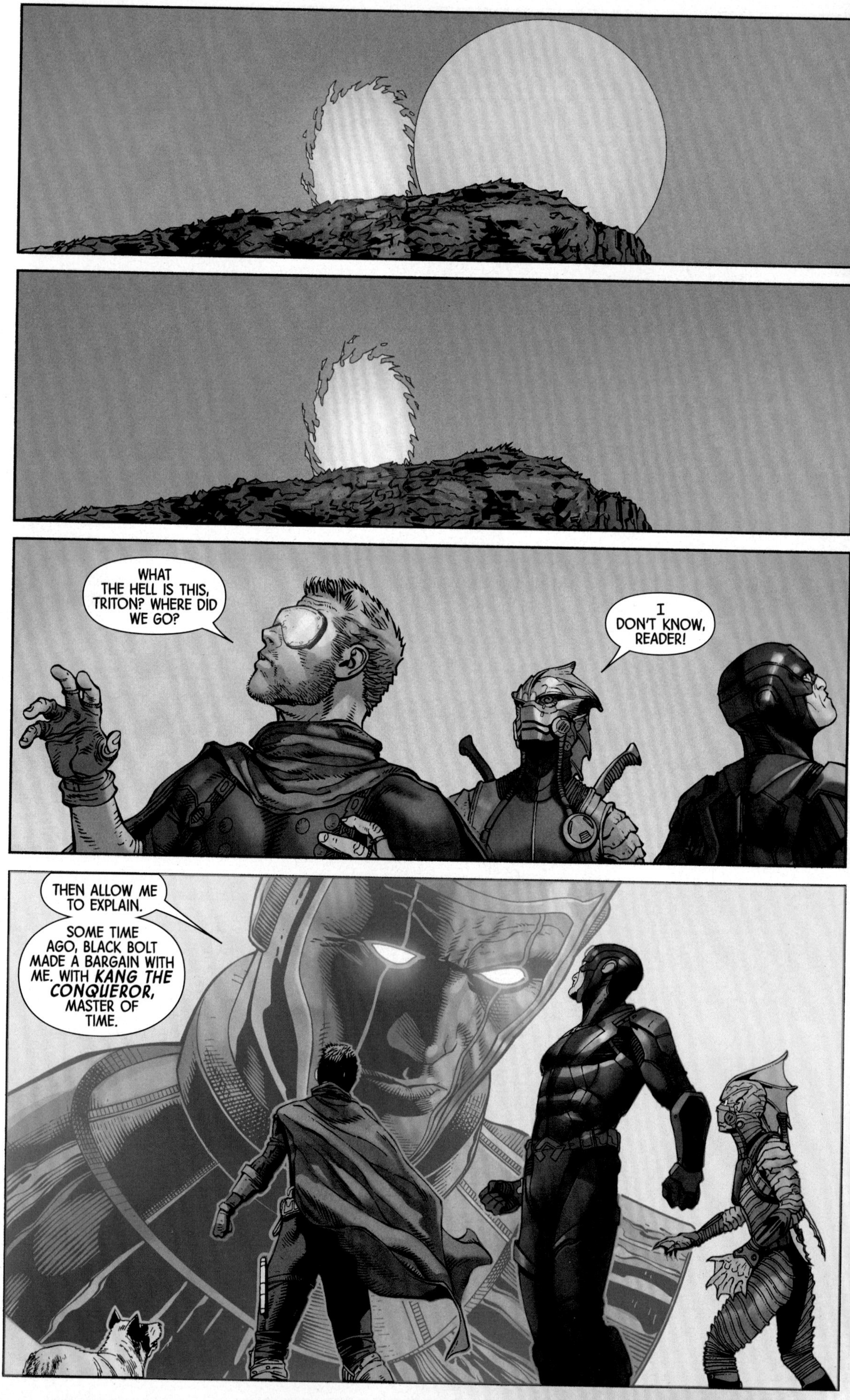
WHAT THE HELL IS THIS, TRITON? WHERE DID WE GO?
I DON'T KNOW, READER!
THEN ALLOW ME TO EXPLAIN.
SOME TIME AGO, BLACK BOLT MADE A BARGAIN WITH ME. WITH *KANG THE CONQUEROR,* MASTER OF TIME.

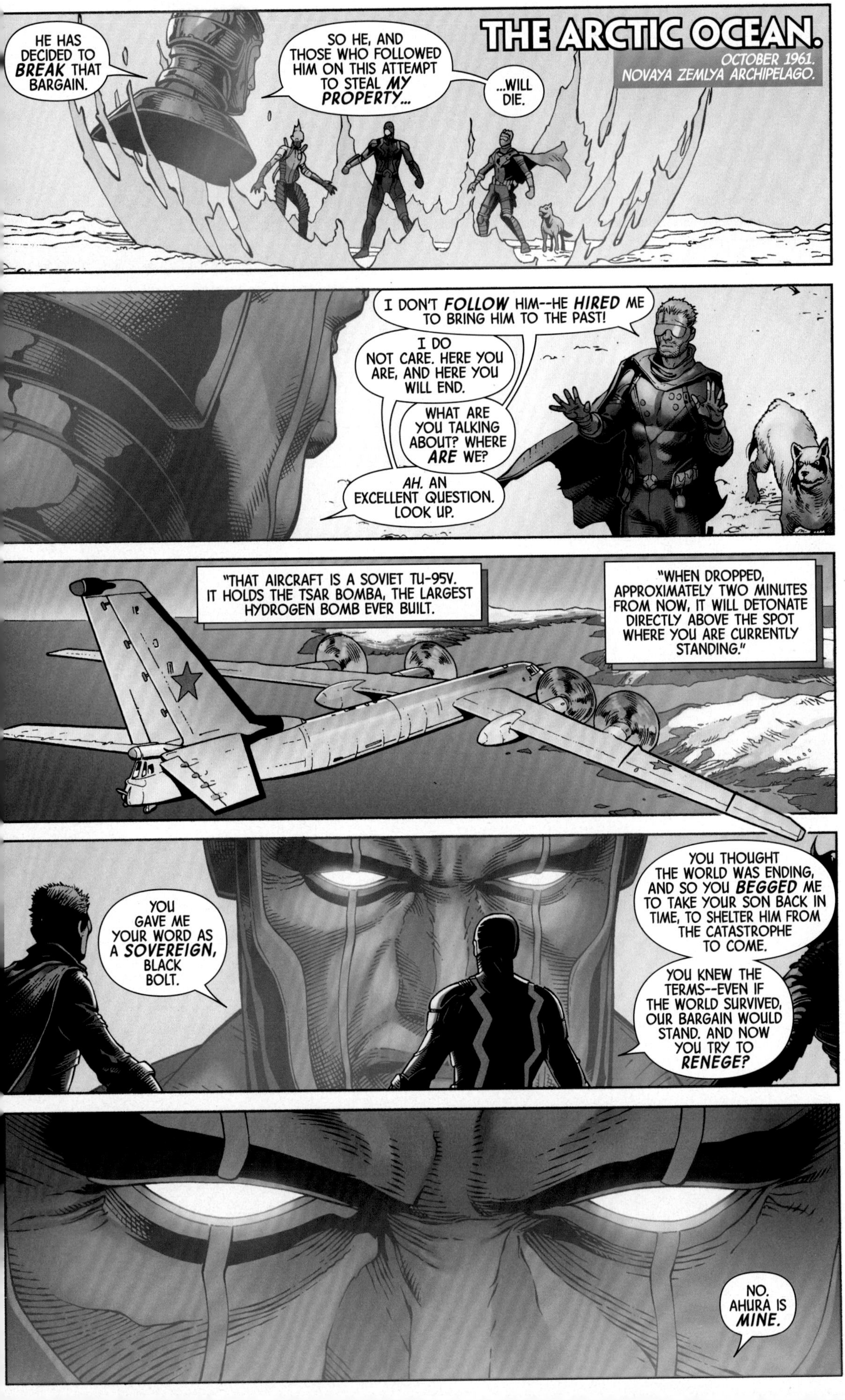
THE ARCTIC OCEAN.
OCTOBER 1961.
NOVAYA ZEMLYA ARCHIPELAGO.
HE HAS DECIDED TO BREAK THAT BARGAIN.
SO HE, AND THOSE WHO FOLLOWED HIM ON THIS ATTEMPT TO STEAL MY PROPERTY...
...WILL DIE.
I DON'T FOLLOW HIM--HE HIRED ME TO BRING HIM TO THE PAST!
I DO NOT CARE. HERE YOU ARE, AND HERE YOU WILL END.
WHAT ARE YOU TALKING ABOUT? WHERE ARE WE?
AH. AN EXCELLENT QUESTION. LOOK UP.
"THAT AIRCRAFT IS A SOVIET TU-95V. IT HOLDS THE TSAR BOMBA, THE LARGEST HYDROGEN BOMB EVER BUILT.
"WHEN DROPPED, APPROXIMATELY TWO MINUTES FROM NOW, IT WILL DETONATE DIRECTLY ABOVE THE SPOT WHERE YOU ARE CURRENTLY STANDING."
YOU GAVE ME YOUR WORD AS A SOVEREIGN, BLACK BOLT.
YOU THOUGHT THE WORLD WAS ENDING, AND SO YOU BEGGED ME TO TAKE YOUR SON BACK IN TIME, TO SHELTER HIM FROM THE CATASTROPHE TO COME.
YOU KNEW THE TERMS--EVEN IF THE WORLD SURVIVED, OUR BARGAIN WOULD STAND. AND NOW YOU TRY TO RENEGE?
NO. AHURA IS MINE.

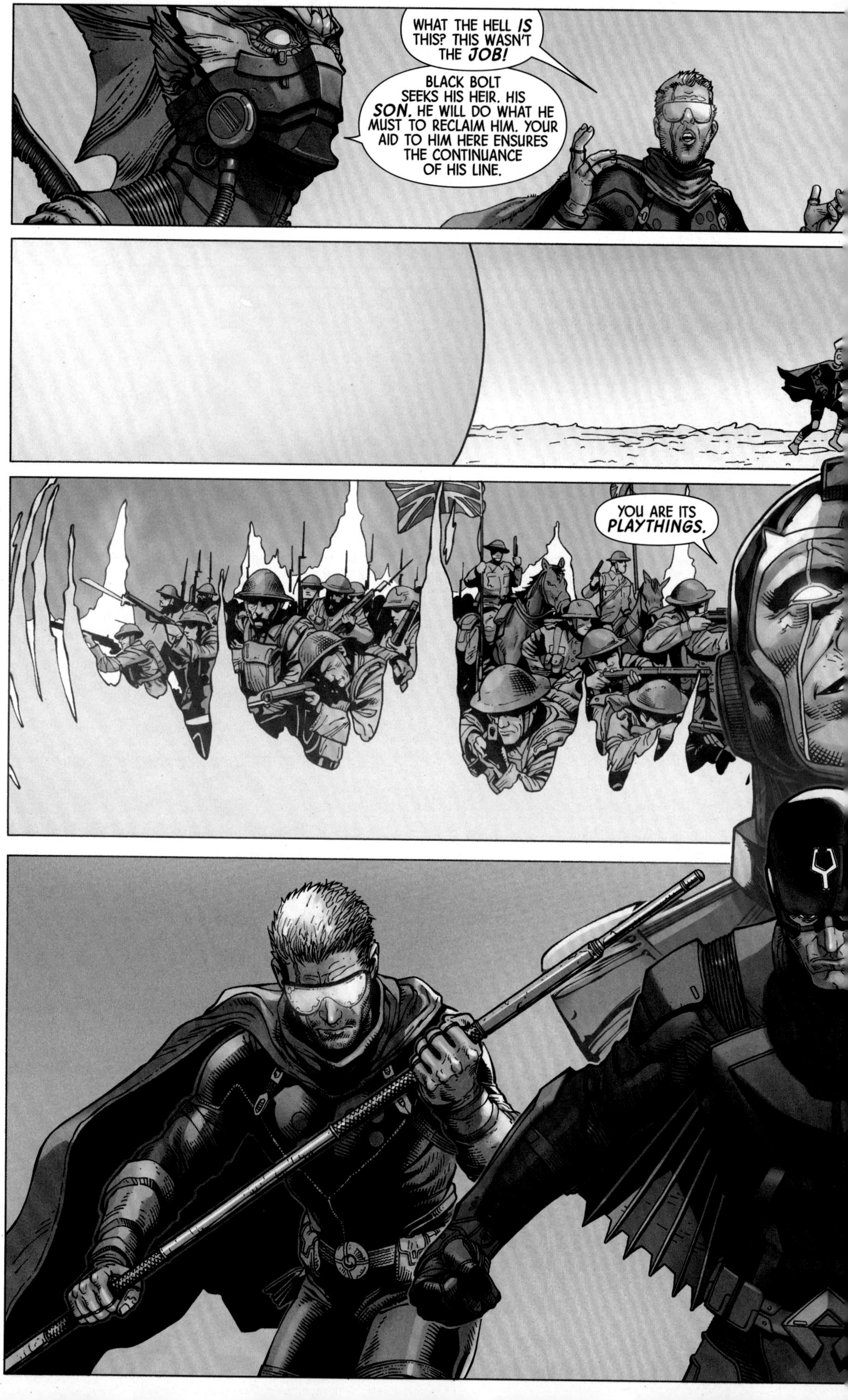
WHAT THE HELL *IS* THIS? THIS WASN'T THE *JOB!*
BLACK BOLT SEEKS HIS HEIR. HIS *SON.* HE WILL DO WHAT HE MUST TO RECLAIM HIM. YOUR AID TO HIM HERE ENSURES THE CONTINUANCE OF HIS LINE.
YOU ARE ITS *PLAYTHINGS.*

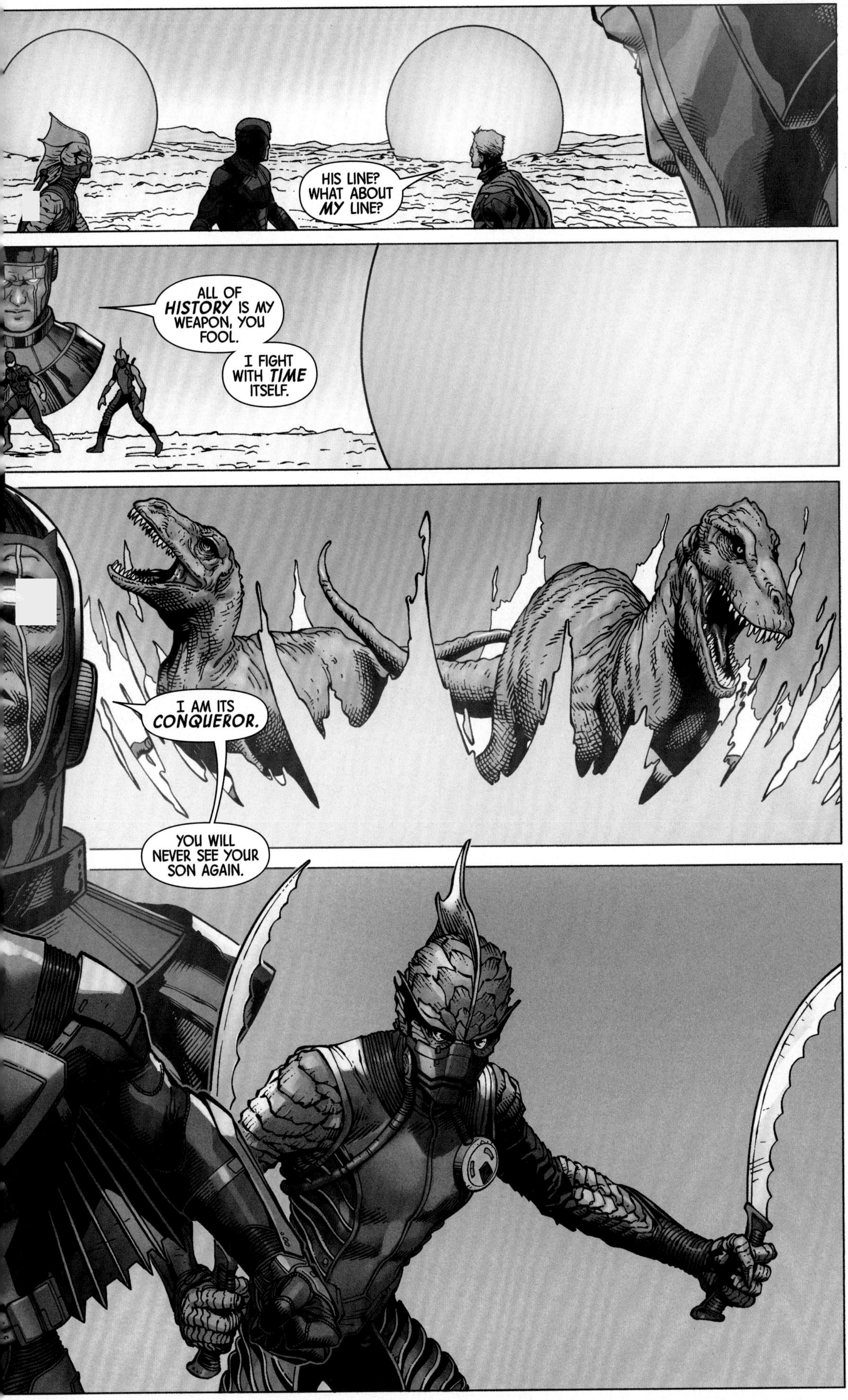
HIS LINE? WHAT ABOUT MY LINE?
ALL OF HISTORY IS MY WEAPON, YOU FOOL.
I FIGHT WITH TIME ITSELF.
I AM ITS CONQUEROR.
YOU WILL NEVER SEE YOUR SON AGAIN.

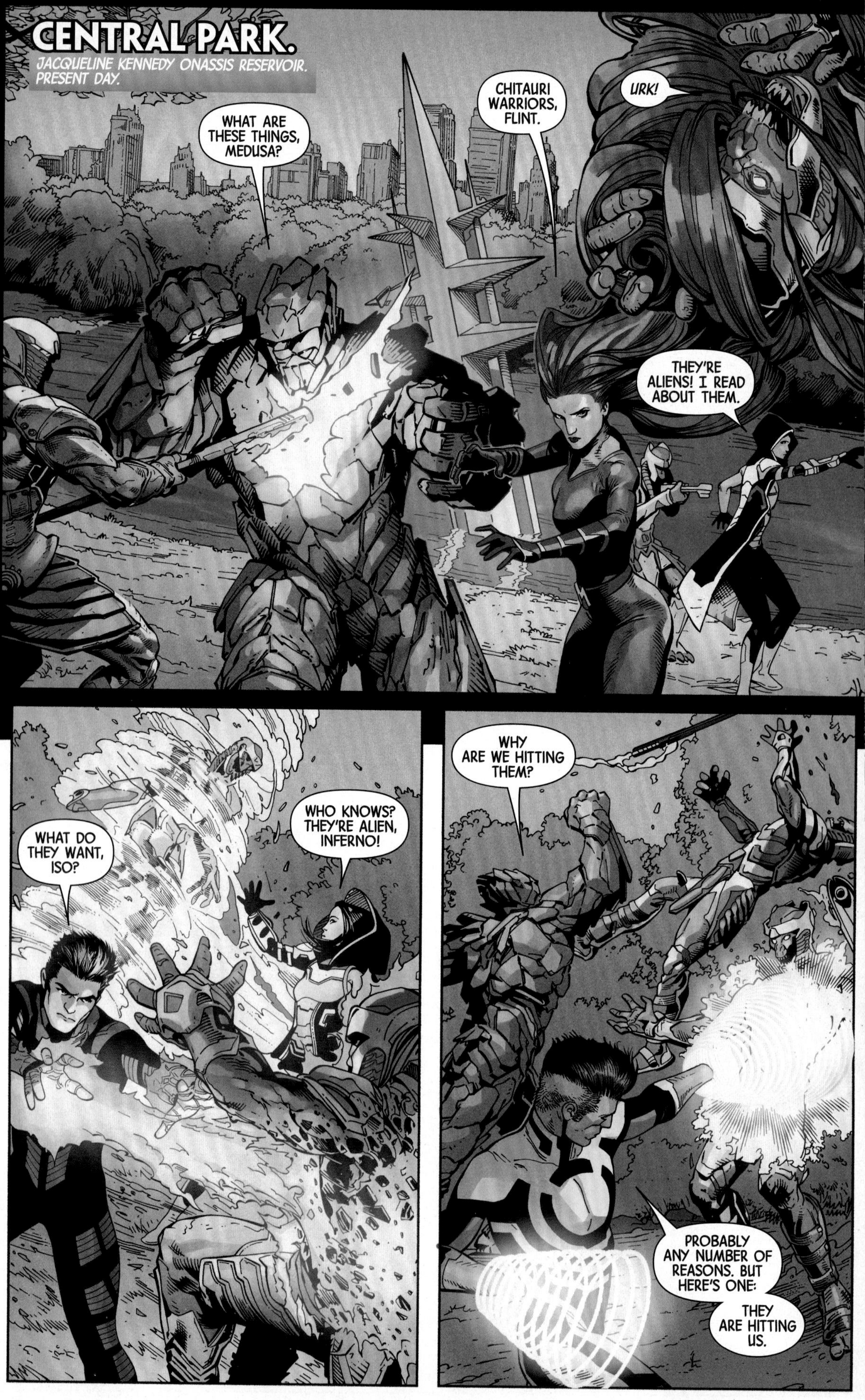
CENTRAL PARK.
JACQUELINE KENNEDY ONASSIS RESERVOIR. PRESENT DAY.
WHAT ARE THESE THINGS, MEDUSA?
CHITAURI WARRIORS, FLINT.
URK!
THEY'RE ALIENS! I READ ABOUT THEM.
WHAT DO THEY WANT, ISO?
WHO KNOWS? THEY'RE ALIEN, INFERNO!
WHY ARE WE HITTING THEM?
PROBABLY ANY NUMBER OF REASONS. BUT HERE'S ONE:
THEY ARE HITTING US.

I HOPE THERE'S MORE TO IT THAN THAT, GRID.

THERE IS. THEY WERE AFTER THE SKYSPEAR. WE'LL SEE MORE OF THIS, I THINK.

BUT FOR RIGHT NOW-- ALL OF YOU-- GAME FACES.

WE HAVE COMPANY.

THE CRISIS HAS PASSED. THE CHITAURI CREATURES WILL TROUBLE YOUR CITY NO LONGER.

QUEEN MEDUSA! ONE QUESTION!

YOU HAVE YOUR OWN CITY--NEW ATTILAN. WHY WOULD YOU PUT YOUR INHUMANS IN DANGER TO PROTECT NEW YORK?

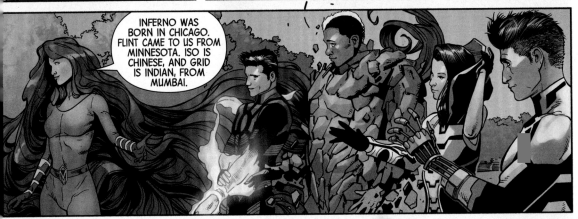

INFERNO WAS BORN IN CHICAGO. FLINT CAME TO US FROM MINNESOTA. ISO IS CHINESE, AND GRID IS INDIAN, FROM MUMBAI.

YOUR WORLD IS OUR WORLD.

WE WILL ALWAYS FIGHT TO KEEP IT SAFE.

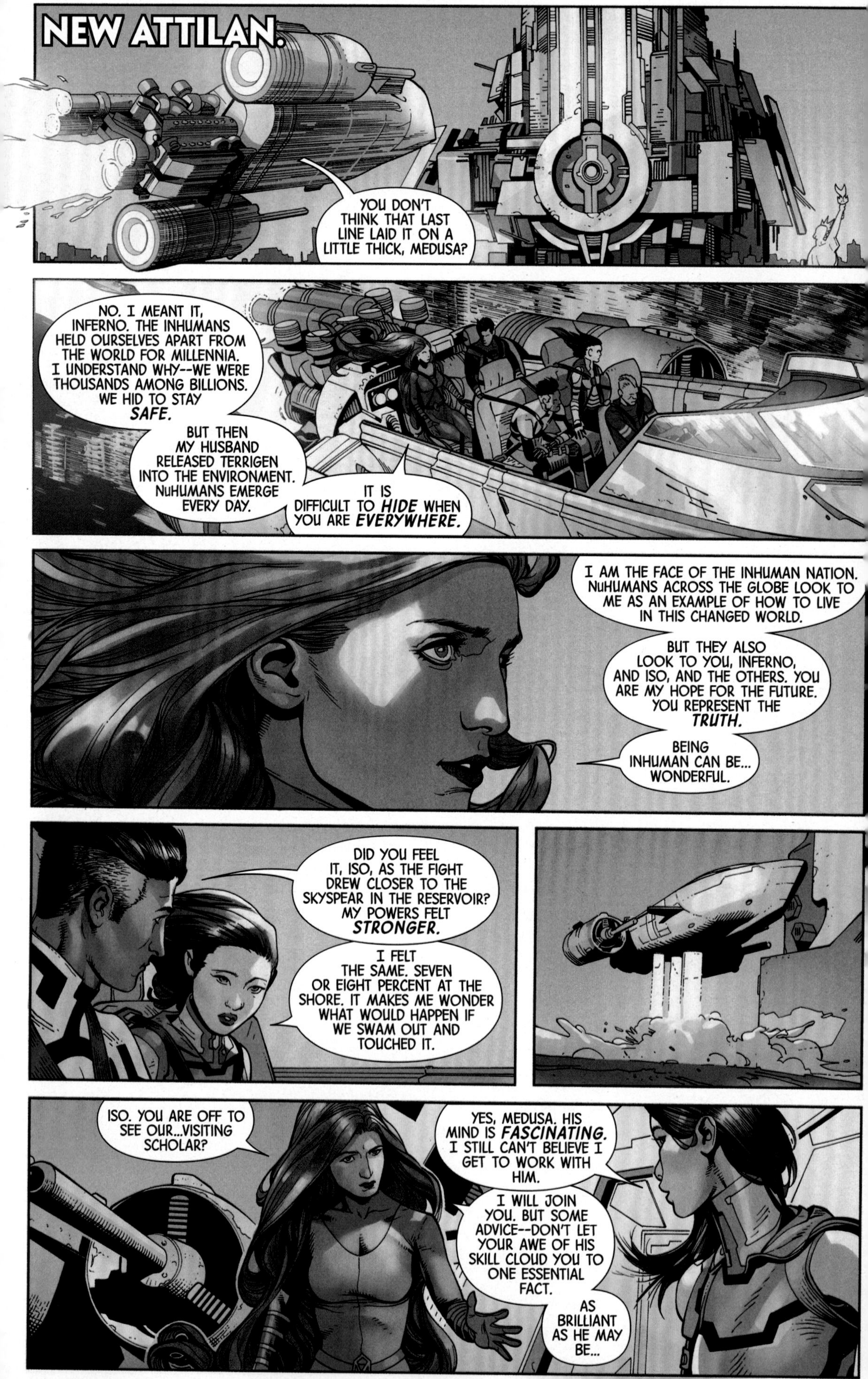
NEW ATTILAN.
YOU DON'T THINK THAT LAST LINE LAID IT ON A LITTLE THICK, MEDUSA?
NO. I MEANT IT, INFERNO. THE INHUMANS HELD OURSELVES APART FROM THE WORLD FOR MILLENNIA. I UNDERSTAND WHY--WE WERE THOUSANDS AMONG BILLIONS. WE HID TO STAY SAFE.
BUT THEN MY HUSBAND RELEASED TERRIGEN INTO THE ENVIRONMENT. NuHUMANS EMERGE EVERY DAY.
IT IS DIFFICULT TO HIDE WHEN YOU ARE EVERYWHERE.
I AM THE FACE OF THE INHUMAN NATION. NuHUMANS ACROSS THE GLOBE LOOK TO ME AS AN EXAMPLE OF HOW TO LIVE IN THIS CHANGED WORLD.
BUT THEY ALSO LOOK TO YOU, INFERNO, AND ISO, AND THE OTHERS. YOU ARE MY HOPE FOR THE FUTURE. YOU REPRESENT THE TRUTH.
BEING INHUMAN CAN BE... WONDERFUL.
DID YOU FEEL IT, ISO, AS THE FIGHT DREW CLOSER TO THE SKYSPEAR IN THE RESERVOIR? MY POWERS FELT STRONGER.
I FELT THE SAME. SEVEN OR EIGHT PERCENT AT THE SHORE. IT MAKES ME WONDER WHAT WOULD HAPPEN IF WE SWAM OUT AND TOUCHED IT.
ISO. YOU ARE OFF TO SEE OUR...VISITING SCHOLAR?
YES, MEDUSA. HIS MIND IS FASCINATING. I STILL CAN'T BELIEVE I GET TO WORK WITH HIM.
I WILL JOIN YOU. BUT SOME ADVICE--DON'T LET YOUR AWE OF HIS SKILL CLOUD YOU TO ONE ESSENTIAL FACT.
AS BRILLIANT AS HE MAY BE...

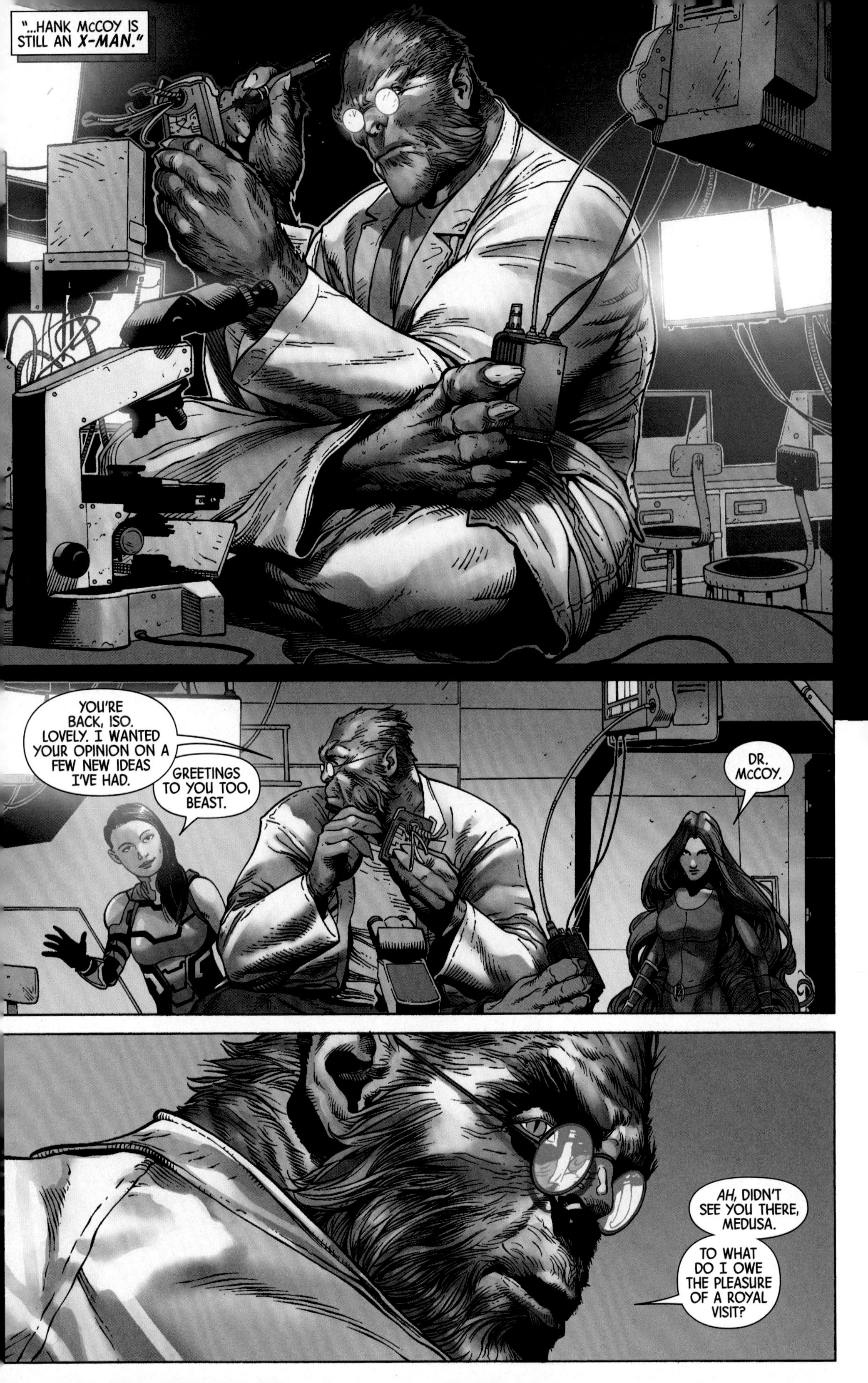
"...HANK McCOY IS STILL AN X-MAN."
YOU'RE BACK, ISO. LOVELY. I WANTED YOUR OPINION ON A FEW NEW IDEAS I'VE HAD.
GREETINGS TO YOU TOO, BEAST.
DR. McCOY.
AH, DIDN'T SEE YOU THERE, MEDUSA.
TO WHAT DO I OWE THE PLEASURE OF A ROYAL VISIT?

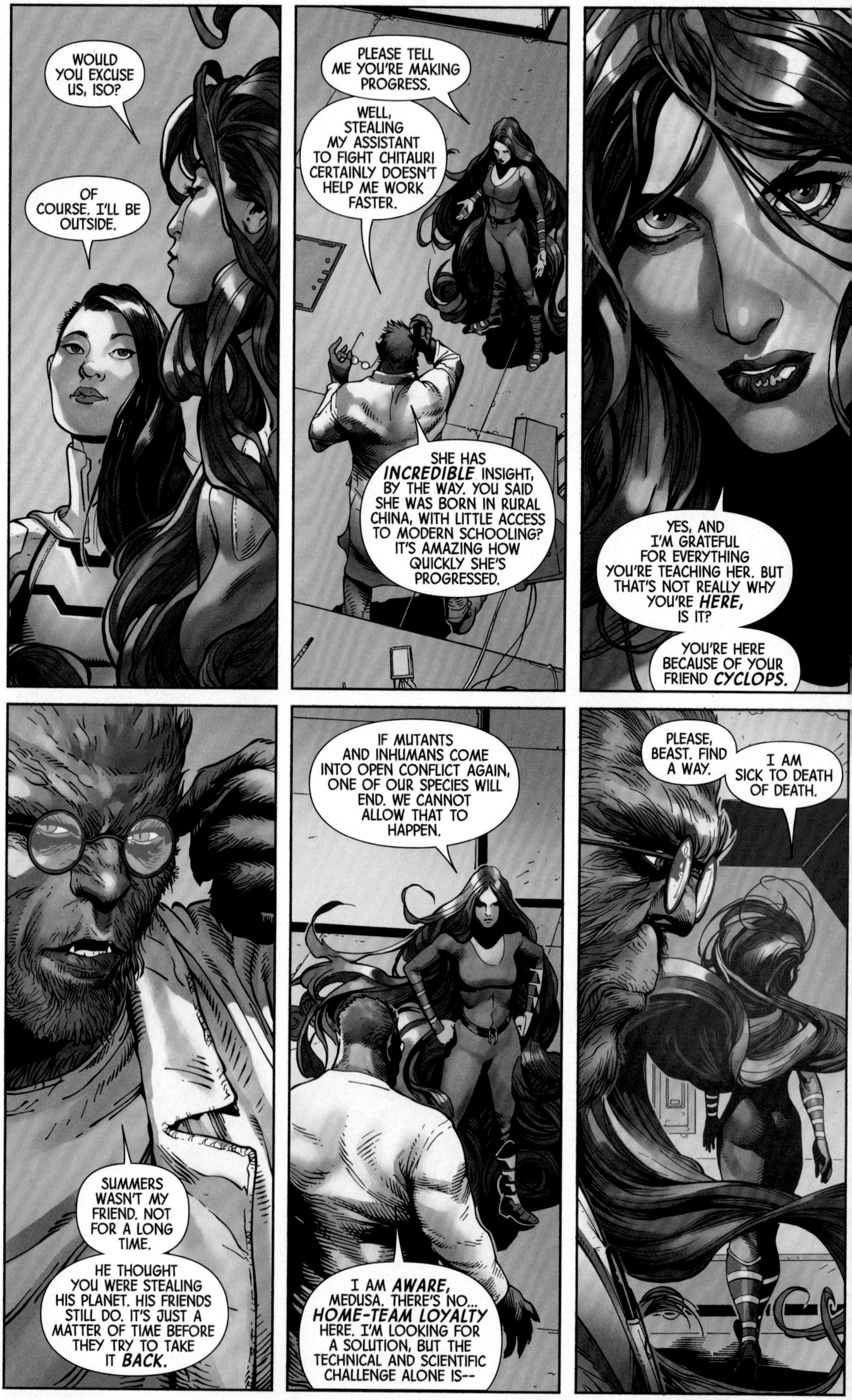
WOULD YOU EXCUSE US, ISO?
OF COURSE. I'LL BE OUTSIDE.
PLEASE TELL ME YOU'RE MAKING PROGRESS.
WELL, STEALING MY ASSISTANT TO FIGHT CHITAURI CERTAINLY DOESN'T HELP ME WORK FASTER.
SHE HAS INCREDIBLE INSIGHT, BY THE WAY. YOU SAID SHE WAS BORN IN RURAL CHINA, WITH LITTLE ACCESS TO MODERN SCHOOLING? IT'S AMAZING HOW QUICKLY SHE'S PROGRESSED.
YES, AND I'M GRATEFUL FOR EVERYTHING YOU'RE TEACHING HER. BUT THAT'S NOT REALLY WHY YOU'RE HERE, IS IT?
YOU'RE HERE BECAUSE OF YOUR FRIEND CYCLOPS.
SUMMERS WASN'T MY FRIEND. NOT FOR A LONG TIME.
HE THOUGHT YOU WERE STEALING HIS PLANET. HIS FRIENDS STILL DO. IT'S JUST A MATTER OF TIME BEFORE THEY TRY TO TAKE IT BACK.
IF MUTANTS AND INHUMANS COME INTO OPEN CONFLICT AGAIN, ONE OF OUR SPECIES WILL END. WE CANNOT ALLOW THAT TO HAPPEN.
I AM AWARE, MEDUSA. THERE'S NO... HOME-TEAM LOYALTY HERE. I'M LOOKING FOR A SOLUTION, BUT THE TECHNICAL AND SCIENTIFIC CHALLENGE ALONE IS--
PLEASE, BEAST. FIND A WAY.
I AM SICK TO DEATH OF DEATH.

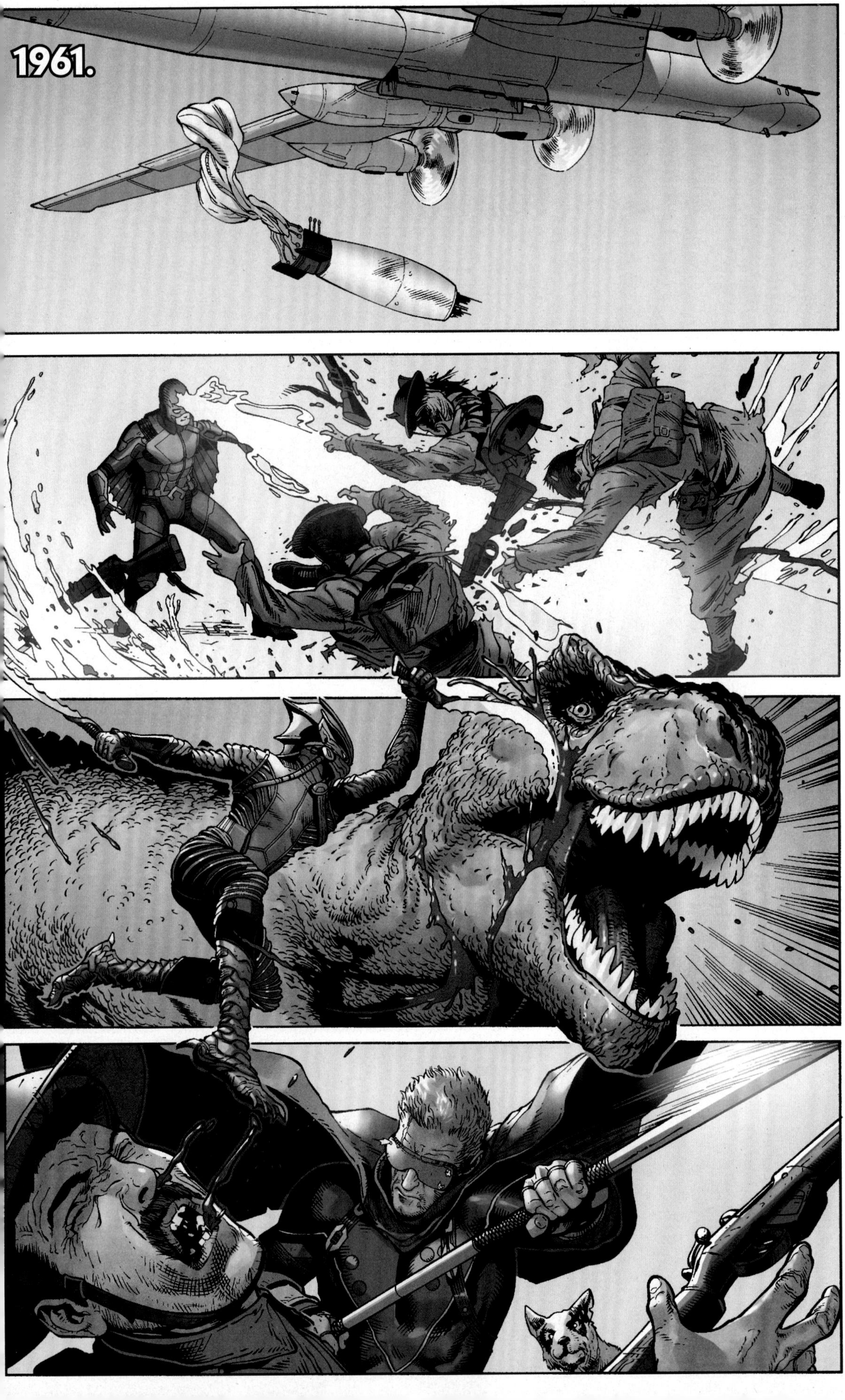
1961.

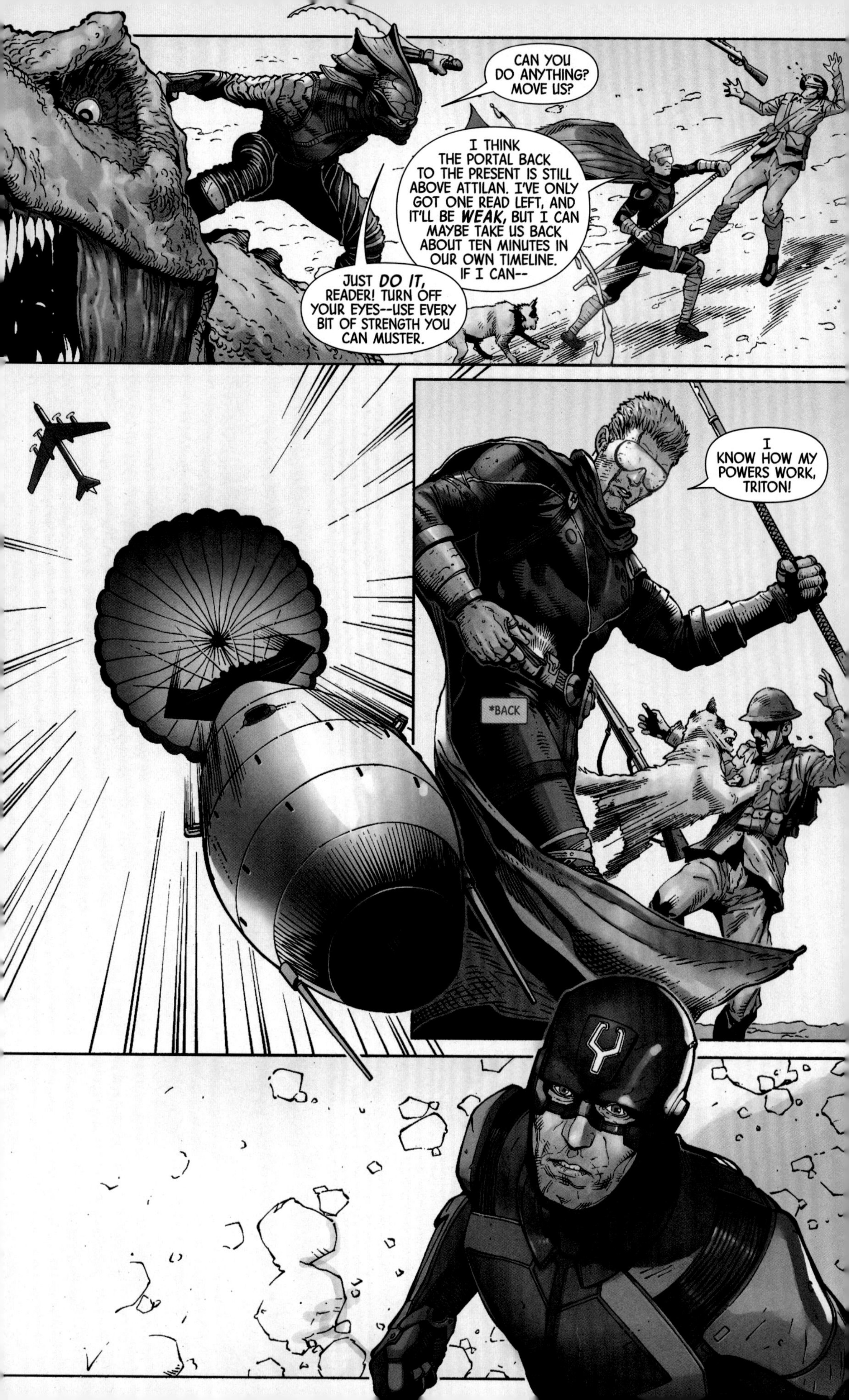
CAN YOU DO ANYTHING? MOVE US?
I THINK THE PORTAL BACK TO THE PRESENT IS STILL ABOVE ATTILAN. I'VE ONLY GOT ONE READ LEFT, AND IT'LL BE WEAK, BUT I CAN MAYBE TAKE US BACK ABOUT TEN MINUTES IN OUR OWN TIMELINE. IF I CAN--
JUST DO IT, READER! TURN OFF YOUR EYES--USE EVERY BIT OF STRENGTH YOU CAN MUSTER.
I KNOW HOW MY POWERS WORK, TRITON!
*BACK

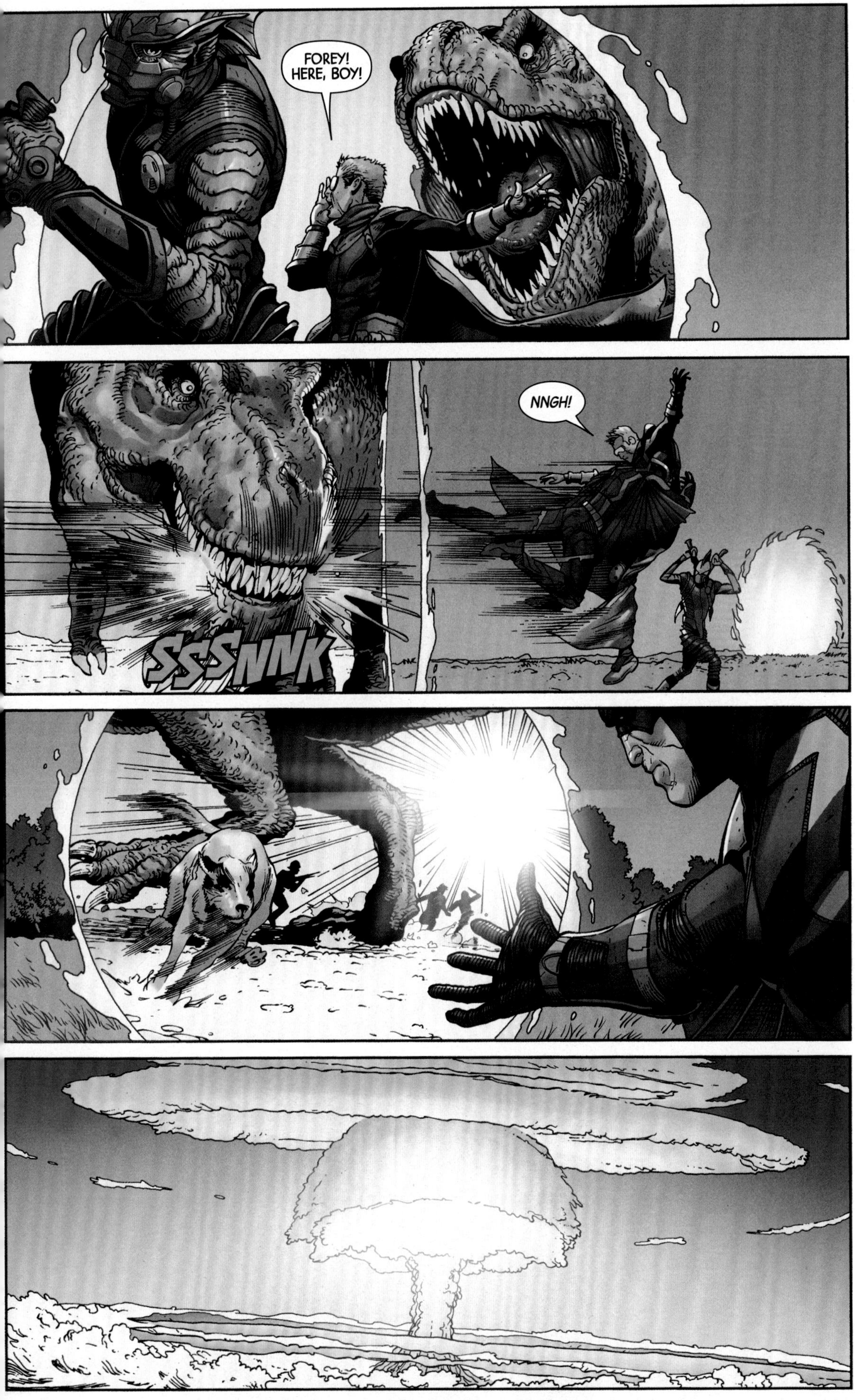
FOREY! HERE, BOY!
NNGH!
SSSNNK

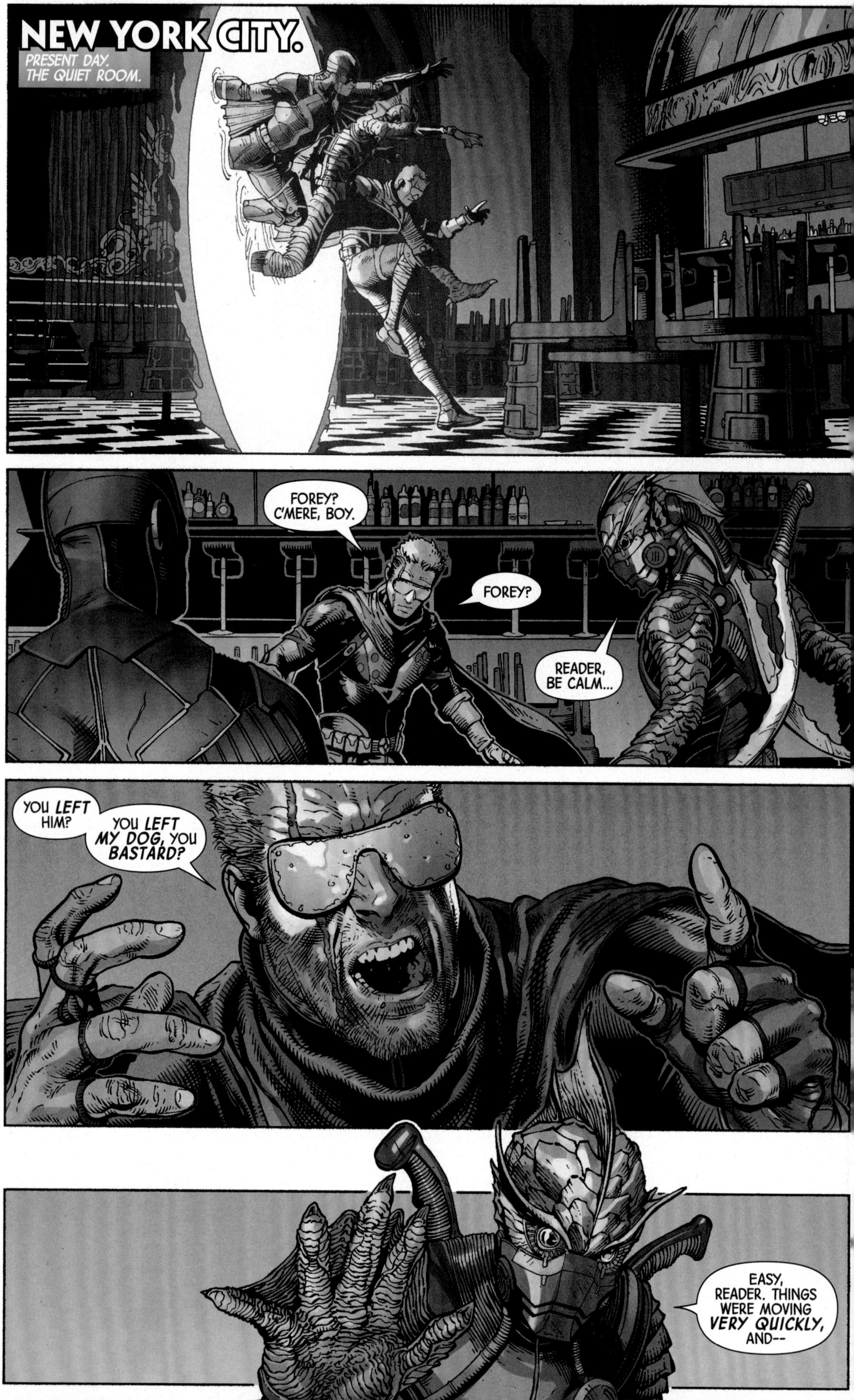
NEW YORK CITY.
PRESENT DAY. THE QUIET ROOM.
FOREY? C'MERE, BOY.
FOREY?
READER, BE CALM...
YOU LEFT HIM?
YOU LEFT MY DOG, YOU BASTARD?
EASY, READER. THINGS WERE MOVING VERY QUICKLY, AND--

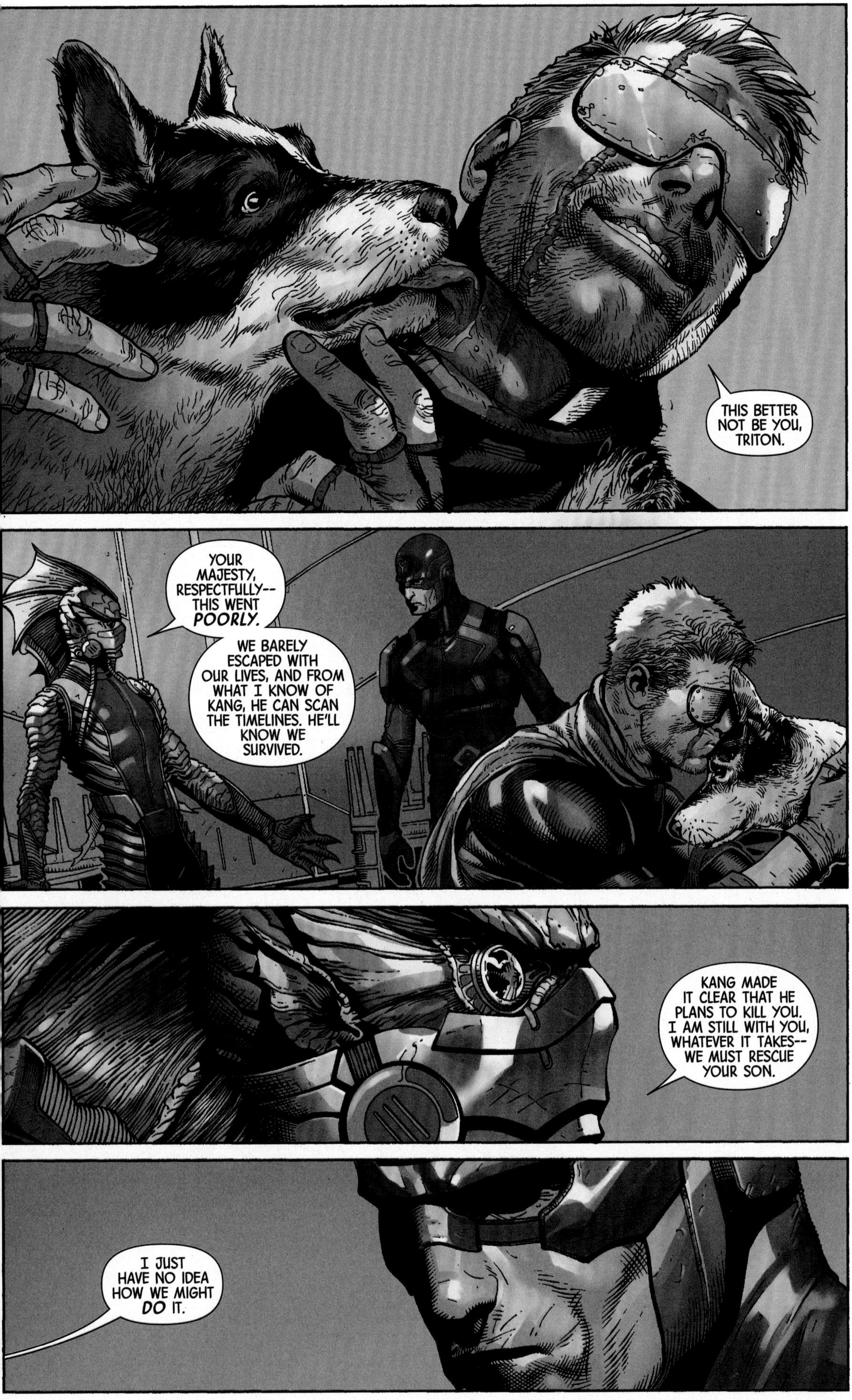
THIS BETTER NOT BE YOU, TRITON.
YOUR MAJESTY, RESPECTFULLY-- THIS WENT POORLY.
WE BARELY ESCAPED WITH OUR LIVES, AND FROM WHAT I KNOW OF KANG, HE CAN SCAN THE TIMELINES. HE'LL KNOW WE SURVIVED.
KANG MADE IT CLEAR THAT HE PLANS TO KILL YOU. I AM STILL WITH YOU, WHATEVER IT TAKES-- WE MUST RESCUE YOUR SON.
I JUST HAVE NO IDEA HOW WE MIGHT DO IT.

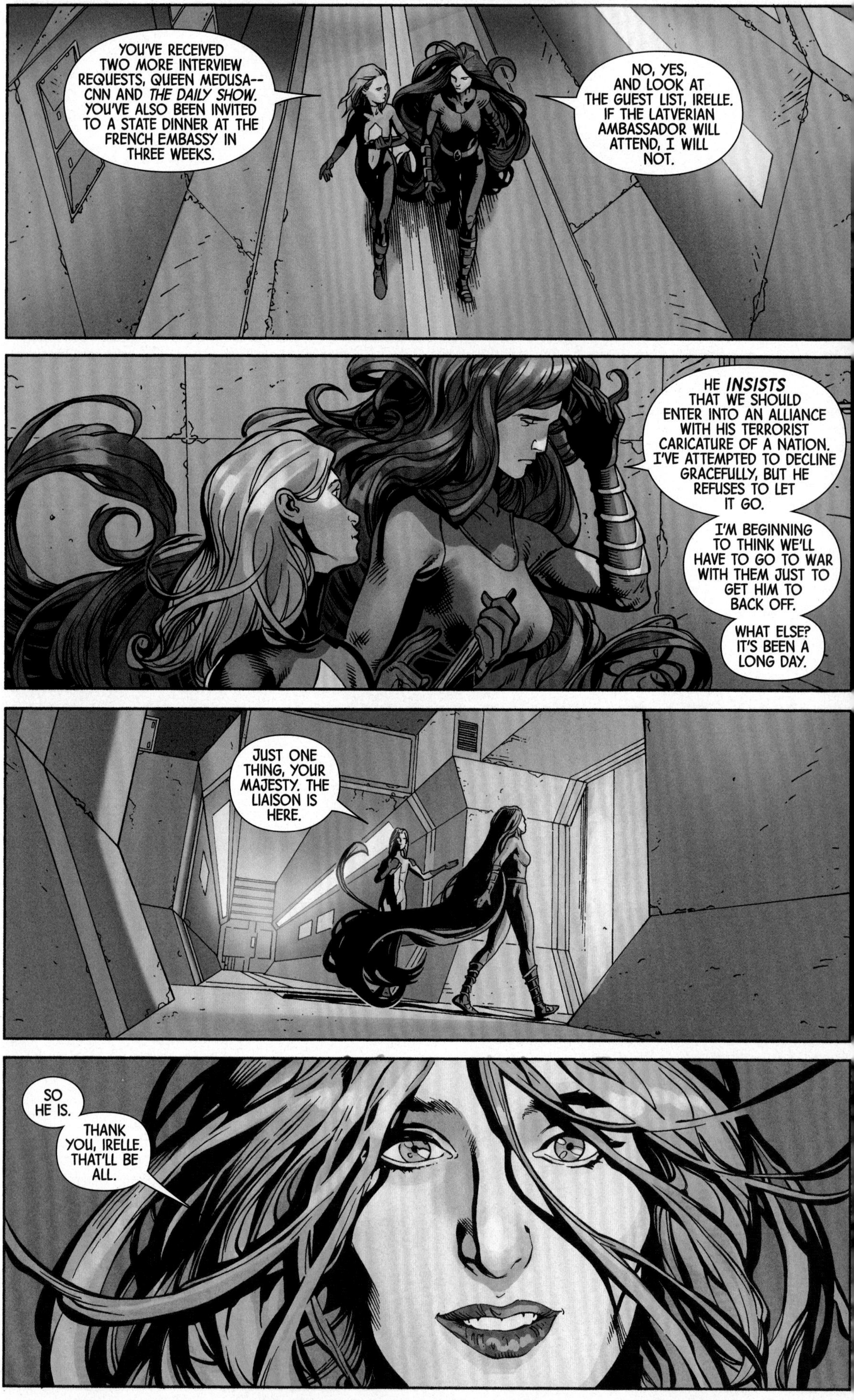
YOU'VE RECEIVED TWO MORE INTERVIEW REQUESTS, QUEEN MEDUSA-- CNN AND *THE DAILY SHOW.* YOU'VE ALSO BEEN INVITED TO A STATE DINNER AT THE FRENCH EMBASSY IN THREE WEEKS.
NO, YES, AND LOOK AT THE GUEST LIST, IRELLE. IF THE LATVERIAN AMBASSADOR WILL ATTEND, I WILL NOT.
HE ***INSISTS*** THAT WE SHOULD ENTER INTO AN ALLIANCE WITH HIS TERRORIST CARICATURE OF A NATION. I'VE ATTEMPTED TO DECLINE GRACEFULLY, BUT HE REFUSES TO LET IT GO.
I'M BEGINNING TO THINK WE'LL HAVE TO GO TO WAR WITH THEM JUST TO GET HIM TO BACK OFF.
WHAT ELSE? IT'S BEEN A LONG DAY.
JUST ONE THING, YOUR MAJESTY. THE LIAISON IS HERE.
SO HE IS.
THANK YOU, IRELLE. THAT'LL BE ALL.

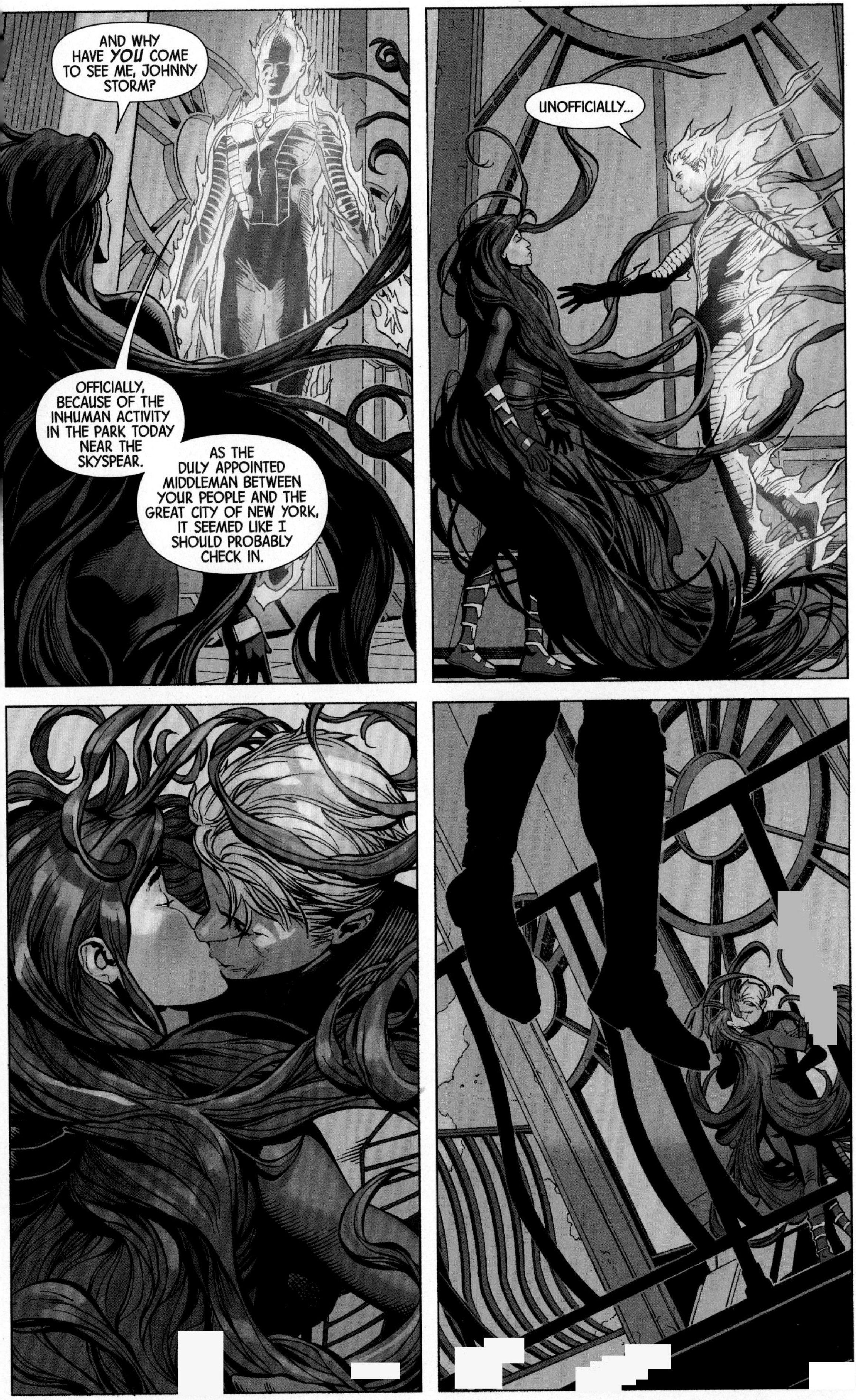
AND WHY HAVE YOU COME TO SEE ME, JOHNNY STORM?
OFFICIALLY, BECAUSE OF THE INHUMAN ACTIVITY IN THE PARK TODAY NEAR THE SKYSPEAR.
AS THE DULY APPOINTED MIDDLEMAN BETWEEN YOUR PEOPLE AND THE GREAT CITY OF NEW YORK, IT SEEMED LIKE I SHOULD PROBABLY CHECK IN.
UNOFFICIALLY...

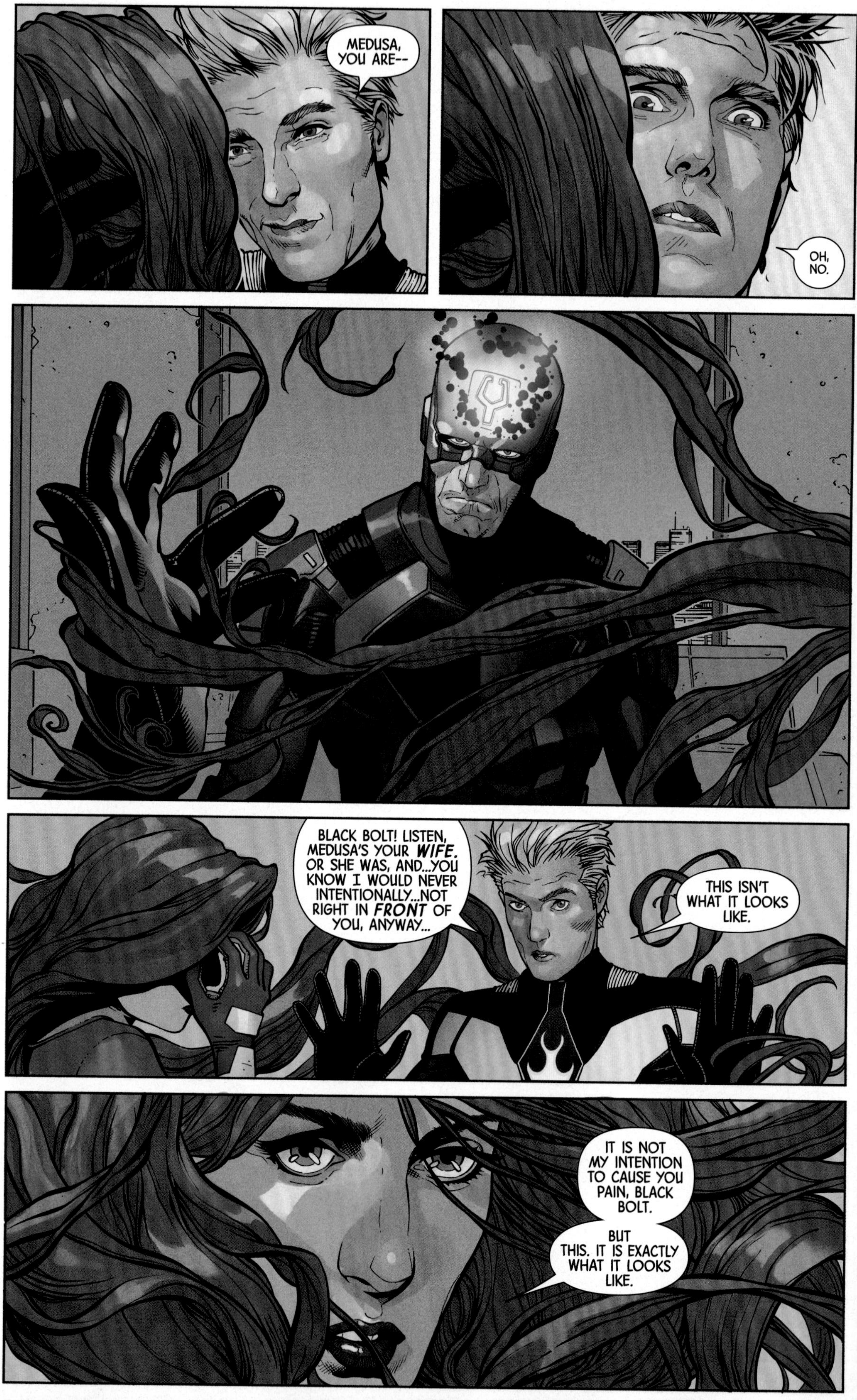
MEDUSA, YOU ARE--
OH, NO.
BLACK BOLT! LISTEN, MEDUSA'S YOUR *WIFE.* OR SHE WAS, AND...YOU KNOW I WOULD NEVER INTENTIONALLY...NOT RIGHT IN *FRONT* OF YOU, ANYWAY...
THIS ISN'T WHAT IT LOOKS LIKE.
IT IS NOT MY INTENTION TO CAUSE YOU PAIN, BLACK BOLT.
BUT THIS. IT IS EXACTLY WHAT IT LOOKS LIKE.

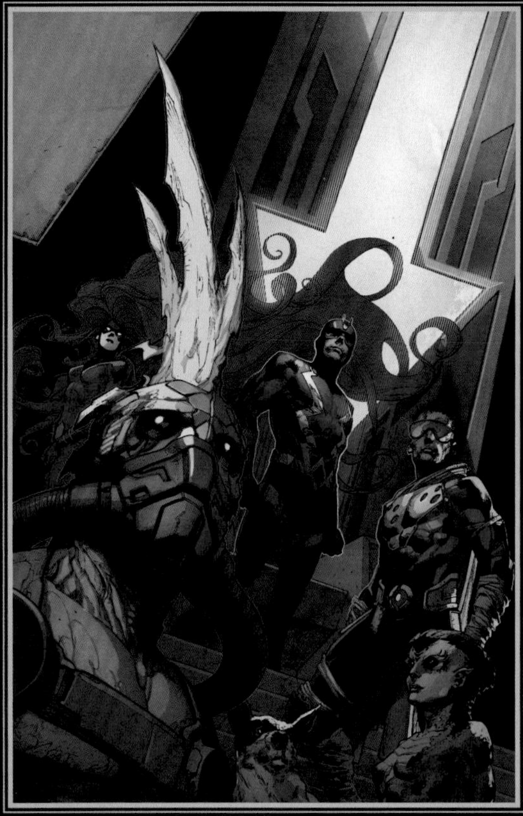

#0 50 YEARS OF INHUMANS VARIANT
BY JEROME OPEÑA & MARTE GRACIA

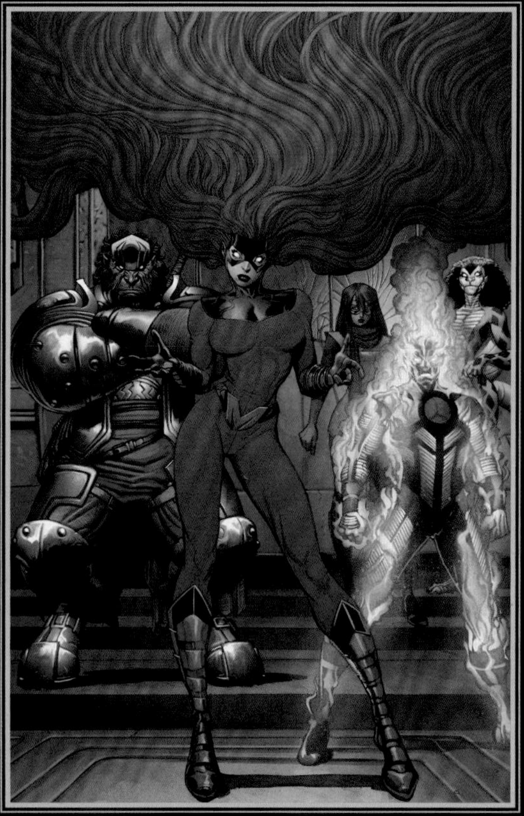

#1 50 YEARS OF INHUMANS VARIANT
BY ART ADAMS & RICHARD ISANOVE

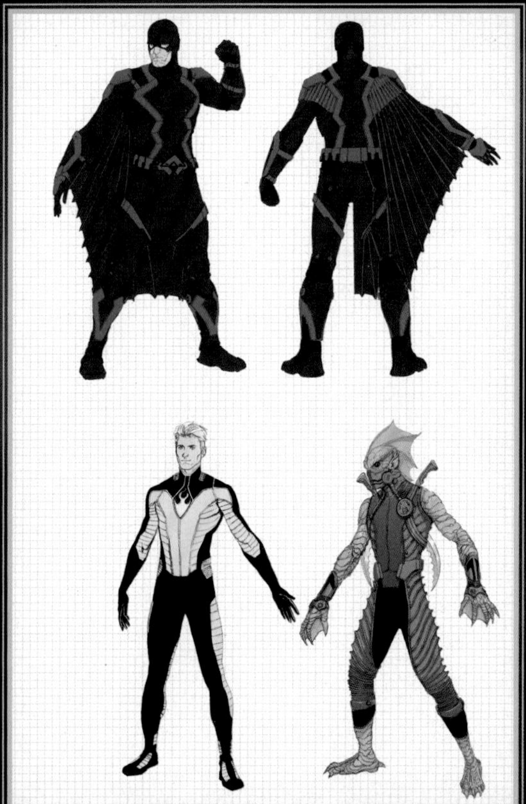

#1 DESIGN VARIANT
BY STEVE MCNIVEN

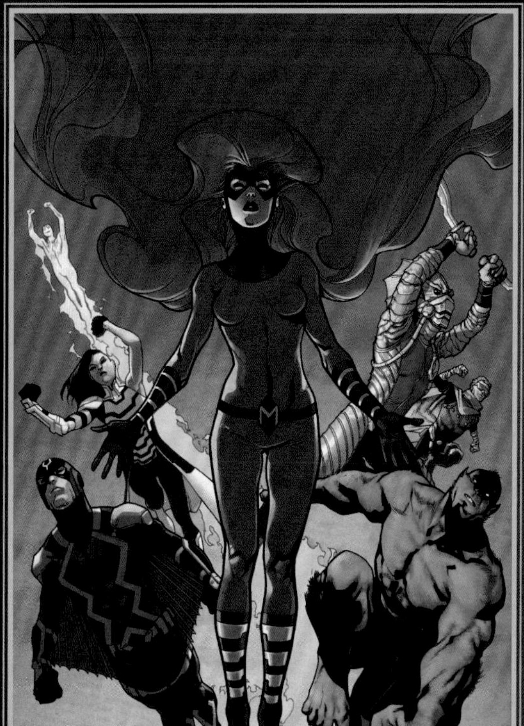

#2 VARIANT
BY MAHMUD ASRAR & NOLAN WOODARD

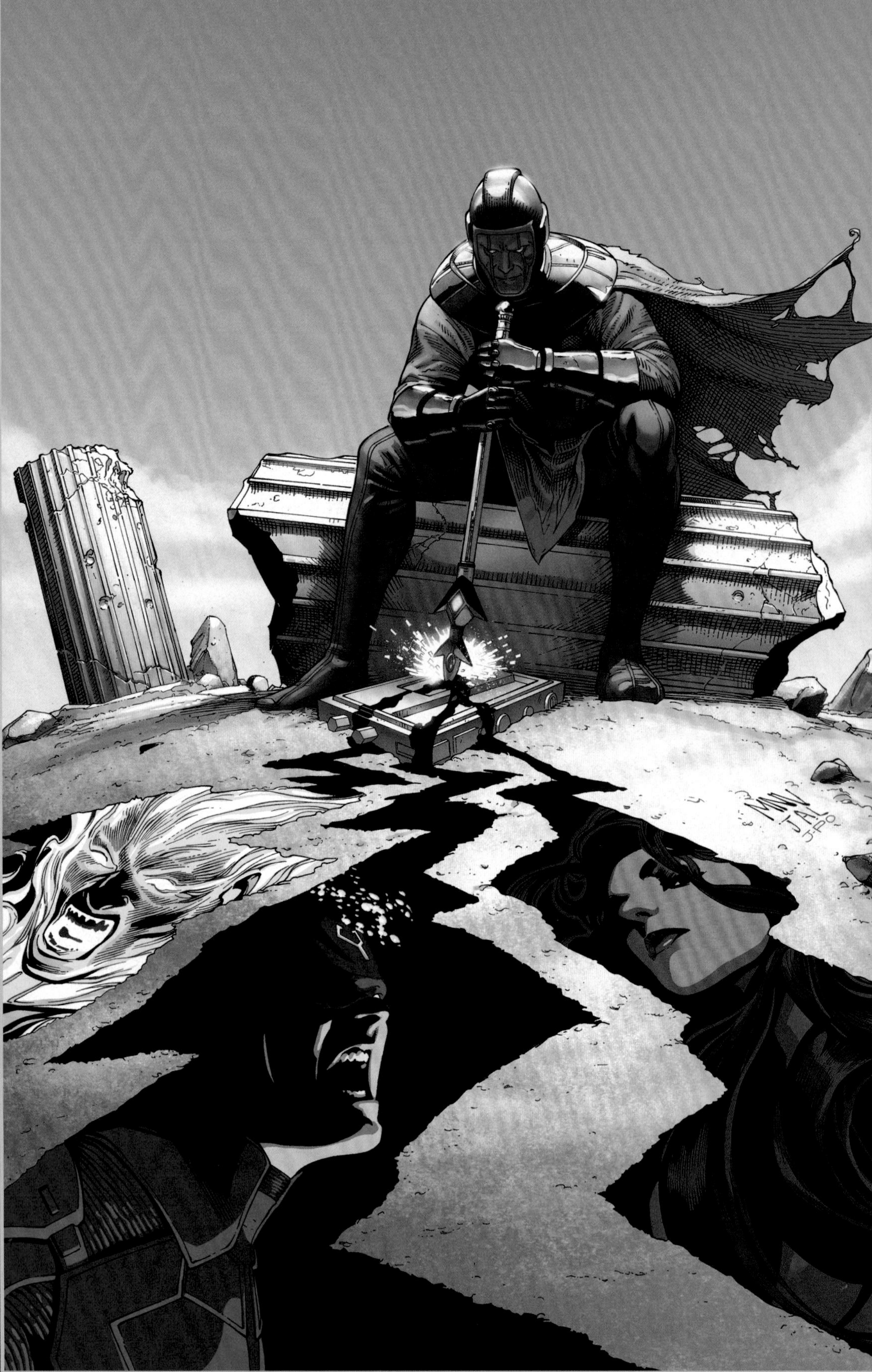

2

JOHNNY, *DON'T!* CALM DOWN.

MEDUSA, YOUR EX-HUSBAND, WHO COULD LITERALLY *CRACK THE MOON IN HALF*, JUST WALKED IN ON YOU AND YOUR NEW BOYFRIEND—WHO IS *ME*—MAKING OUT.

WHY DON'T YOU TELL *HIM* TO CALM DOWN?

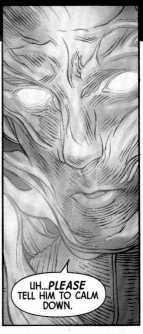

UH...*PLEASE* TELL HIM TO CALM DOWN.

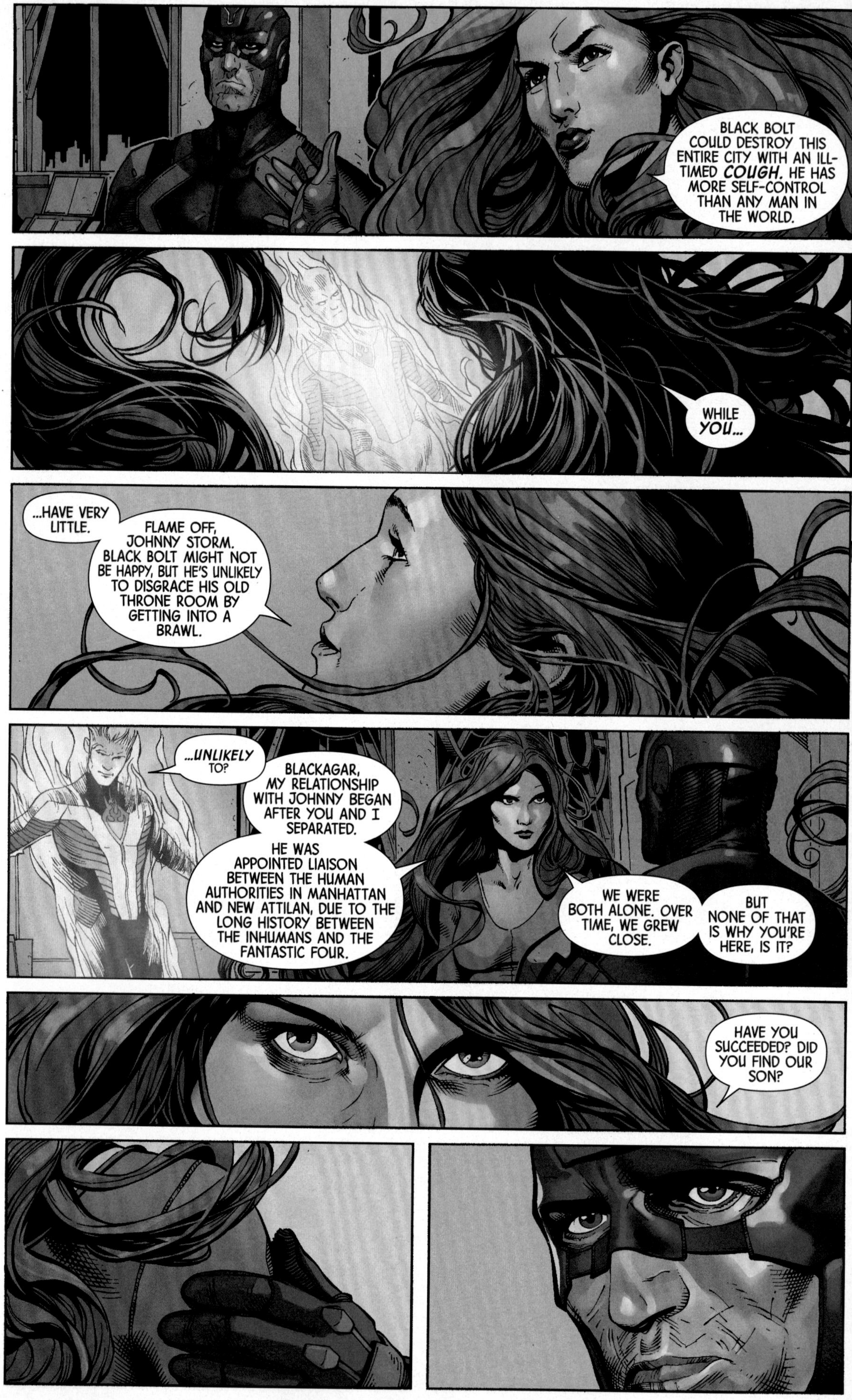
BLACK BOLT COULD DESTROY THIS ENTIRE CITY WITH AN ILL-TIMED COUGH. HE HAS MORE SELF-CONTROL THAN ANY MAN IN THE WORLD.
WHILE YOU...
...HAVE VERY LITTLE.
FLAME OFF, JOHNNY STORM. BLACK BOLT MIGHT NOT BE HAPPY, BUT HE'S UNLIKELY TO DISGRACE HIS OLD THRONE ROOM BY GETTING INTO A BRAWL.
...UNLIKELY TO?
BLACKAGAR, MY RELATIONSHIP WITH JOHNNY BEGAN AFTER YOU AND I SEPARATED.
HE WAS APPOINTED LIAISON BETWEEN THE HUMAN AUTHORITIES IN MANHATTAN AND NEW ATTILAN, DUE TO THE LONG HISTORY BETWEEN THE INHUMANS AND THE FANTASTIC FOUR.
WE WERE BOTH ALONE. OVER TIME, WE GREW CLOSE.
BUT NONE OF THAT IS WHY YOU'RE HERE, IS IT?
HAVE YOU SUCCEEDED? DID YOU FIND OUR SON?

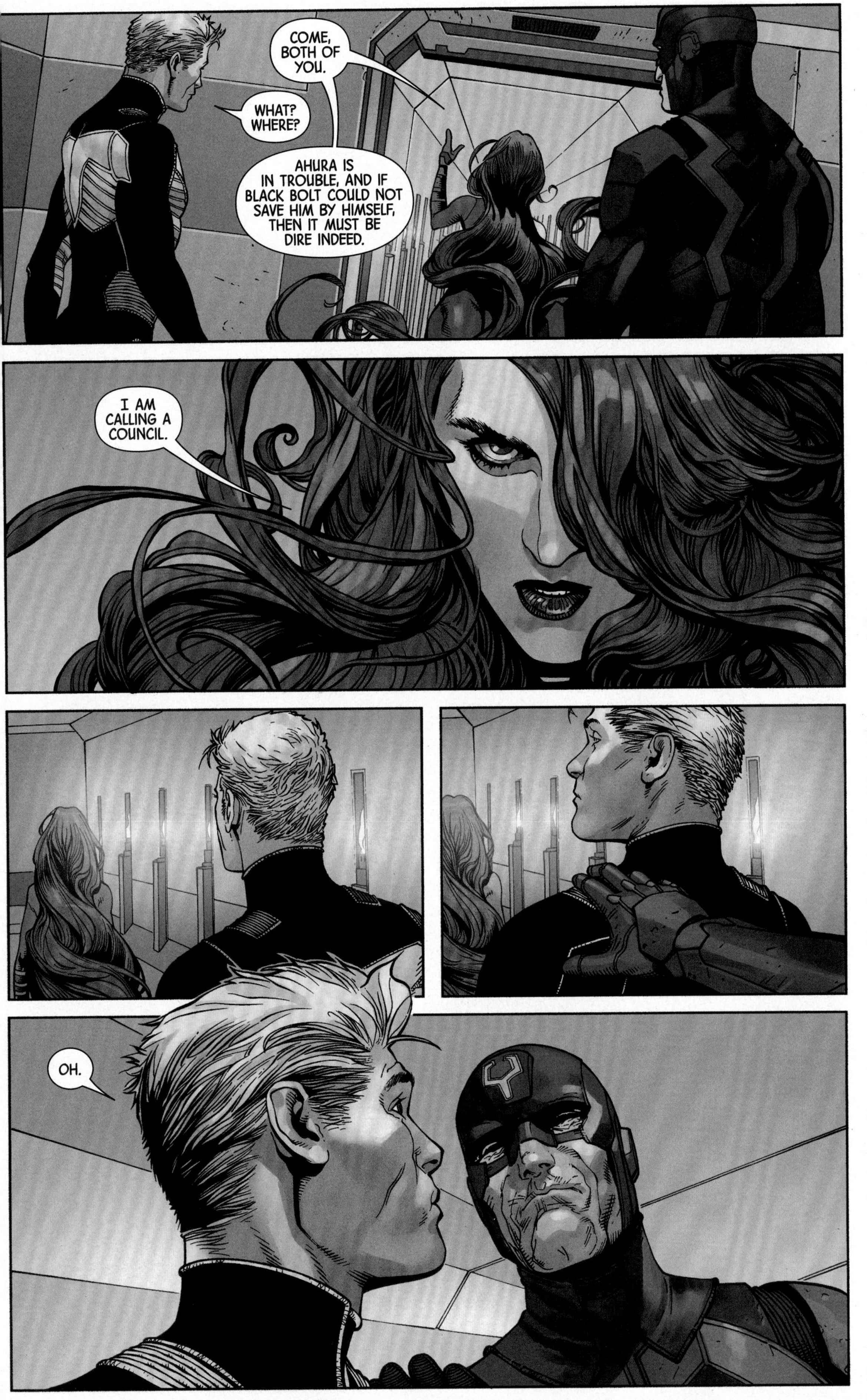
COME, BOTH OF YOU.
WHAT? WHERE?
AHURA IS IN TROUBLE, AND IF BLACK BOLT COULD NOT SAVE HIM BY HIMSELF, THEN IT MUST BE DIRE INDEED.
I AM CALLING A COUNCIL.
OH.

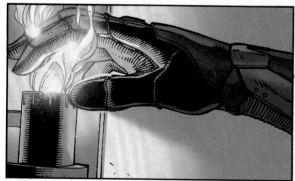

HUH. *THAT* SEEMS PRETTY CLEAR.

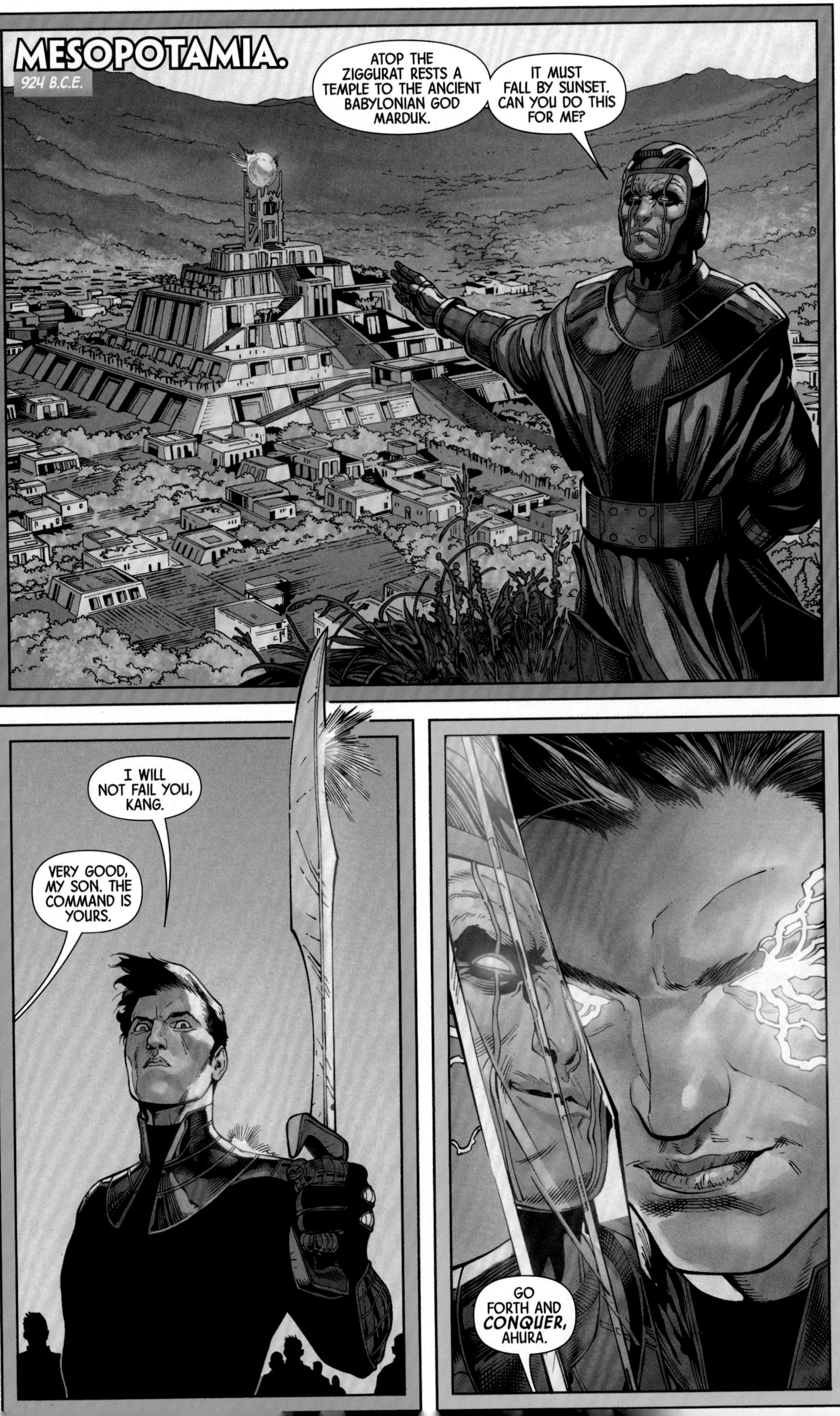
MESOPOTAMIA.
924 B.C.E.
ATOP THE ZIGGURAT RESTS A TEMPLE TO THE ANCIENT BABYLONIAN GOD MARDUK.
IT MUST FALL BY SUNSET. CAN YOU DO THIS FOR ME?
I WILL NOT FAIL YOU, KANG.
VERY GOOD, MY SON. THE COMMAND IS YOURS.
GO FORTH AND CONQUER, AHURA.

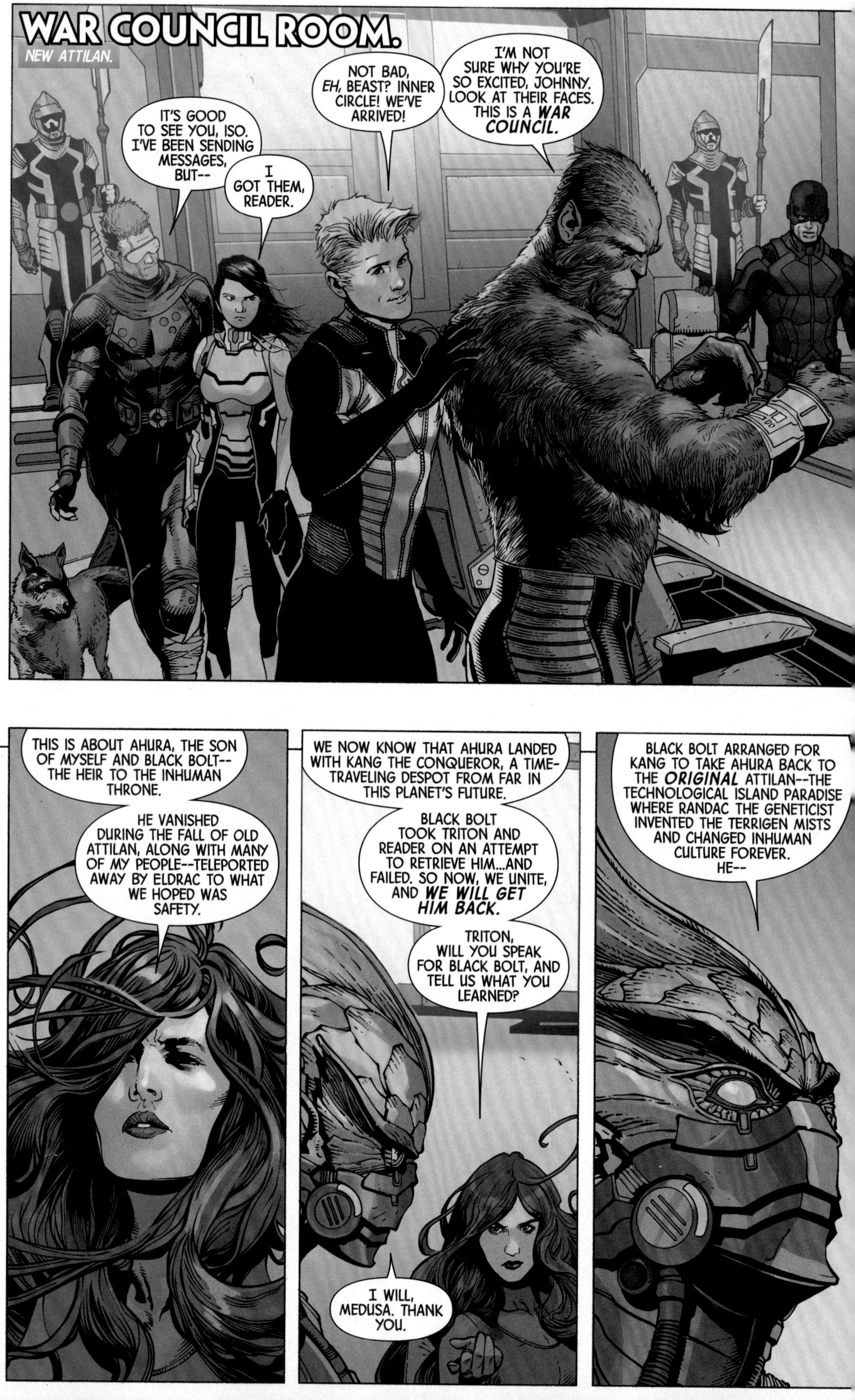

WAR COUNCIL ROOM.
NEW ATTILAN.
IT'S GOOD TO SEE YOU, ISO. I'VE BEEN SENDING MESSAGES, BUT--
I GOT THEM, READER.
NOT BAD, EH, BEAST? INNER CIRCLE! WE'VE ARRIVED!
I'M NOT SURE WHY YOU'RE SO EXCITED, JOHNNY. LOOK AT THEIR FACES. THIS IS A WAR COUNCIL.
THIS IS ABOUT AHURA, THE SON OF MYSELF AND BLACK BOLT-- THE HEIR TO THE INHUMAN THRONE.
HE VANISHED DURING THE FALL OF OLD ATTILAN, ALONG WITH MANY OF MY PEOPLE--TELEPORTED AWAY BY ELDRAC TO WHAT WE HOPED WAS SAFETY.
WE NOW KNOW THAT AHURA LANDED WITH KANG THE CONQUEROR, A TIME-TRAVELING DESPOT FROM FAR IN THIS PLANET'S FUTURE.
BLACK BOLT TOOK TRITON AND READER ON AN ATTEMPT TO RETRIEVE HIM...AND FAILED. SO NOW, WE UNITE, AND WE WILL GET HIM BACK.
TRITON, WILL YOU SPEAK FOR BLACK BOLT, AND TELL US WHAT YOU LEARNED?
I WILL, MEDUSA. THANK YOU.
BLACK BOLT ARRANGED FOR KANG TO TAKE AHURA BACK TO THE ORIGINAL ATTILAN--THE TECHNOLOGICAL ISLAND PARADISE WHERE RANDAC THE GENETICIST INVENTED THE TERRIGEN MISTS AND CHANGED INHUMAN CULTURE FOREVER. HE--

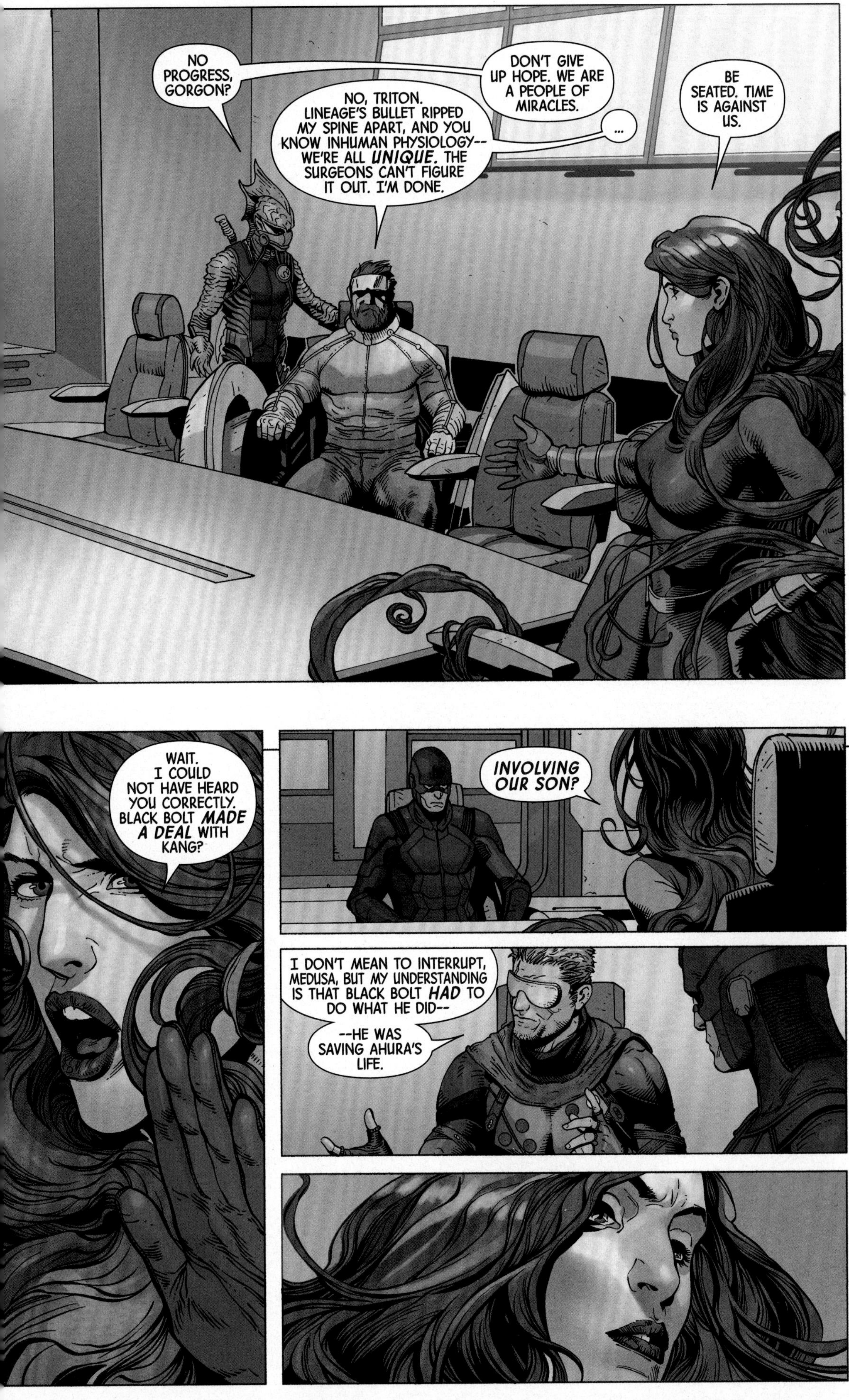
NO PROGRESS, GORGON?
NO, TRITON. LINEAGE'S BULLET RIPPED MY SPINE APART, AND YOU KNOW INHUMAN PHYSIOLOGY-- WE'RE ALL *UNIQUE.* THE SURGEONS CAN'T FIGURE IT OUT. I'M DONE.
DON'T GIVE UP HOPE. WE ARE A PEOPLE OF MIRACLES.
...
BE SEATED. TIME IS AGAINST US.
WAIT. I COULD NOT HAVE HEARD YOU CORRECTLY. BLACK BOLT *MADE A DEAL* WITH KANG?
INVOLVING OUR SON?
I DON'T MEAN TO INTERRUPT, MEDUSA, BUT MY UNDERSTANDING IS THAT BLACK BOLT *HAD* TO DO WHAT HE DID--
--HE WAS SAVING AHURA'S LIFE.

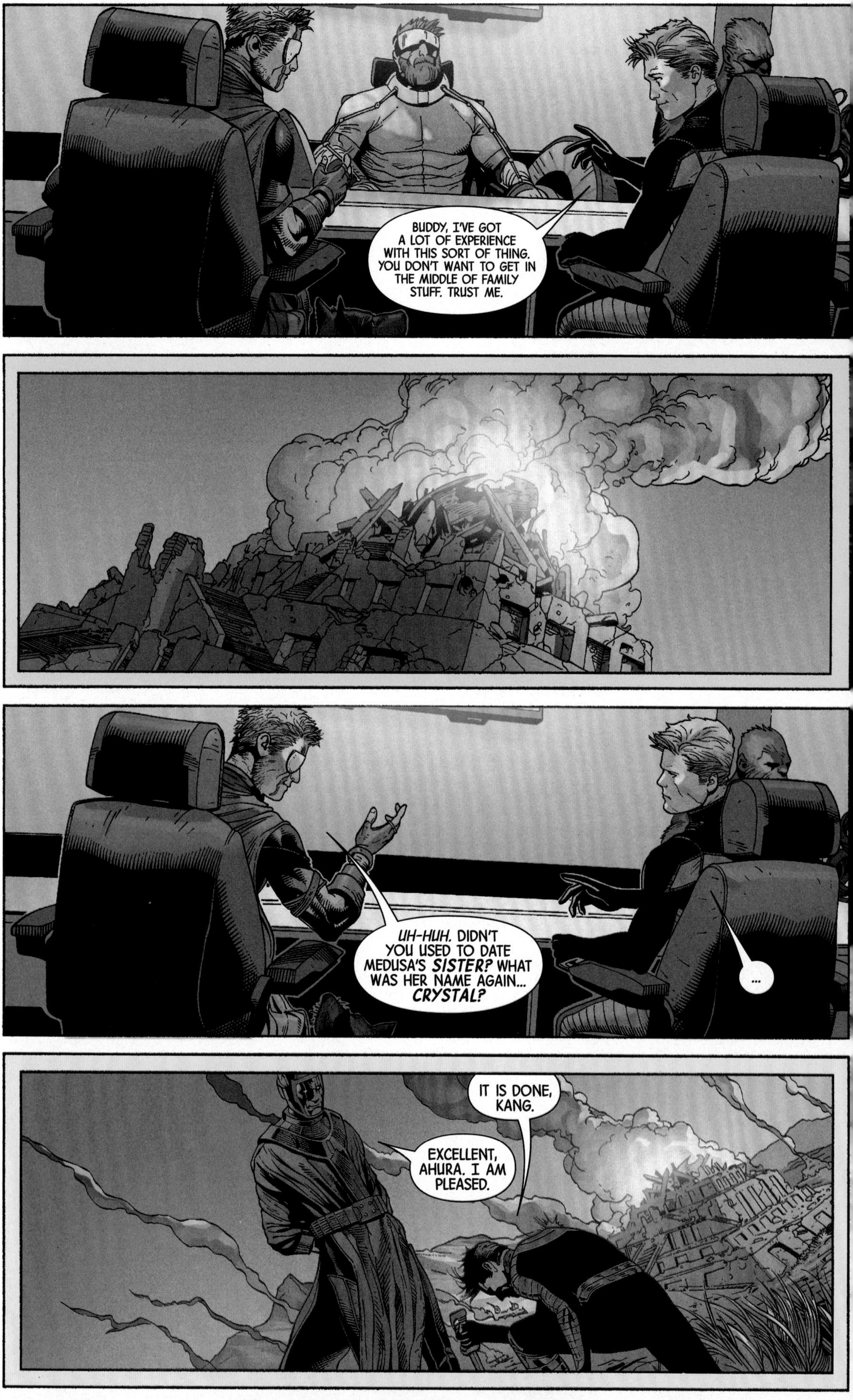
BUDDY, I'VE GOT A LOT OF EXPERIENCE WITH THIS SORT OF THING. YOU DON'T WANT TO GET IN THE MIDDLE OF FAMILY STUFF. TRUST ME.
UH-HUH. DIDN'T YOU USED TO DATE MEDUSA'S SISTER? WHAT WAS HER NAME AGAIN... CRYSTAL?
...
IT IS DONE, KANG.
EXCELLENT, AHURA. I AM PLEASED.

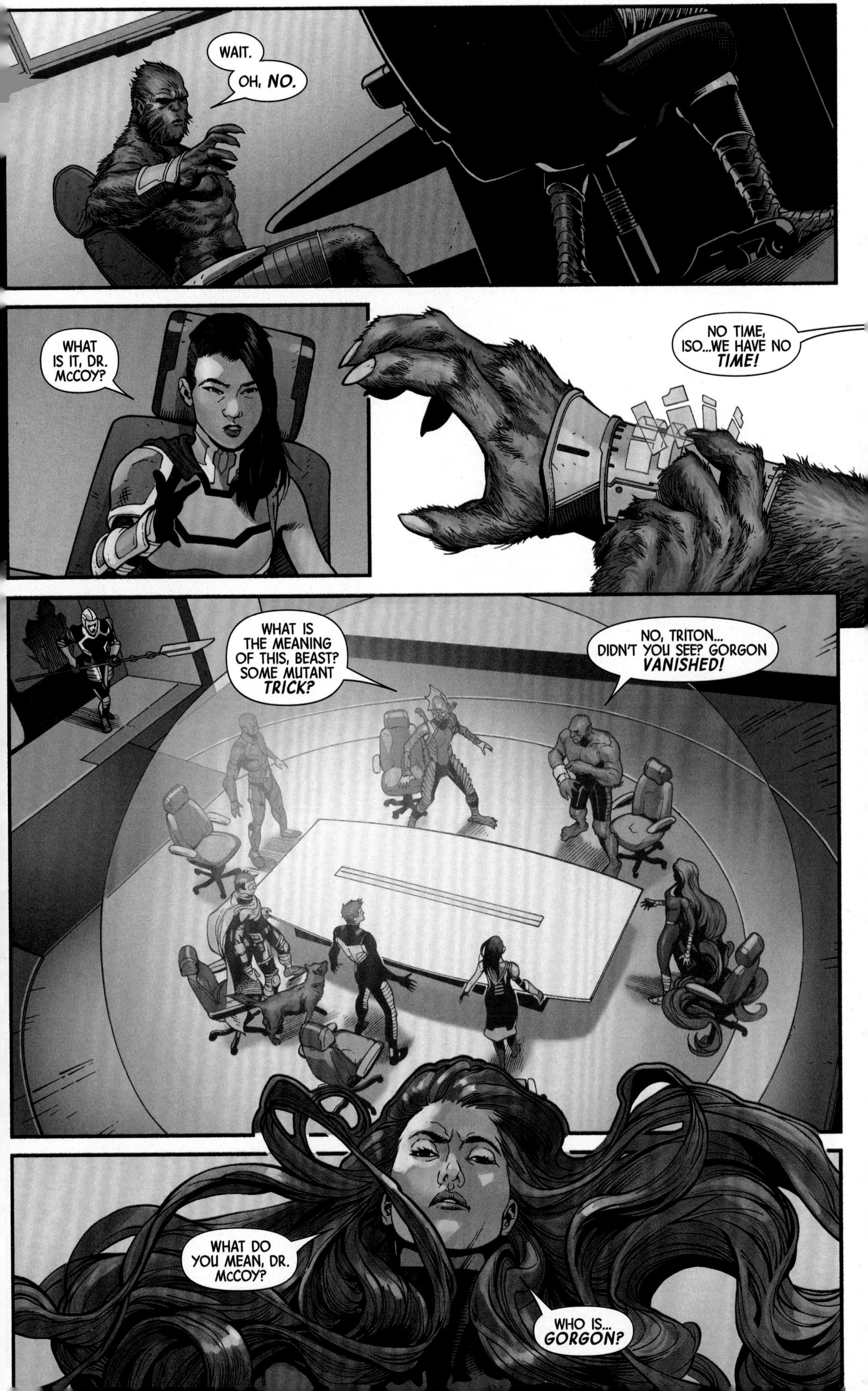
WAIT.
OH, NO.
WHAT IS IT, DR. McCOY?
NO TIME, ISO...WE HAVE NO TIME!
WHAT IS THE MEANING OF THIS, BEAST? SOME MUTANT TRICK?
NO, TRITON... DIDN'T YOU SEE? GORGON VANISHED!
WHAT DO YOU MEAN, DR. McCOY?
WHO IS... GORGON?

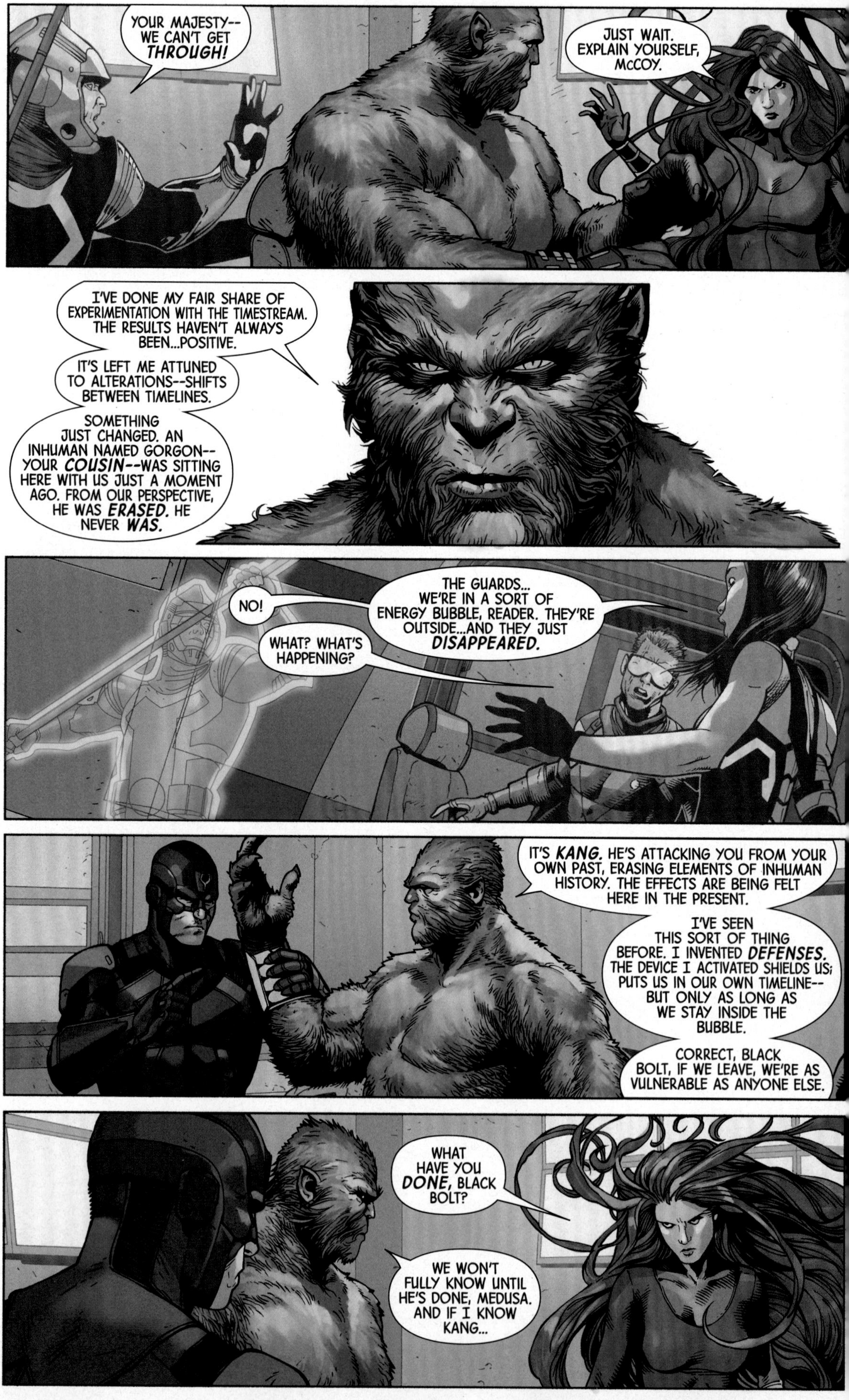
YOUR MAJESTY-- WE CAN'T GET THROUGH!
JUST WAIT. EXPLAIN YOURSELF, McCOY.
I'VE DONE MY FAIR SHARE OF EXPERIMENTATION WITH THE TIMESTREAM. THE RESULTS HAVEN'T ALWAYS BEEN...POSITIVE.
IT'S LEFT ME ATTUNED TO ALTERATIONS--SHIFTS BETWEEN TIMELINES.
SOMETHING JUST CHANGED. AN INHUMAN NAMED GORGON-- YOUR COUSIN--WAS SITTING HERE WITH US JUST A MOMENT AGO. FROM OUR PERSPECTIVE, HE WAS ERASED. HE NEVER WAS.
NO!
WHAT? WHAT'S HAPPENING?
THE GUARDS... WE'RE IN A SORT OF ENERGY BUBBLE, READER. THEY'RE OUTSIDE...AND THEY JUST DISAPPEARED.
IT'S KANG. HE'S ATTACKING YOU FROM YOUR OWN PAST, ERASING ELEMENTS OF INHUMAN HISTORY. THE EFFECTS ARE BEING FELT HERE IN THE PRESENT.
I'VE SEEN THIS SORT OF THING BEFORE. I INVENTED DEFENSES. THE DEVICE I ACTIVATED SHIELDS US; PUTS US IN OUR OWN TIMELINE-- BUT ONLY AS LONG AS WE STAY INSIDE THE BUBBLE.
CORRECT, BLACK BOLT, IF WE LEAVE, WE'RE AS VULNERABLE AS ANYONE ELSE.
WHAT HAVE YOU DONE, BLACK BOLT?
WE WON'T FULLY KNOW UNTIL HE'S DONE, MEDUSA. AND IF I KNOW KANG...

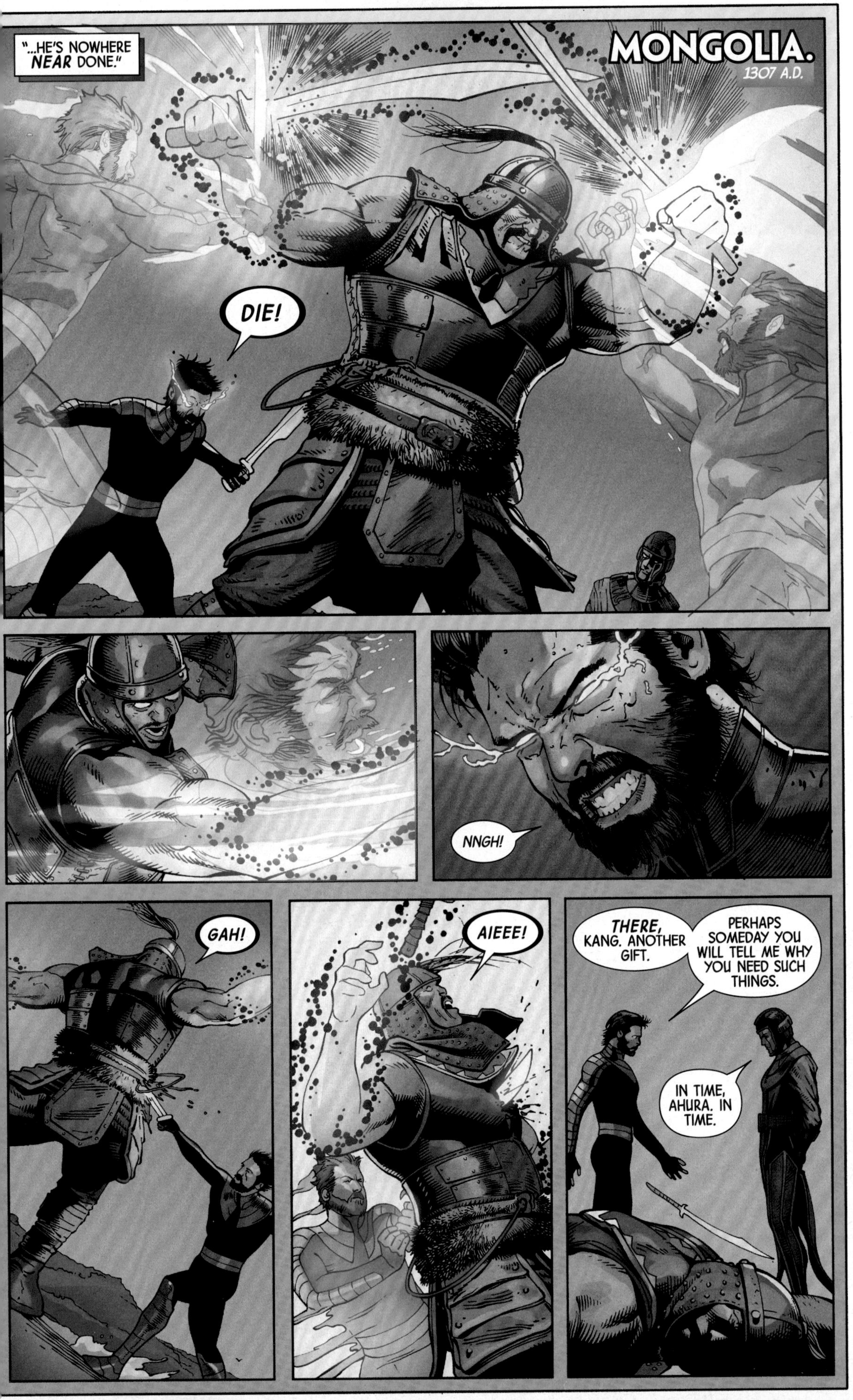
"...HE'S NOWHERE NEAR DONE."
MONGOLIA.
1307 A.D.
DIE!
NNGH!
GAH!
AIEEE!
THERE, KANG. ANOTHER GIFT.
PERHAPS SOMEDAY YOU WILL TELL ME WHY YOU NEED SUCH THINGS.
IN TIME, AHURA. IN TIME.

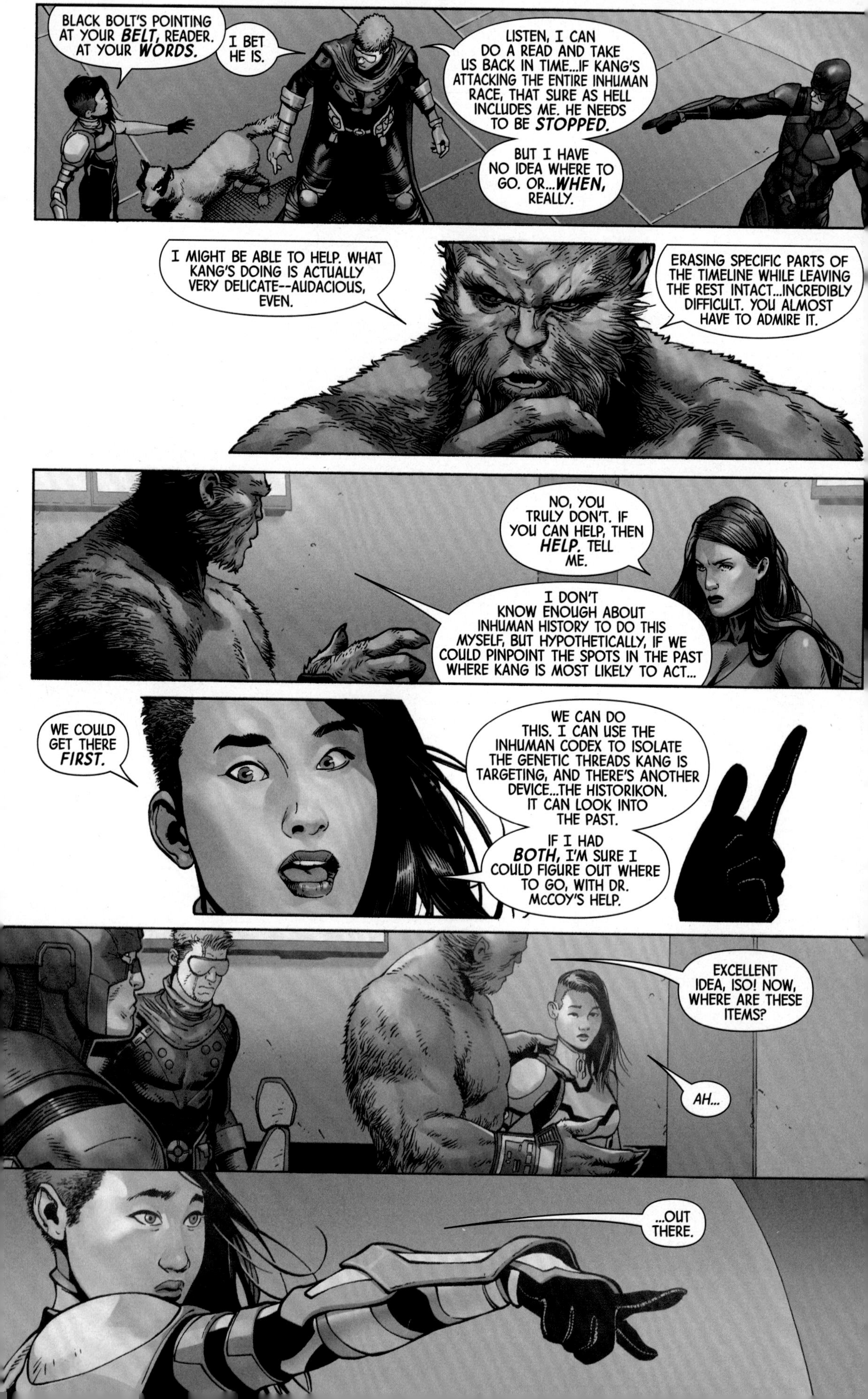
BLACK BOLT'S POINTING AT YOUR BELT, READER. AT YOUR WORDS.
I BET HE IS.
LISTEN, I CAN DO A READ AND TAKE US BACK IN TIME...IF KANG'S ATTACKING THE ENTIRE INHUMAN RACE, THAT SURE AS HELL INCLUDES ME. HE NEEDS TO BE STOPPED.
BUT I HAVE NO IDEA WHERE TO GO. OR...WHEN, REALLY.
I MIGHT BE ABLE TO HELP. WHAT KANG'S DOING IS ACTUALLY VERY DELICATE--AUDACIOUS, EVEN.
ERASING SPECIFIC PARTS OF THE TIMELINE WHILE LEAVING THE REST INTACT...INCREDIBLY DIFFICULT. YOU ALMOST HAVE TO ADMIRE IT.
NO, YOU TRULY DON'T. IF YOU CAN HELP, THEN HELP. TELL ME.
I DON'T KNOW ENOUGH ABOUT INHUMAN HISTORY TO DO THIS MYSELF, BUT HYPOTHETICALLY, IF WE COULD PINPOINT THE SPOTS IN THE PAST WHERE KANG IS MOST LIKELY TO ACT...
WE COULD GET THERE FIRST.
WE CAN DO THIS. I CAN USE THE INHUMAN CODEX TO ISOLATE THE GENETIC THREADS KANG IS TARGETING, AND THERE'S ANOTHER DEVICE...THE HISTORIKON. IT CAN LOOK INTO THE PAST.
IF I HAD BOTH, I'M SURE I COULD FIGURE OUT WHERE TO GO, WITH DR. McCOY'S HELP.
EXCELLENT IDEA, ISO! NOW, WHERE ARE THESE ITEMS?
AH...
...OUT THERE.

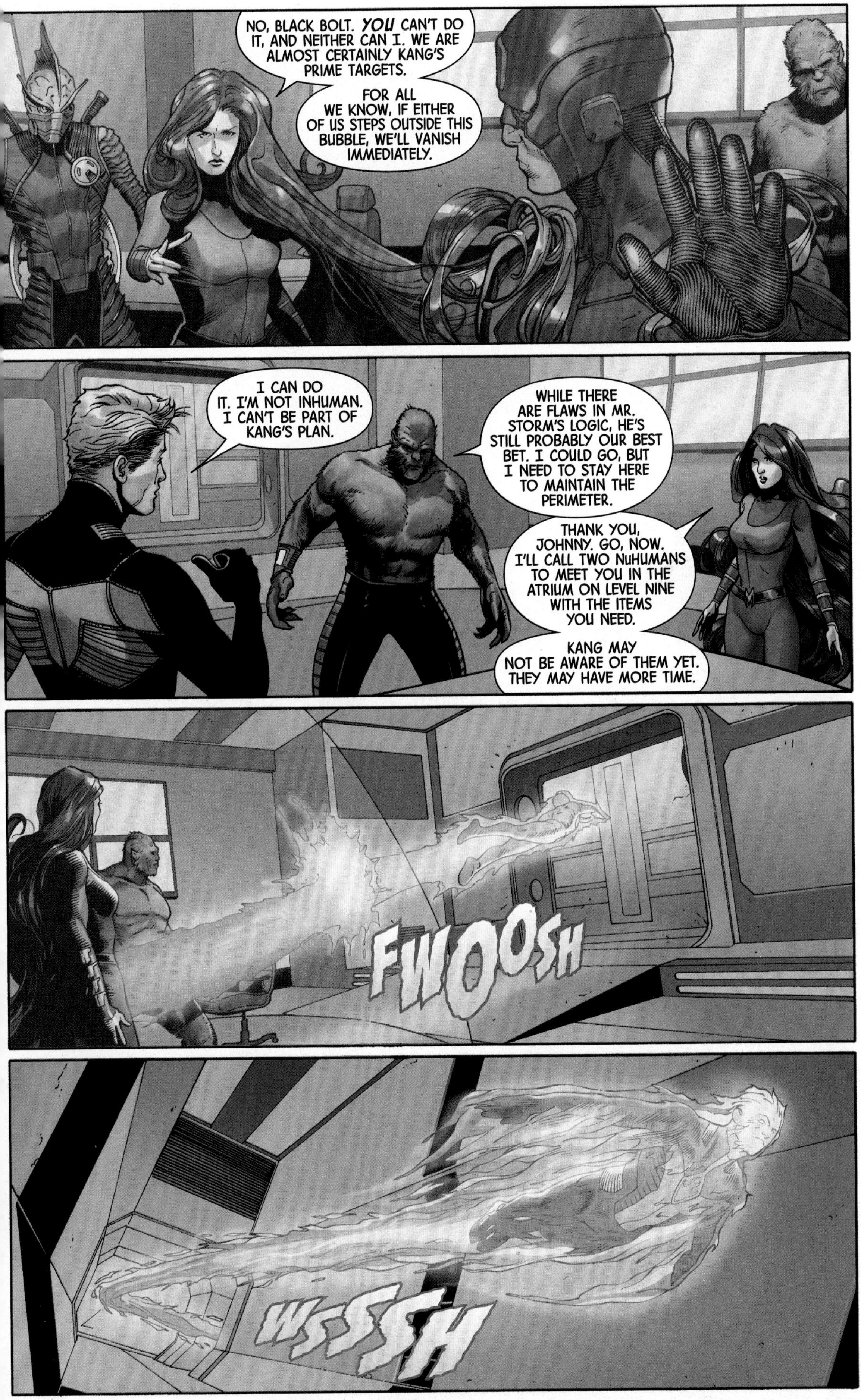
NO, BLACK BOLT. YOU CAN'T DO IT, AND NEITHER CAN I. WE ARE ALMOST CERTAINLY KANG'S PRIME TARGETS.
FOR ALL WE KNOW, IF EITHER OF US STEPS OUTSIDE THIS BUBBLE, WE'LL VANISH IMMEDIATELY.
I CAN DO IT. I'M NOT INHUMAN. I CAN'T BE PART OF KANG'S PLAN.
WHILE THERE ARE FLAWS IN MR. STORM'S LOGIC, HE'S STILL PROBABLY OUR BEST BET. I COULD GO, BUT I NEED TO STAY HERE TO MAINTAIN THE PERIMETER.
THANK YOU, JOHNNY. GO, NOW. I'LL CALL TWO NuHUMANS TO MEET YOU IN THE ATRIUM ON LEVEL NINE WITH THE ITEMS YOU NEED.
KANG MAY NOT BE AWARE OF THEM YET. THEY MAY HAVE MORE TIME.
FWOOSH
WSSSH

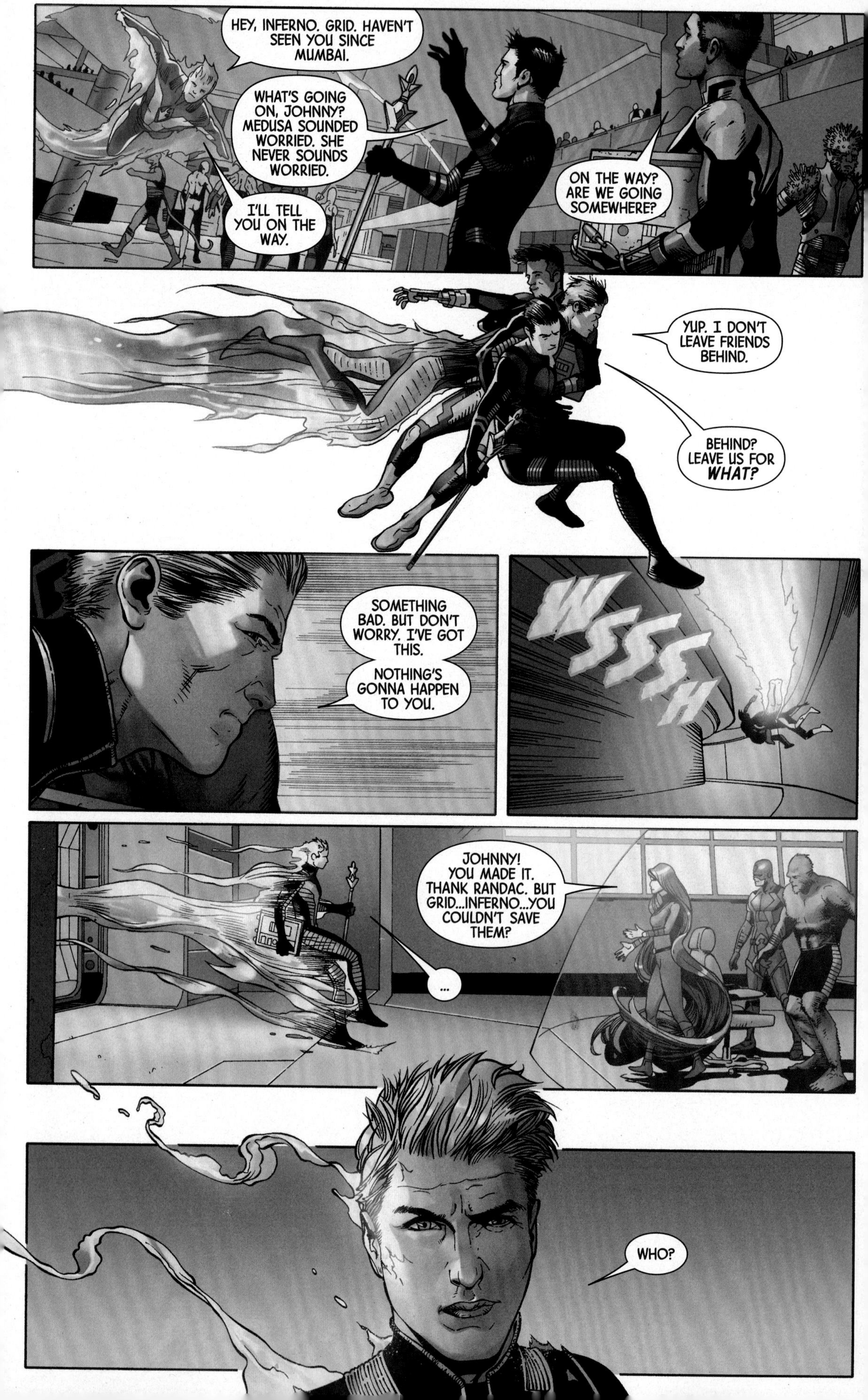
HEY, INFERNO. GRID. HAVEN'T SEEN YOU SINCE MUMBAI.
WHAT'S GOING ON, JOHNNY? MEDUSA SOUNDED WORRIED. SHE NEVER SOUNDS WORRIED.
I'LL TELL YOU ON THE WAY.
ON THE WAY? ARE WE GOING SOMEWHERE?
YUP. I DON'T LEAVE FRIENDS BEHIND.
BEHIND? LEAVE US FOR WHAT?
SOMETHING BAD. BUT DON'T WORRY. I'VE GOT THIS.
NOTHING'S GONNA HAPPEN TO YOU.
WSSSH
JOHNNY! YOU MADE IT. THANK RANDAC. BUT GRID...INFERNO...YOU COULDN'T SAVE THEM?
...
WHO?

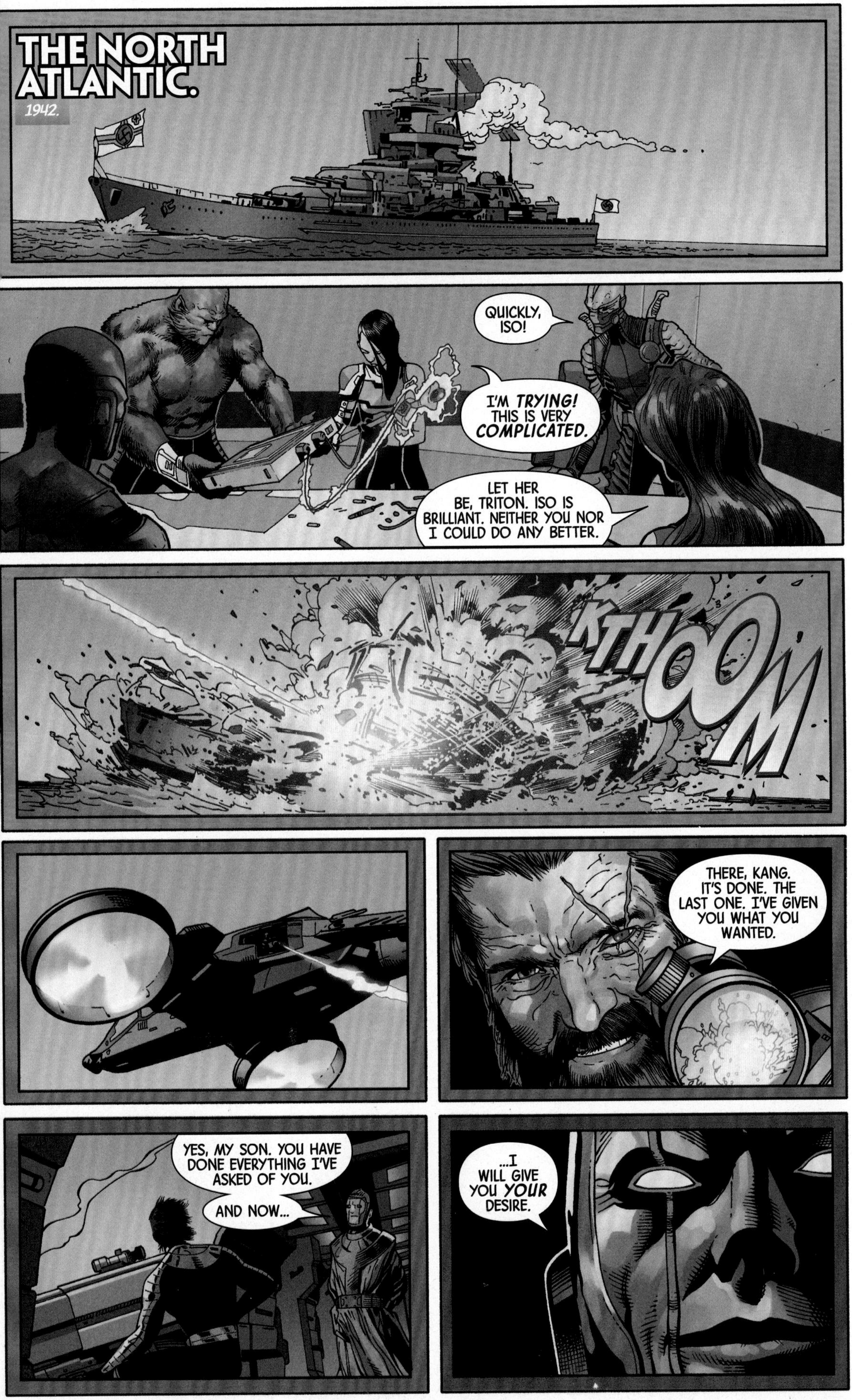
THE NORTH ATLANTIC.
1942.
QUICKLY, ISO!
I'M TRYING! THIS IS VERY COMPLICATED.
LET HER BE, TRITON. ISO IS BRILLIANT. NEITHER YOU NOR I COULD DO ANY BETTER.
KTHOOM
THERE, KANG. IT'S DONE. THE LAST ONE. I'VE GIVEN YOU WHAT YOU WANTED.
YES, MY SON. YOU HAVE DONE EVERYTHING I'VE ASKED OF YOU.
AND NOW...
...I WILL GIVE YOU YOUR DESIRE.

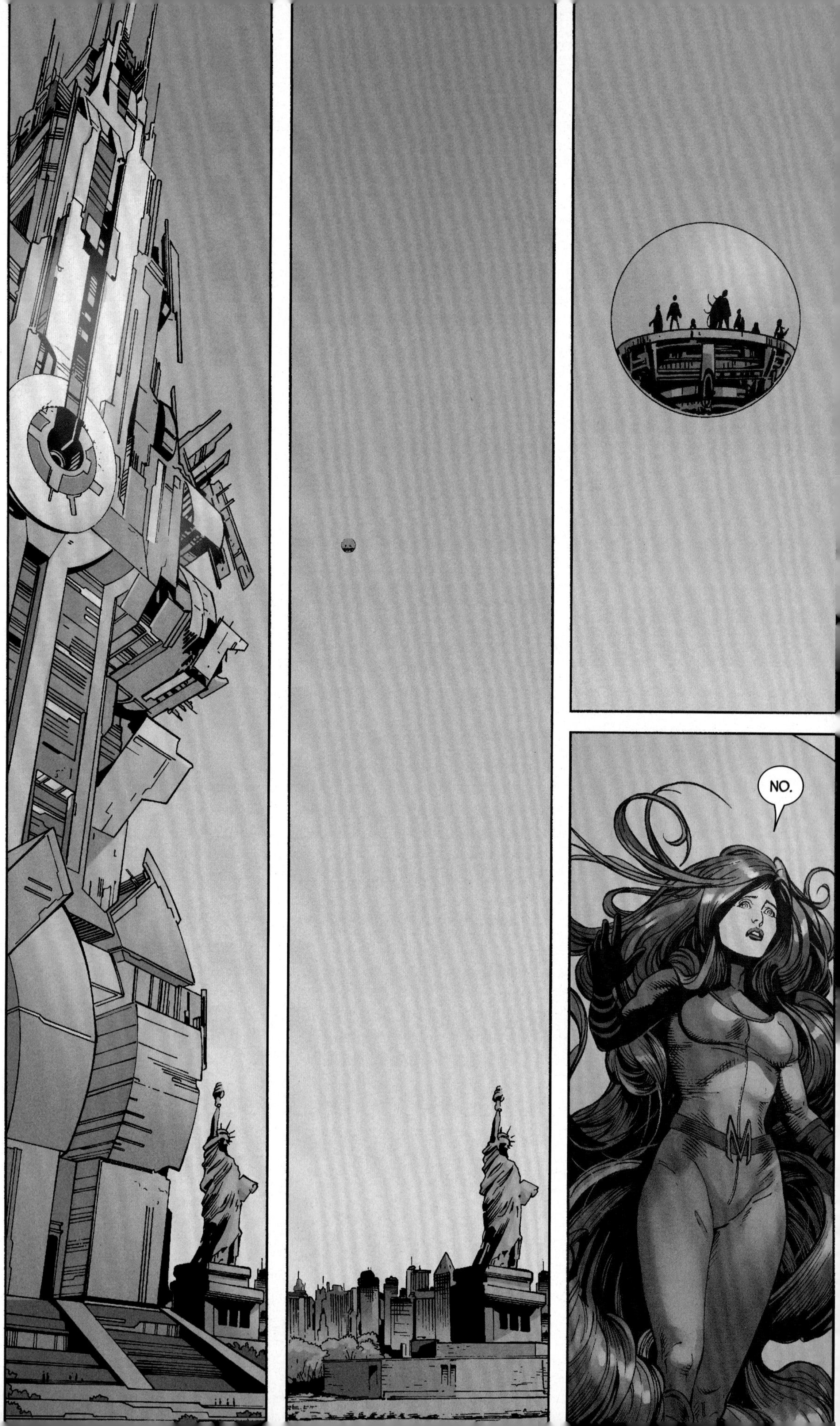
NO.

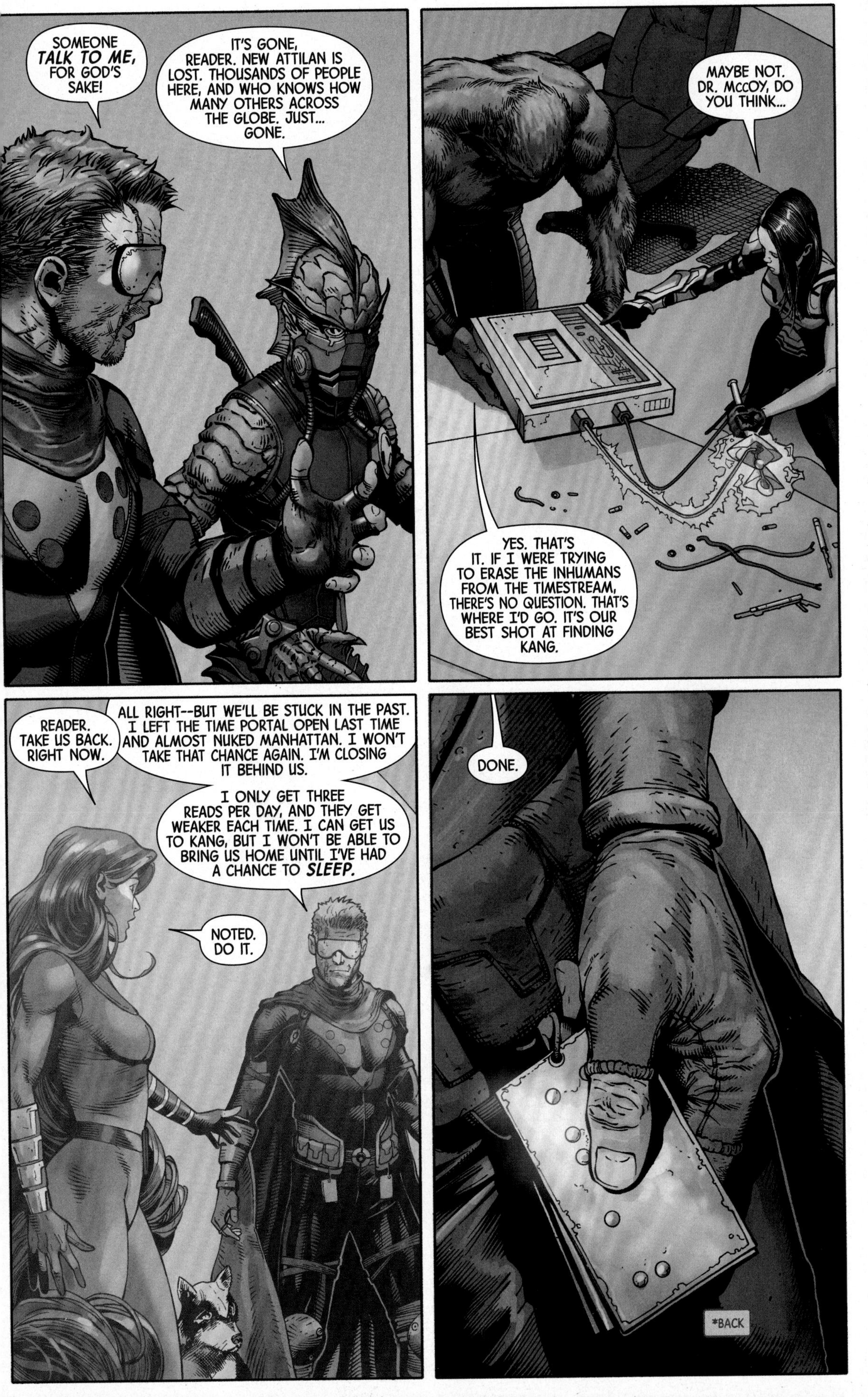
SOMEONE TALK TO ME, FOR GOD'S SAKE!
IT'S GONE, READER. NEW ATTILAN IS LOST. THOUSANDS OF PEOPLE HERE, AND WHO KNOWS HOW MANY OTHERS ACROSS THE GLOBE. JUST... GONE.
MAYBE NOT. DR. McCOY, DO YOU THINK...
YES. THAT'S IT. IF I WERE TRYING TO ERASE THE INHUMANS FROM THE TIMESTREAM, THERE'S NO QUESTION. THAT'S WHERE I'D GO. IT'S OUR BEST SHOT AT FINDING KANG.
READER. TAKE US BACK. RIGHT NOW.
ALL RIGHT--BUT WE'LL BE STUCK IN THE PAST. I LEFT THE TIME PORTAL OPEN LAST TIME AND ALMOST NUKED MANHATTAN. I WON'T TAKE THAT CHANCE AGAIN. I'M CLOSING IT BEHIND US.
I ONLY GET THREE READS PER DAY, AND THEY GET WEAKER EACH TIME. I CAN GET US TO KANG, BUT I WON'T BE ABLE TO BRING US HOME UNTIL I'VE HAD A CHANCE TO SLEEP.
NOTED. DO IT.
DONE.
*BACK

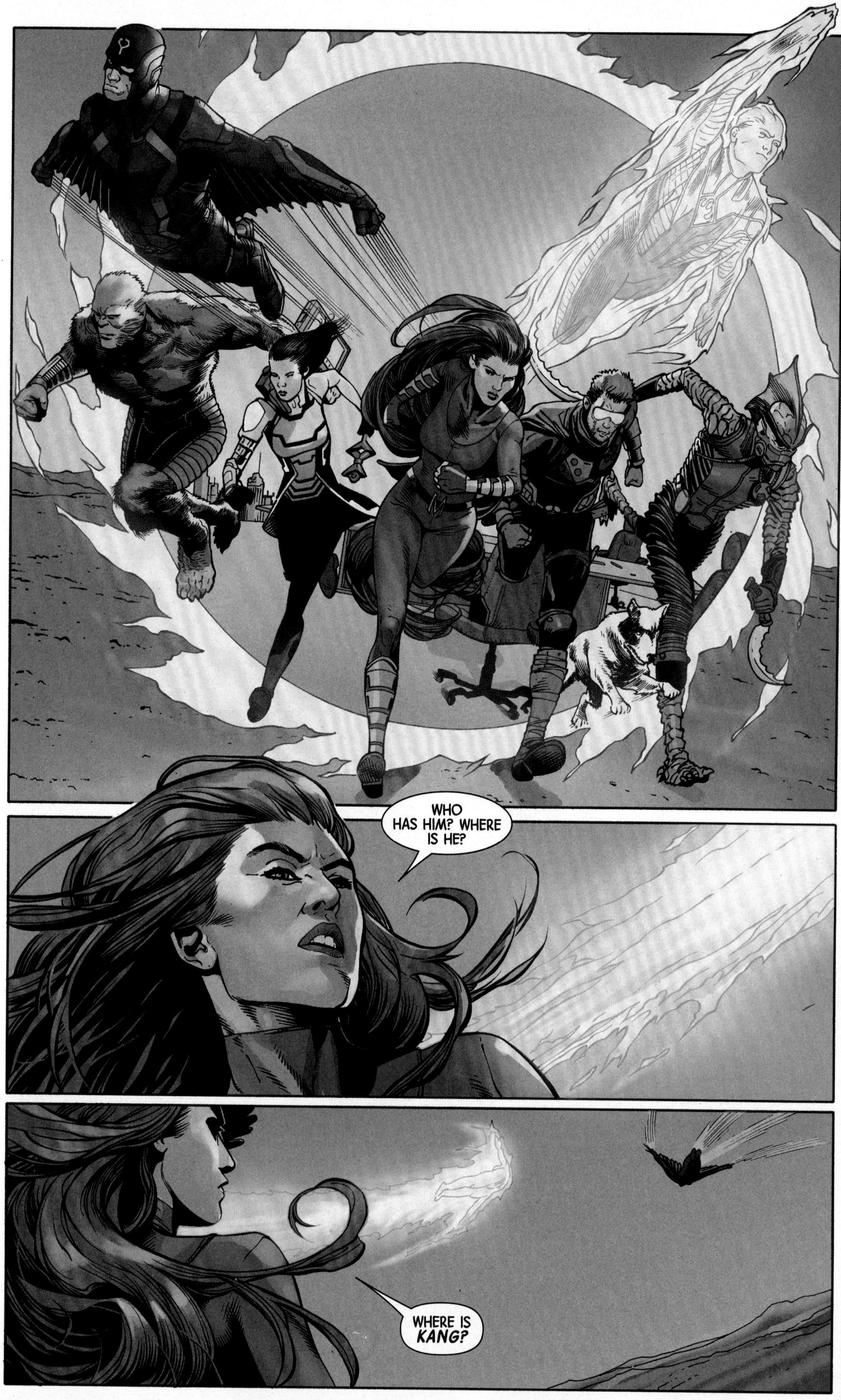
WHO HAS HIM? WHERE IS HE?
WHERE IS KANG?

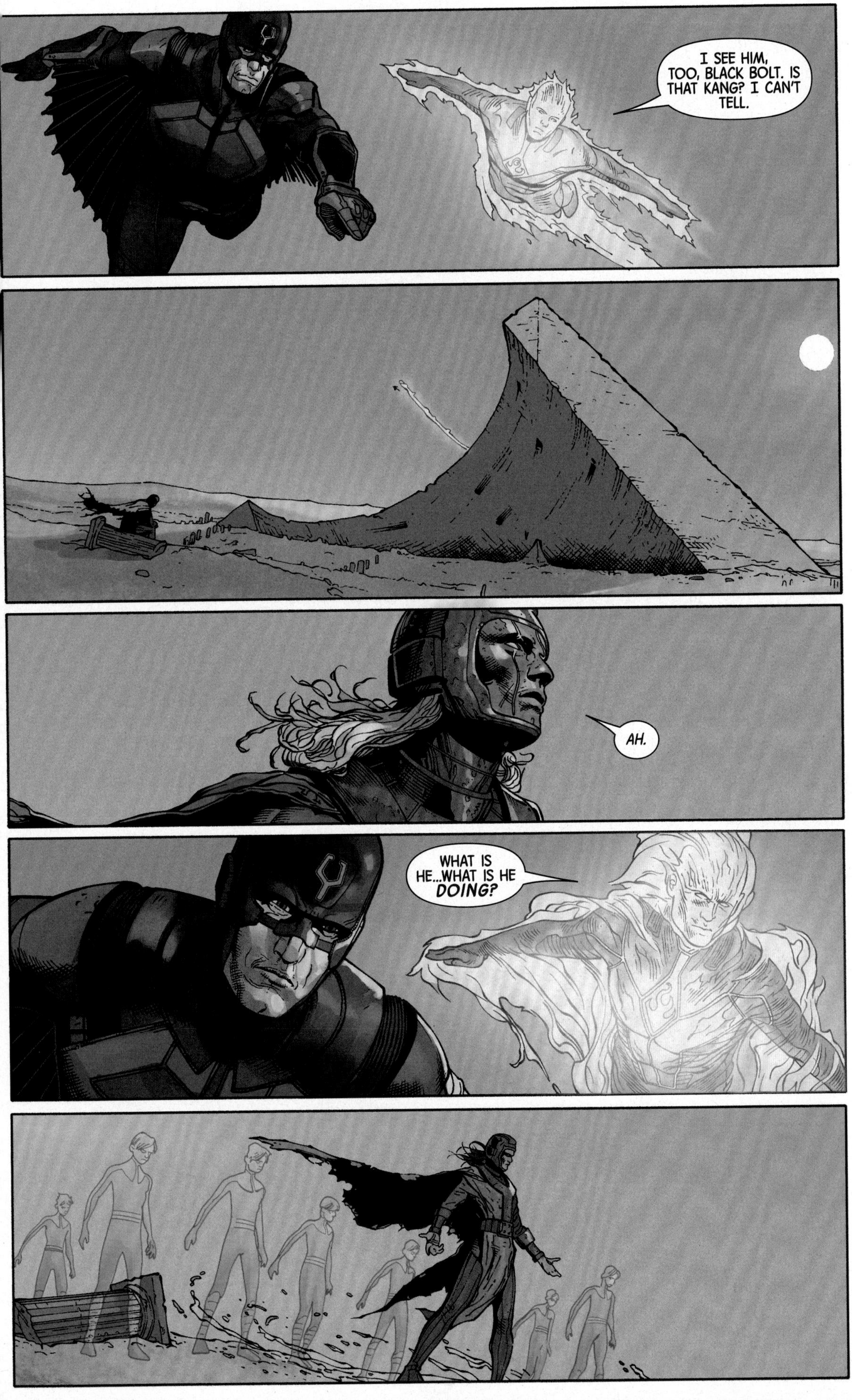
I SEE HIM, TOO, BLACK BOLT. IS THAT KANG? I CAN'T TELL.
AH.
WHAT IS HE...WHAT IS HE *DOING?*

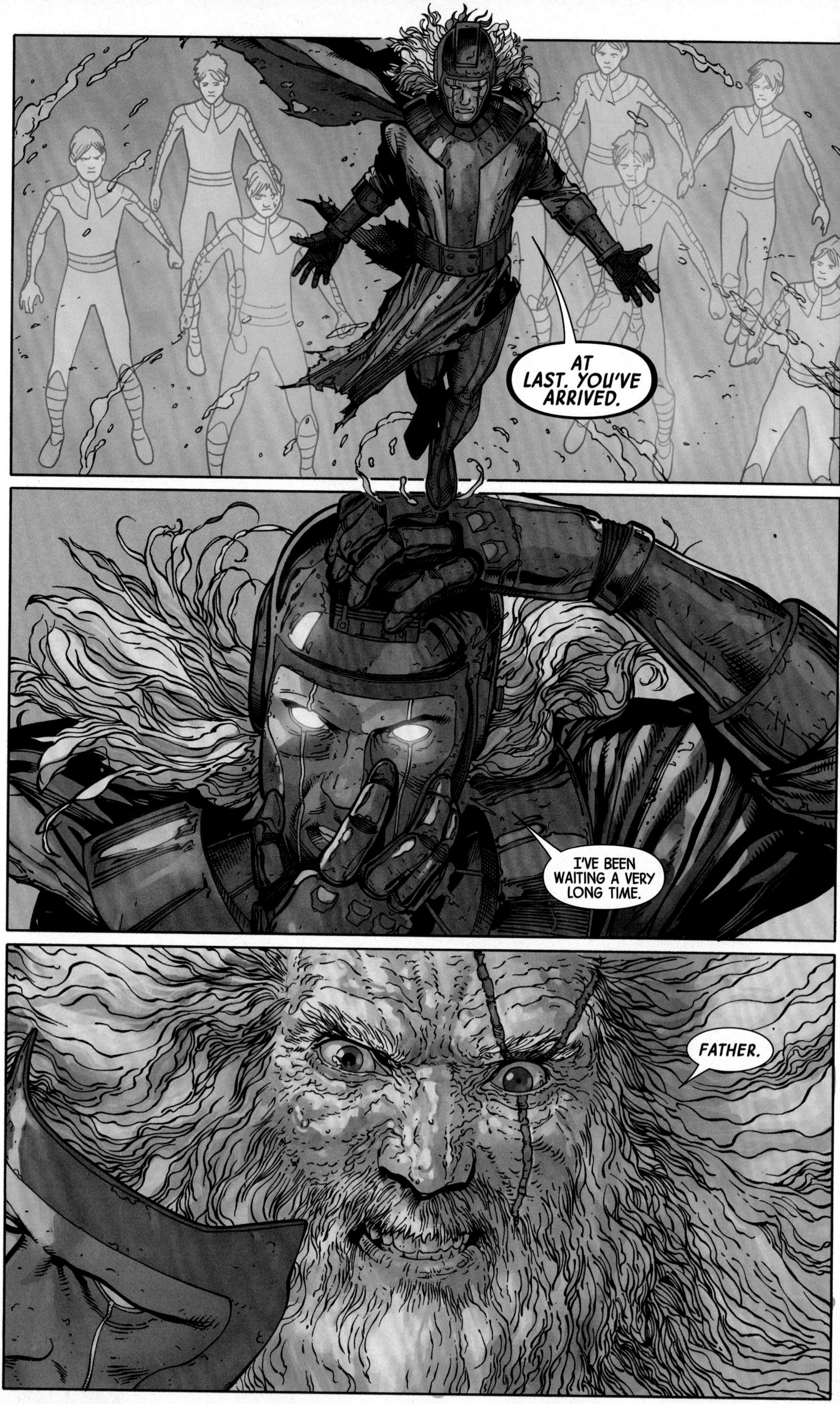
AT LAST. YOU'VE ARRIVED.
I'VE BEEN WAITING A VERY LONG TIME.
FATHER.

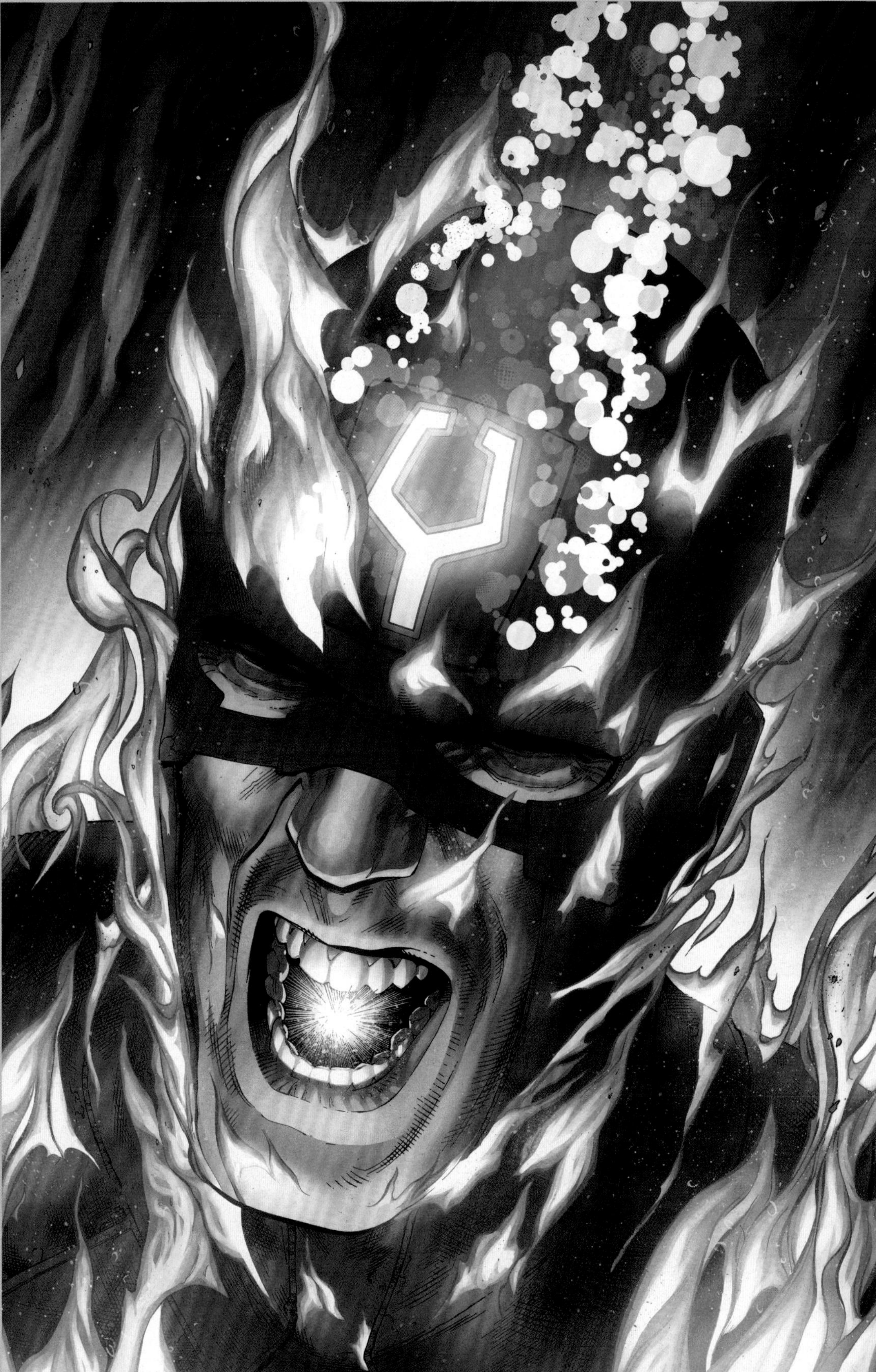

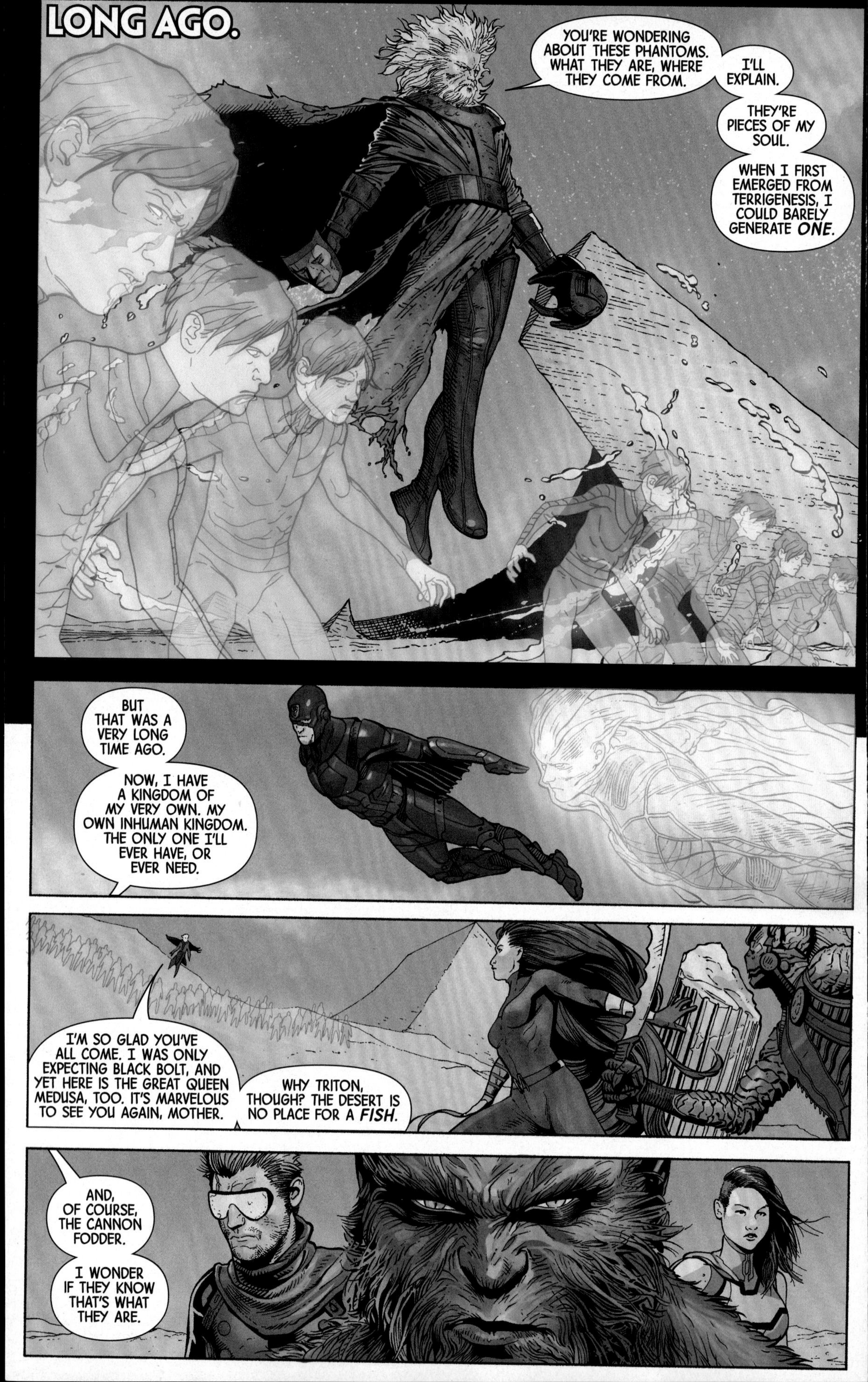
LONG AGO.
YOU'RE WONDERING ABOUT THESE PHANTOMS. WHAT THEY ARE, WHERE THEY COME FROM.
I'LL EXPLAIN.
THEY'RE PIECES OF MY SOUL.
WHEN I FIRST EMERGED FROM TERRIGENESIS, I COULD BARELY GENERATE *ONE*.
BUT THAT WAS A VERY LONG TIME AGO.
NOW, I HAVE A KINGDOM OF MY VERY OWN. MY OWN INHUMAN KINGDOM. THE ONLY ONE I'LL EVER HAVE, OR EVER NEED.
I'M SO GLAD YOU'VE ALL COME. I WAS ONLY EXPECTING BLACK BOLT, AND YET HERE IS THE GREAT QUEEN MEDUSA, TOO. IT'S MARVELOUS TO SEE YOU AGAIN, MOTHER.
WHY TRITON, THOUGH? THE DESERT IS NO PLACE FOR A *FISH*.
AND, OF COURSE, THE CANNON FODDER.
I WONDER IF THEY KNOW THAT'S WHAT THEY ARE.

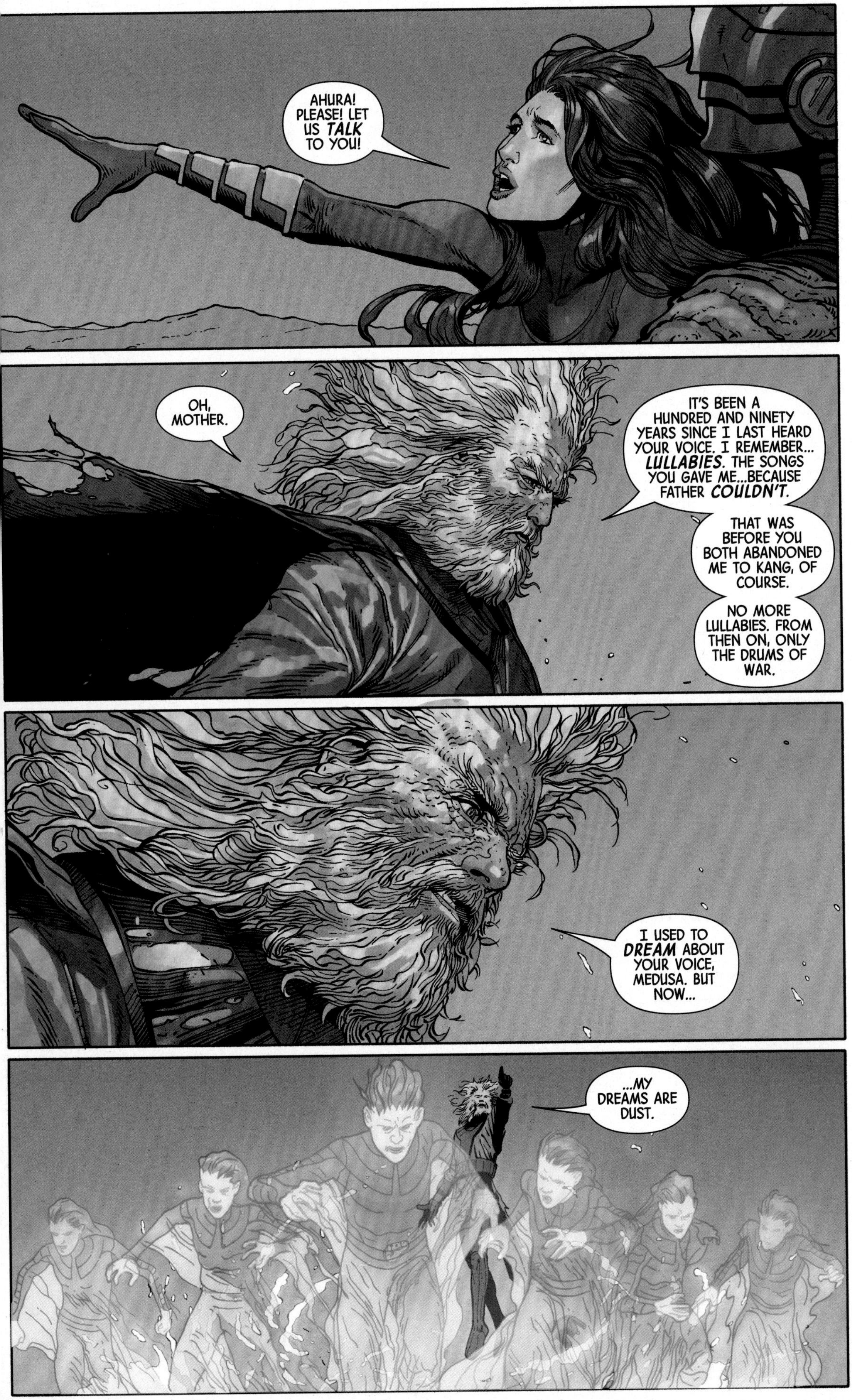
AHURA! PLEASE! LET US TALK TO YOU!
OH, MOTHER.
IT'S BEEN A HUNDRED AND NINETY YEARS SINCE I LAST HEARD YOUR VOICE. I REMEMBER... LULLABIES. THE SONGS YOU GAVE ME...BECAUSE FATHER COULDN'T.
THAT WAS BEFORE YOU BOTH ABANDONED ME TO KANG, OF COURSE.
NO MORE LULLABIES. FROM THEN ON, ONLY THE DRUMS OF WAR.
I USED TO DREAM ABOUT YOUR VOICE, MEDUSA. BUT NOW...
...MY DREAMS ARE DUST.

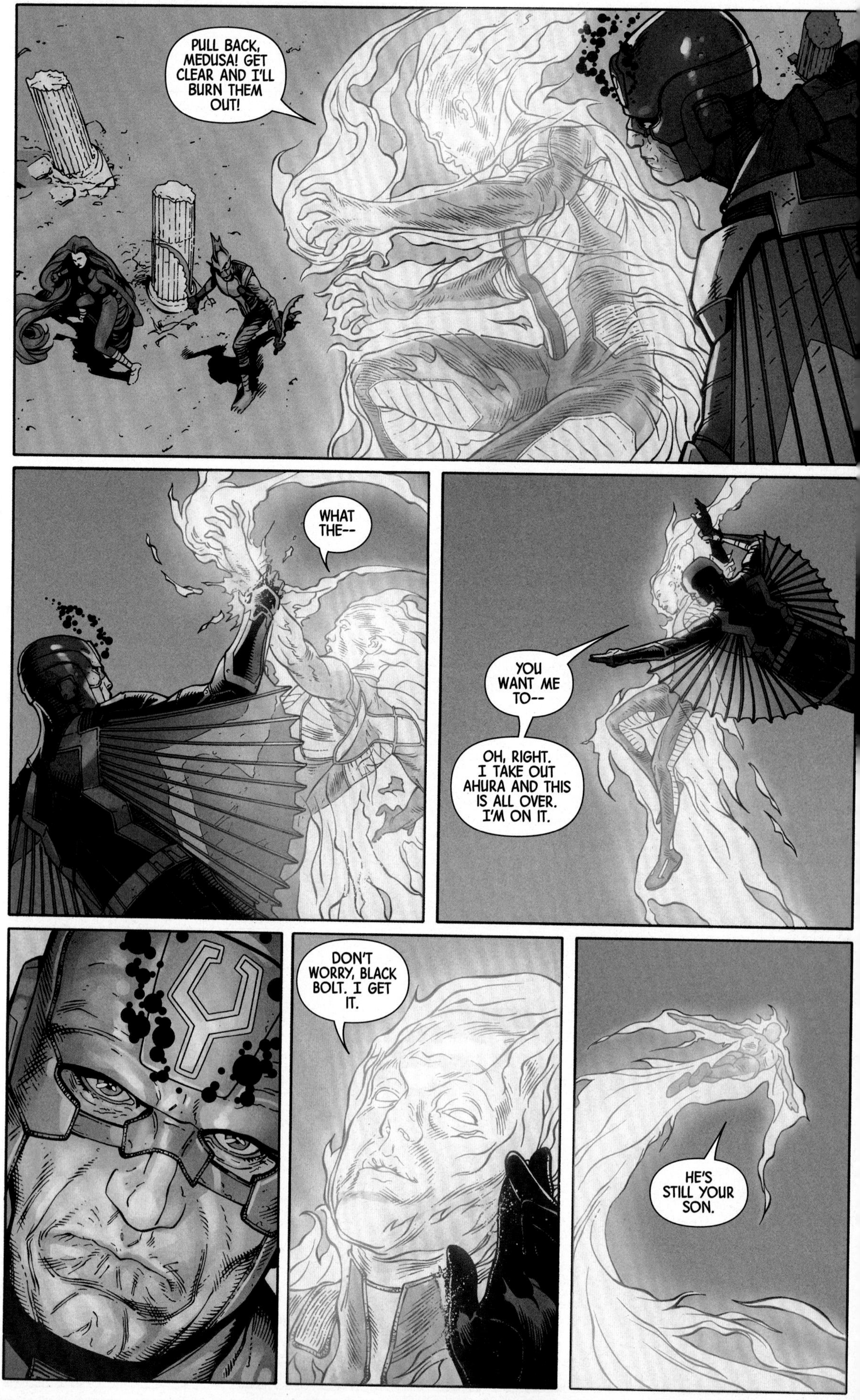
PULL BACK, MEDUSA! GET CLEAR AND I'LL BURN THEM OUT!
WHAT THE--
YOU WANT ME TO--
OH, RIGHT. I TAKE OUT AHURA AND THIS IS ALL OVER. I'M ON IT.
DON'T WORRY, BLACK BOLT. I GET IT.
HE'S STILL YOUR SON.

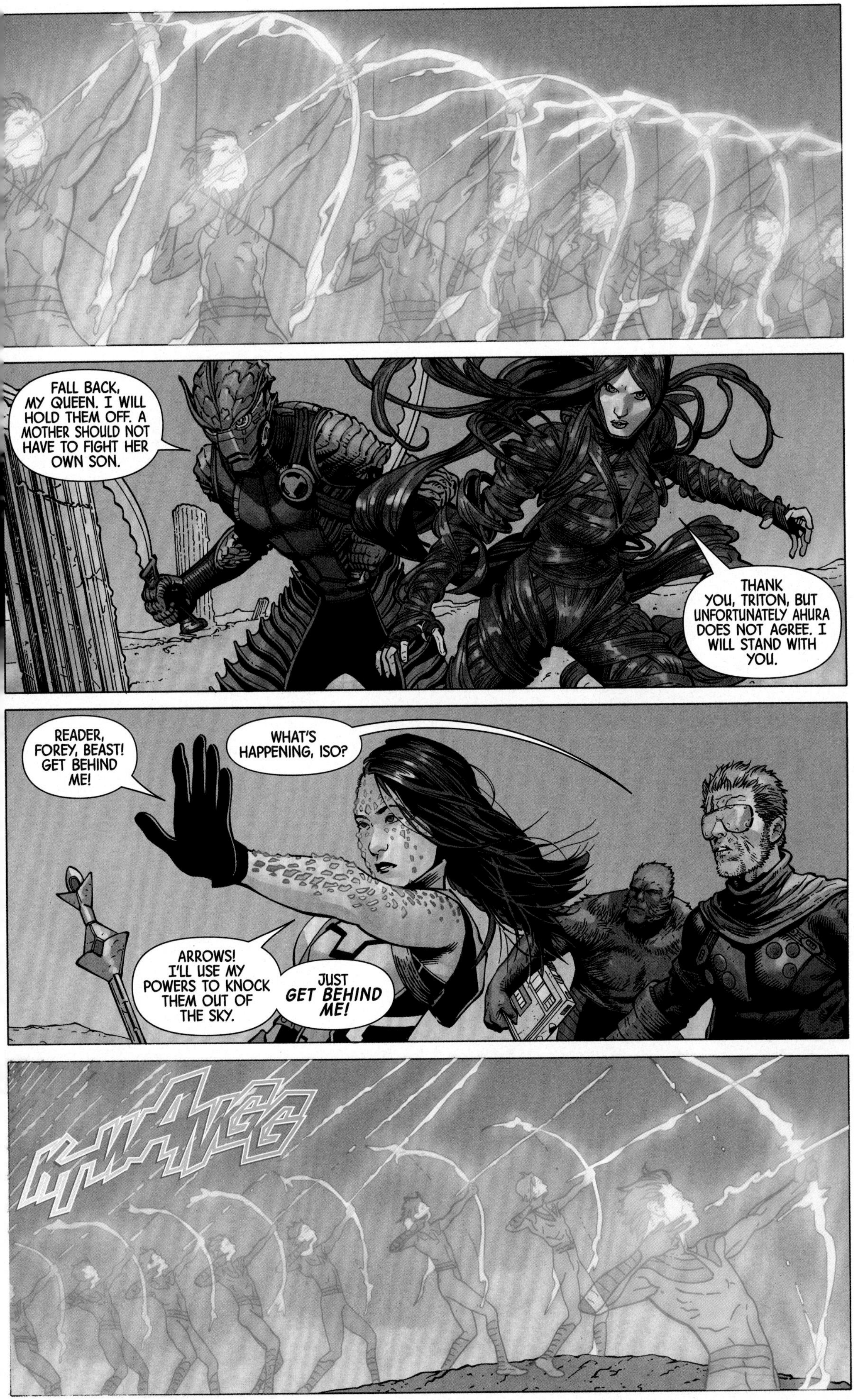
FALL BACK, MY QUEEN. I WILL HOLD THEM OFF. A MOTHER SHOULD NOT HAVE TO FIGHT HER OWN SON.
THANK YOU, TRITON, BUT UNFORTUNATELY AHURA DOES NOT AGREE. I WILL STAND WITH YOU.
READER, FOREY, BEAST! GET BEHIND ME!
WHAT'S HAPPENING, ISO?
ARROWS! I'LL USE MY POWERS TO KNOCK THEM OUT OF THE SKY.
JUST GET BEHIND ME!
KHHAKGG

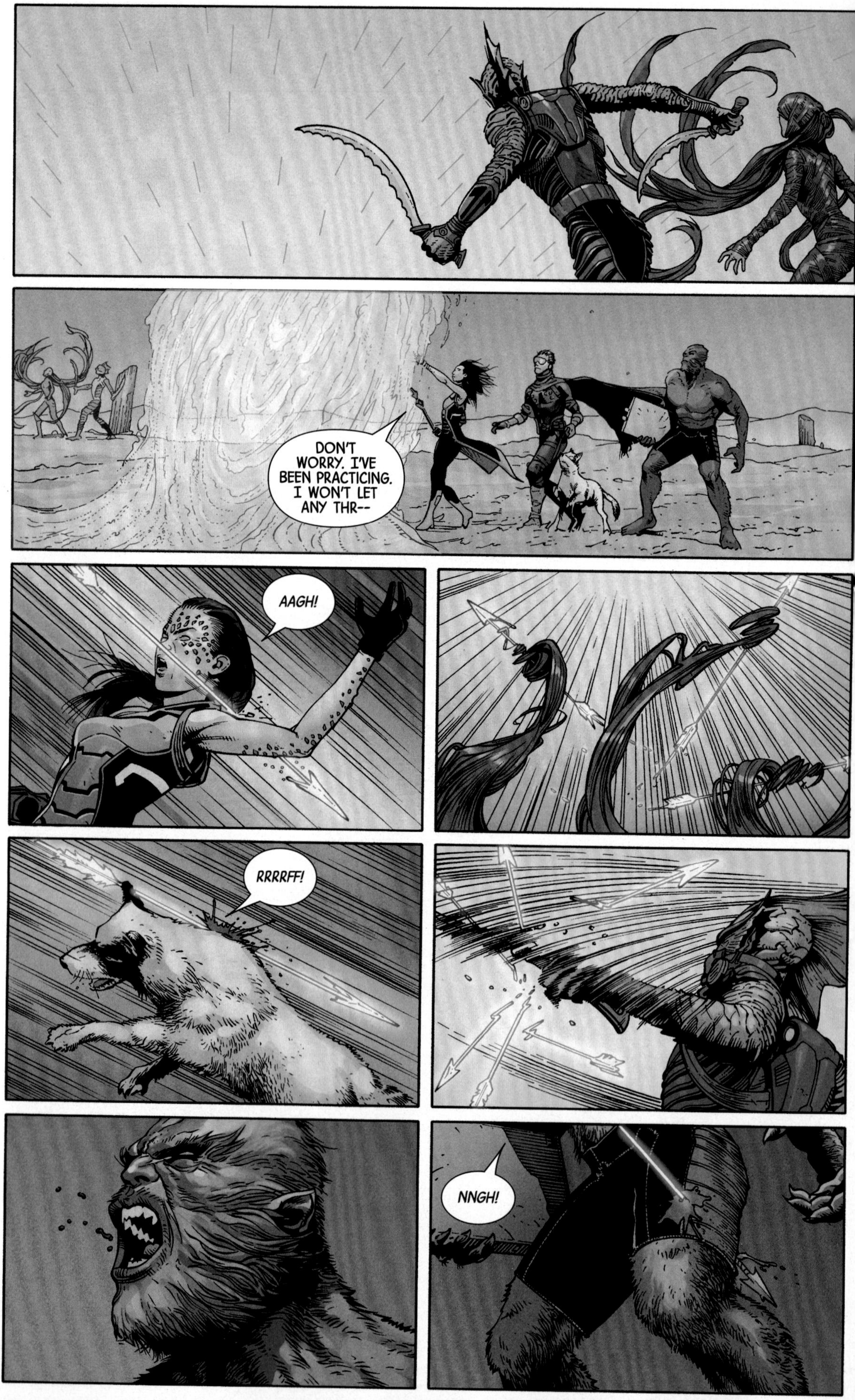
DON'T WORRY. I'VE BEEN PRACTICING. I WON'T LET ANY THR--
AAGH!
RRRRFF!
NNGH!

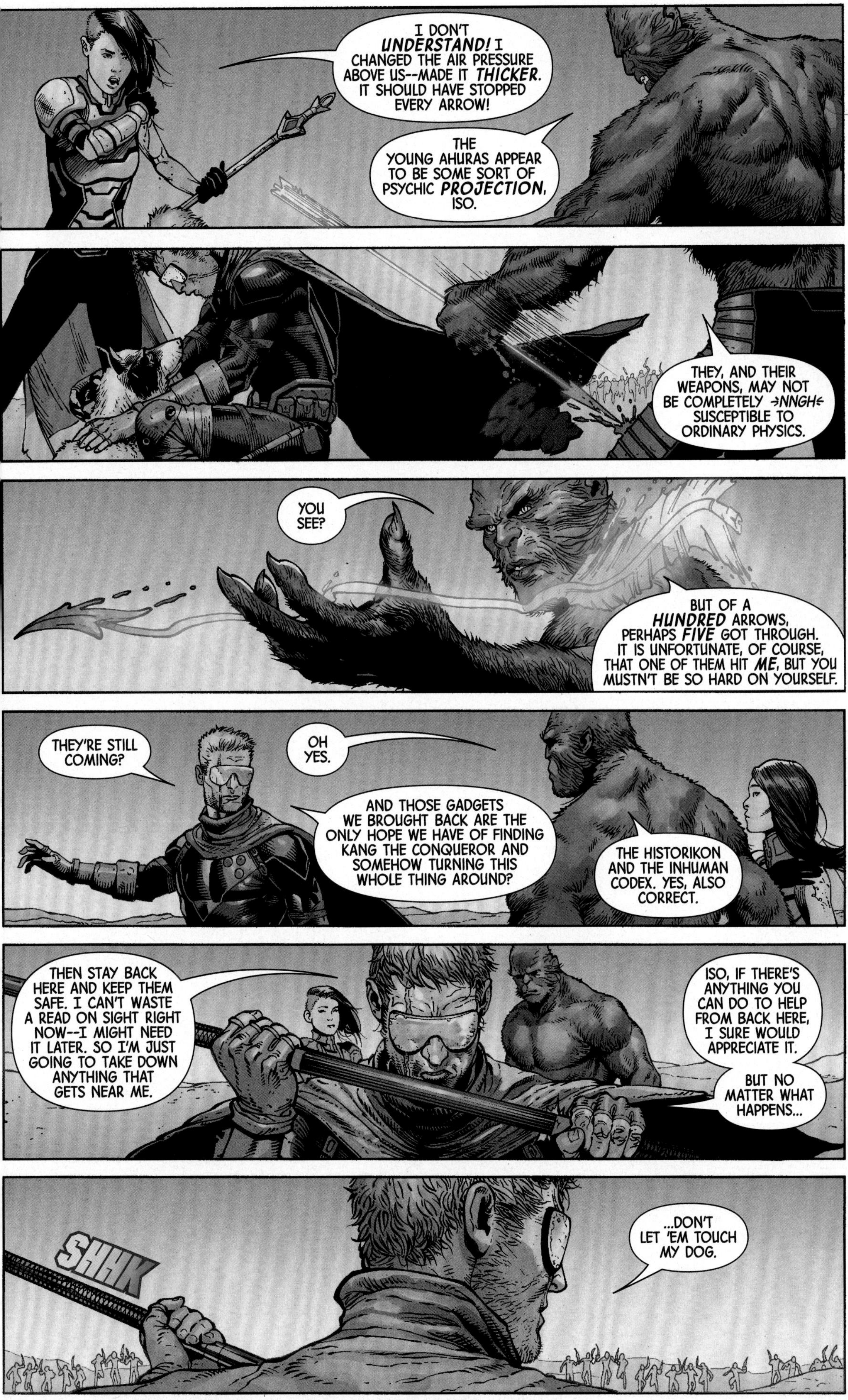
I DON'T UNDERSTAND! I CHANGED THE AIR PRESSURE ABOVE US--MADE IT THICKER. IT SHOULD HAVE STOPPED EVERY ARROW!
THE YOUNG AHURAS APPEAR TO BE SOME SORT OF PSYCHIC PROJECTION, ISO.
THEY, AND THEIR WEAPONS, MAY NOT BE COMPLETELY →NNGH← SUSCEPTIBLE TO ORDINARY PHYSICS.
YOU SEE?
BUT OF A HUNDRED ARROWS, PERHAPS FIVE GOT THROUGH. IT IS UNFORTUNATE, OF COURSE, THAT ONE OF THEM HIT ME, BUT YOU MUSTN'T BE SO HARD ON YOURSELF.
THEY'RE STILL COMING?
OH YES.
AND THOSE GADGETS WE BROUGHT BACK ARE THE ONLY HOPE WE HAVE OF FINDING KANG THE CONQUEROR AND SOMEHOW TURNING THIS WHOLE THING AROUND?
THE HISTORIKON AND THE INHUMAN CODEX. YES, ALSO CORRECT.
THEN STAY BACK HERE AND KEEP THEM SAFE. I CAN'T WASTE A READ ON SIGHT RIGHT NOW--I MIGHT NEED IT LATER. SO I'M JUST GOING TO TAKE DOWN ANYTHING THAT GETS NEAR ME.
ISO, IF THERE'S ANYTHING YOU CAN DO TO HELP FROM BACK HERE, I SURE WOULD APPRECIATE IT.
BUT NO MATTER WHAT HAPPENS...
SHHK
...DON'T LET 'EM TOUCH MY DOG.

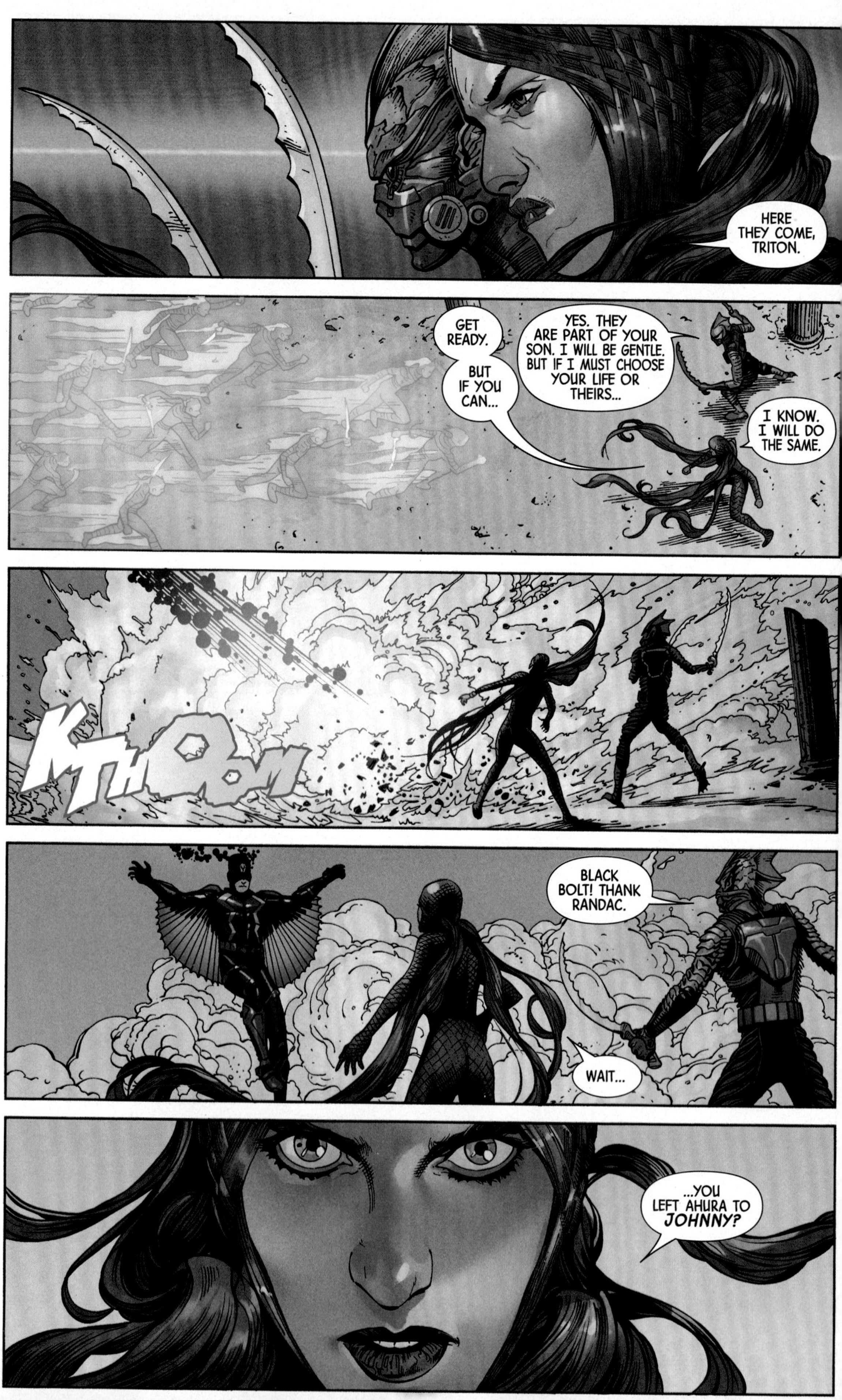
HERE THEY COME, TRITON.
GET READY.
BUT IF YOU CAN...
YES. THEY ARE PART OF YOUR SON. I WILL BE GENTLE. BUT IF I MUST CHOOSE YOUR LIFE OR THEIRS...
I KNOW. I WILL DO THE SAME.
KTHOOM
BLACK BOLT! THANK RANDAC.
WAIT...
...YOU LEFT AHURA TO JOHNNY?

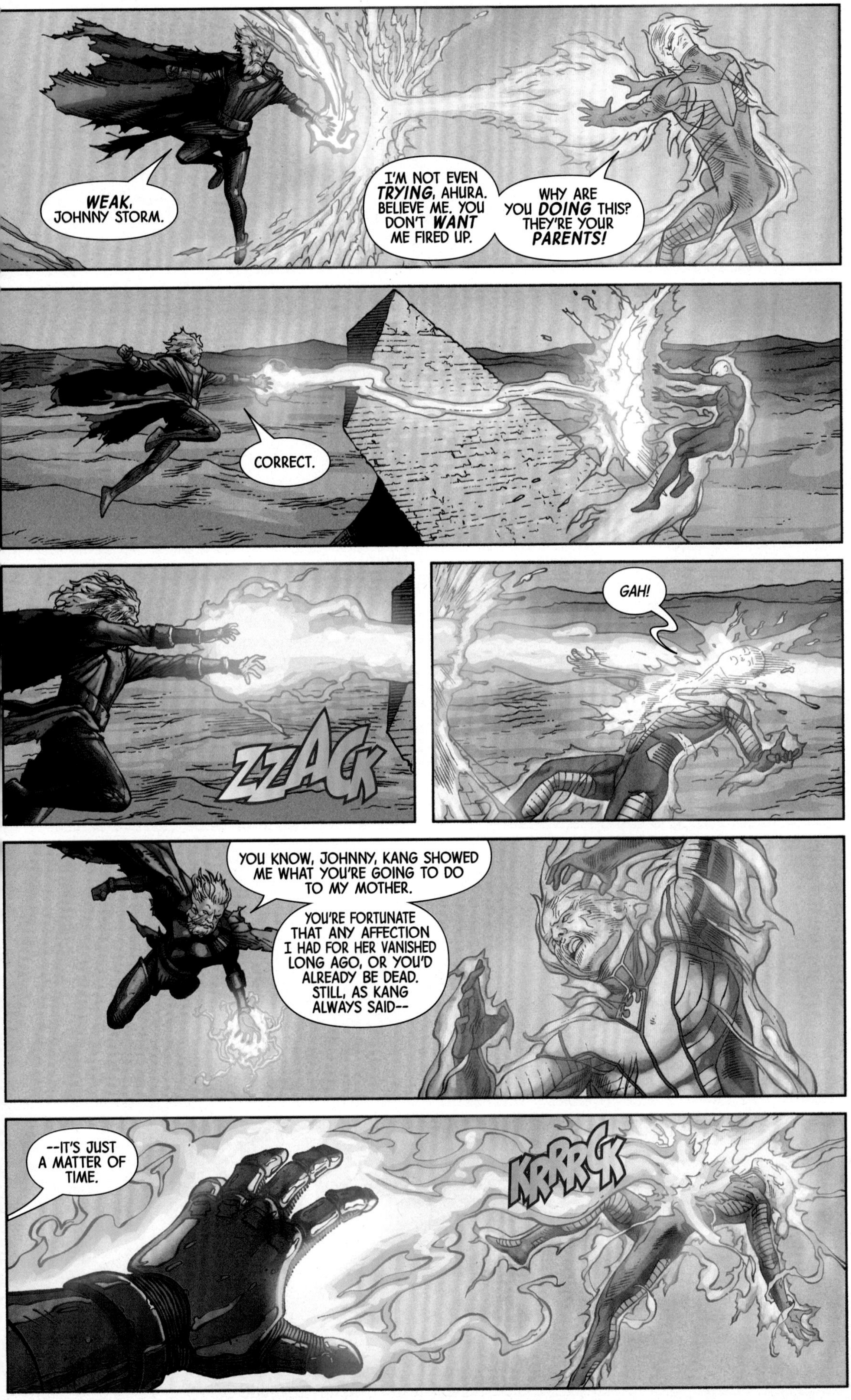
WEAK, JOHNNY STORM.
I'M NOT EVEN TRYING, AHURA. BELIEVE ME. YOU DON'T WANT ME FIRED UP.
WHY ARE YOU DOING THIS? THEY'RE YOUR PARENTS!
CORRECT.
ZZACK
GAH!
YOU KNOW, JOHNNY, KANG SHOWED ME WHAT YOU'RE GOING TO DO TO MY MOTHER.
YOU'RE FORTUNATE THAT ANY AFFECTION I HAD FOR HER VANISHED LONG AGO, OR YOU'D ALREADY BE DEAD. STILL, AS KANG ALWAYS SAID--
--IT'S JUST A MATTER OF TIME.
KRRRCK

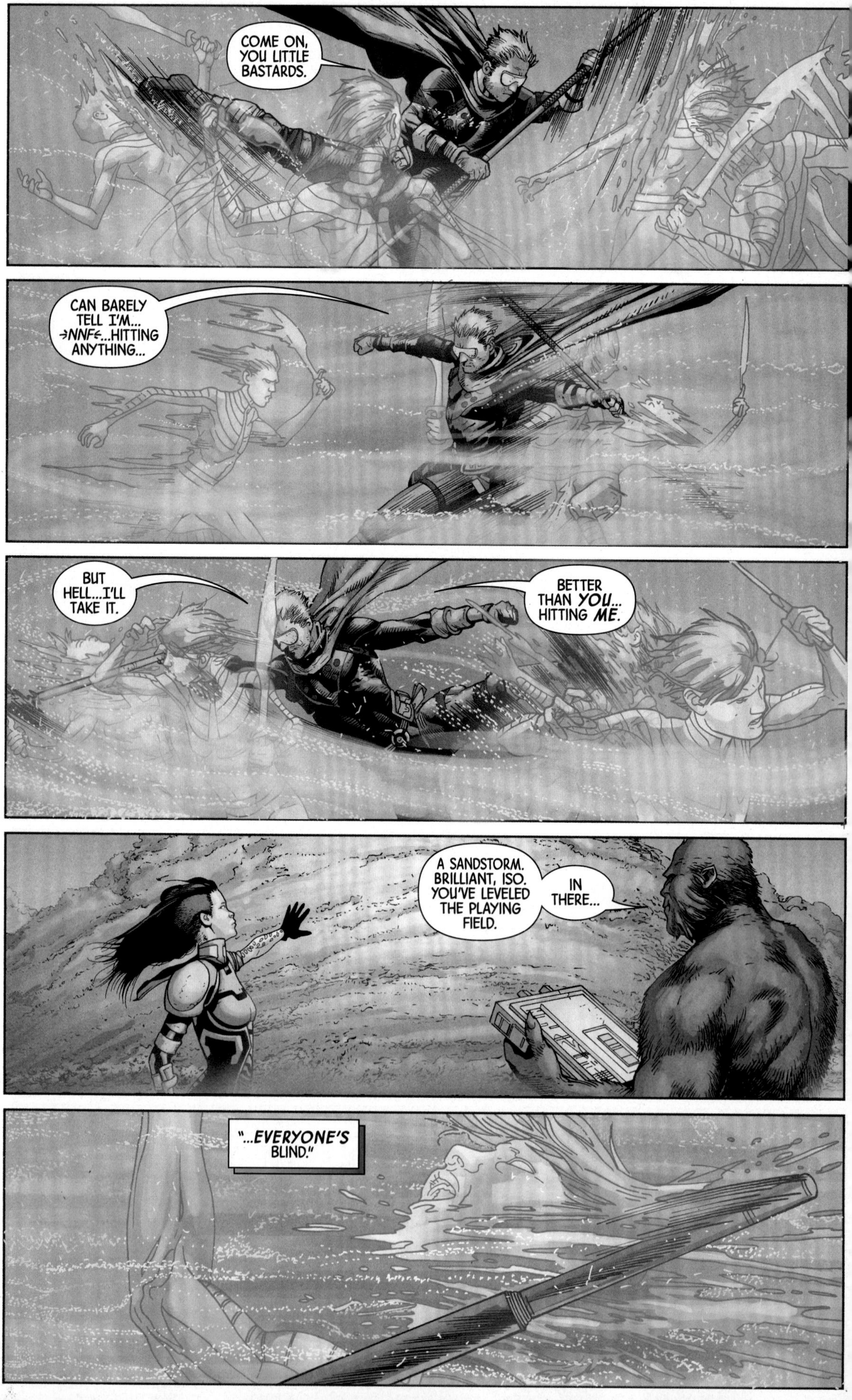
COME ON, YOU LITTLE BASTARDS.
CAN BARELY TELL I'M... ⇒NNF⇐...HITTING ANYTHING...
BUT HELL...I'LL TAKE IT.
BETTER THAN *YOU*... HITTING *ME*.
A SANDSTORM. BRILLIANT, ISO. YOU'VE LEVELED THE PLAYING FIELD.
IN THERE...
"...*EVERYONE'S* BLIND."

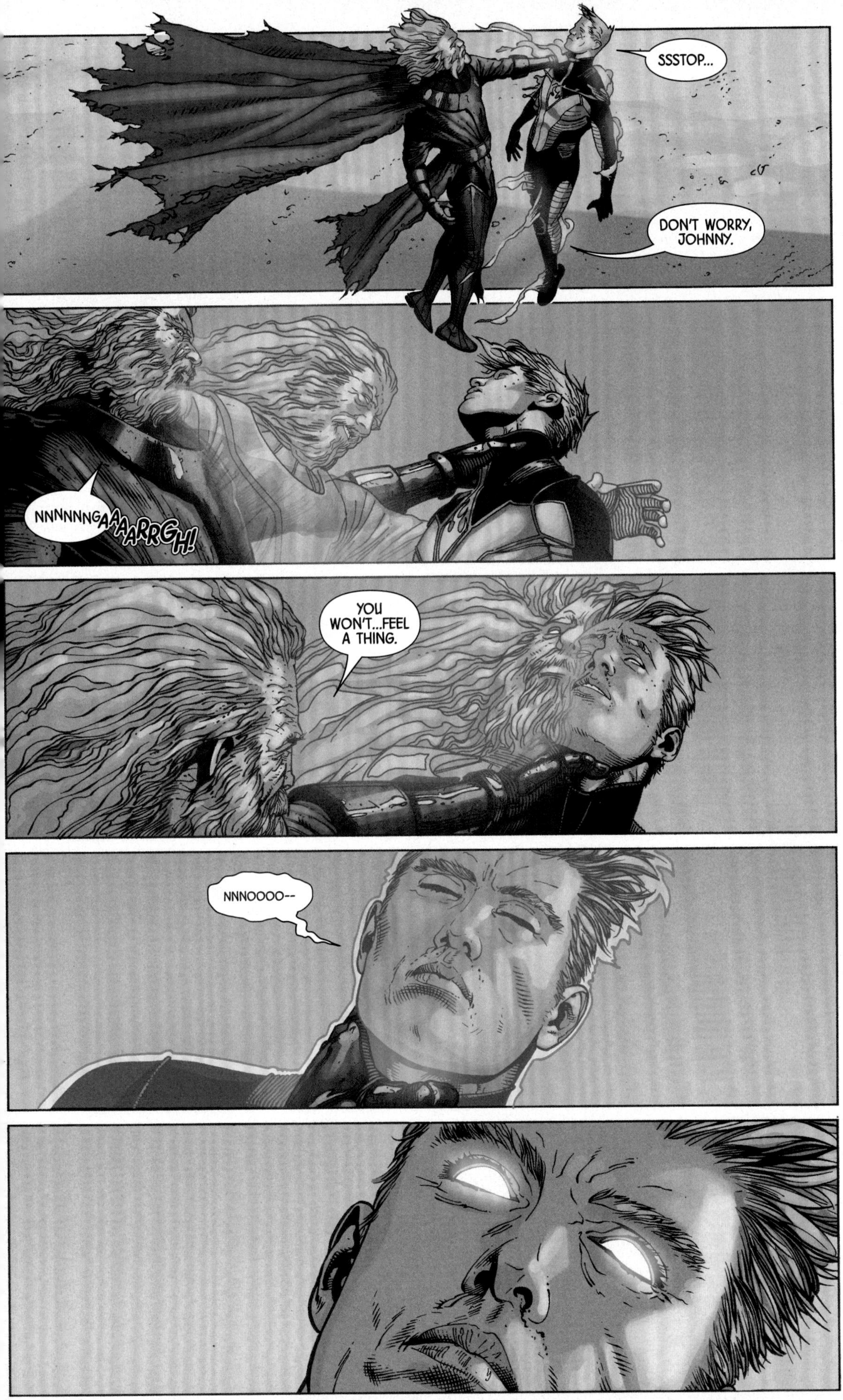
SSSTOP...
DON'T WORRY, JOHNNY.
NNNNNNGAAAARRGH!
YOU WON'T...FEEL A THING.
NNNOOOO--

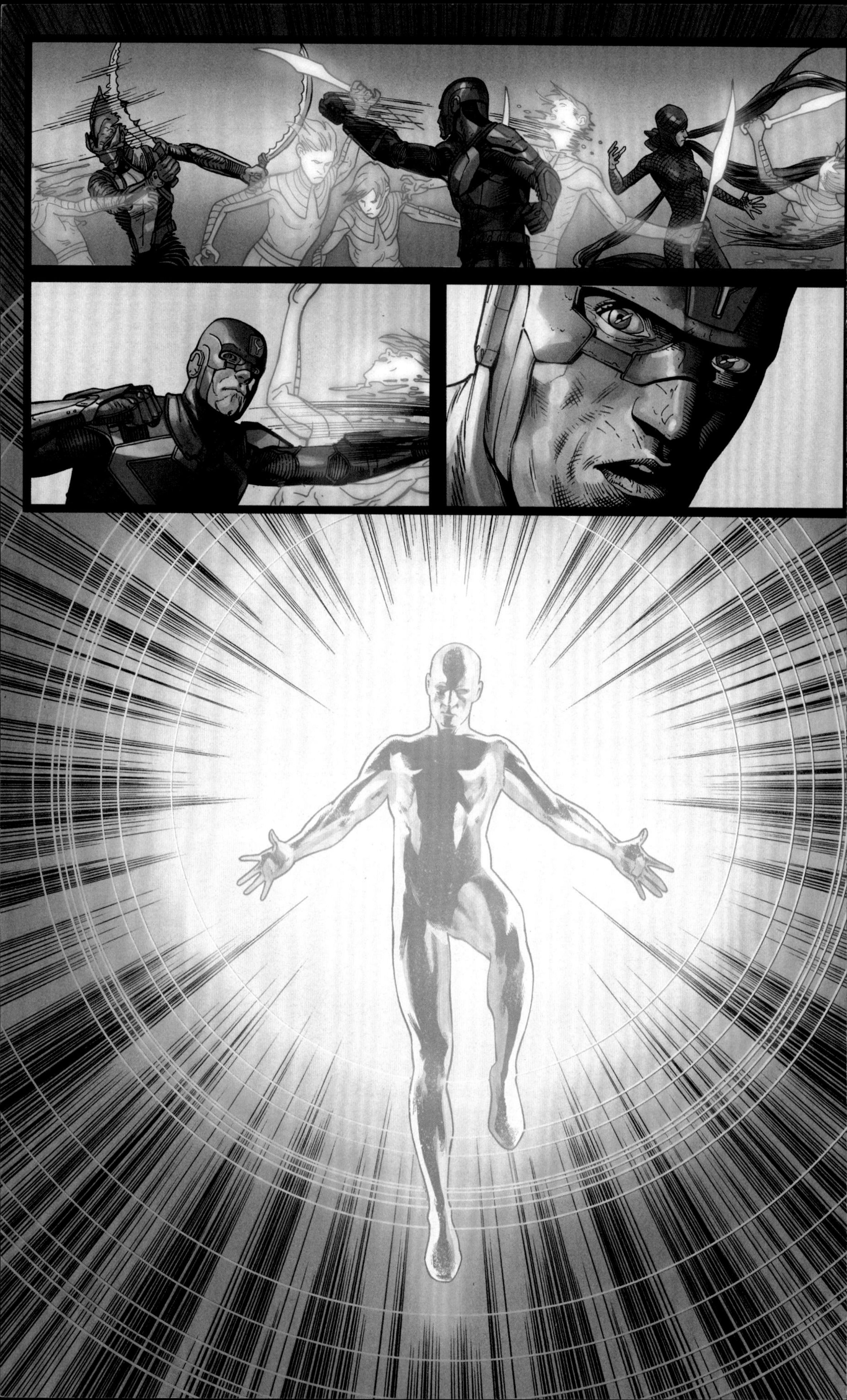

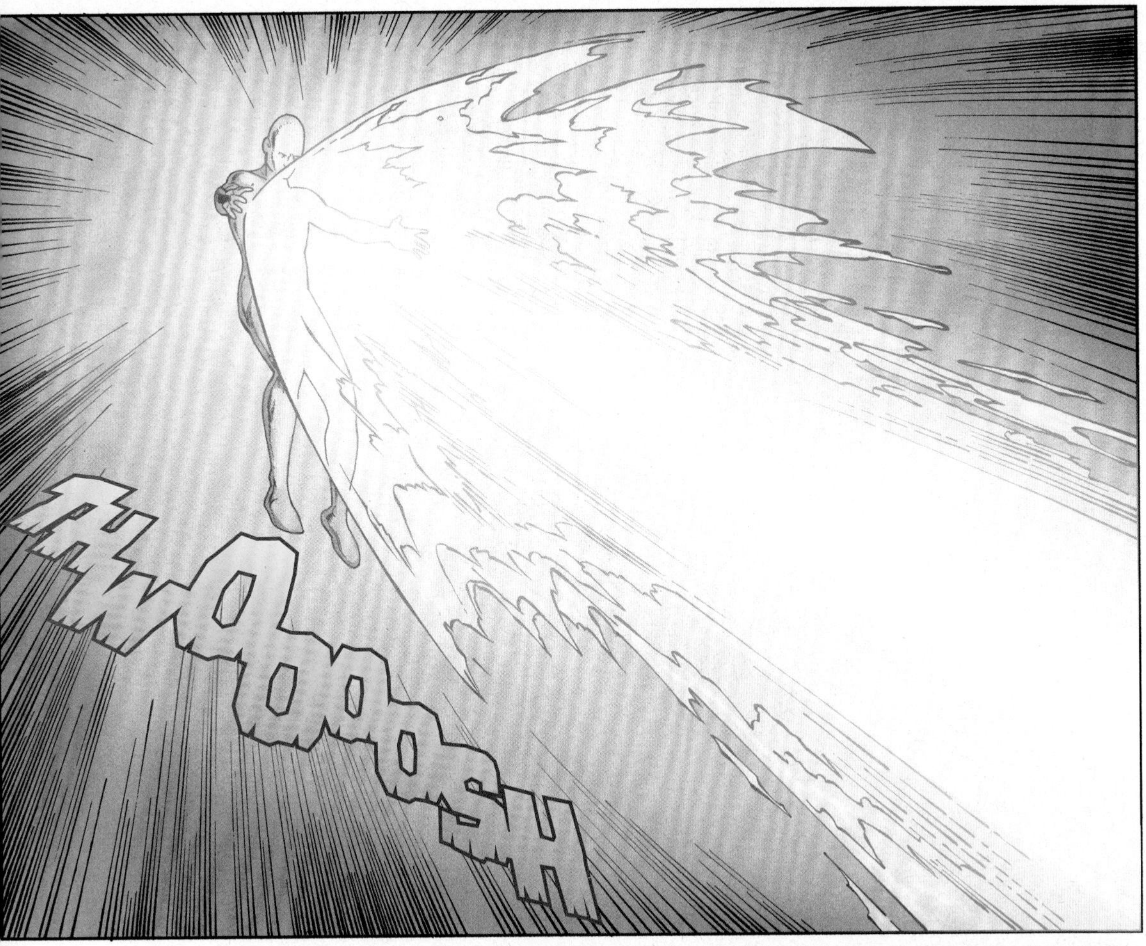
FWOOOOSH

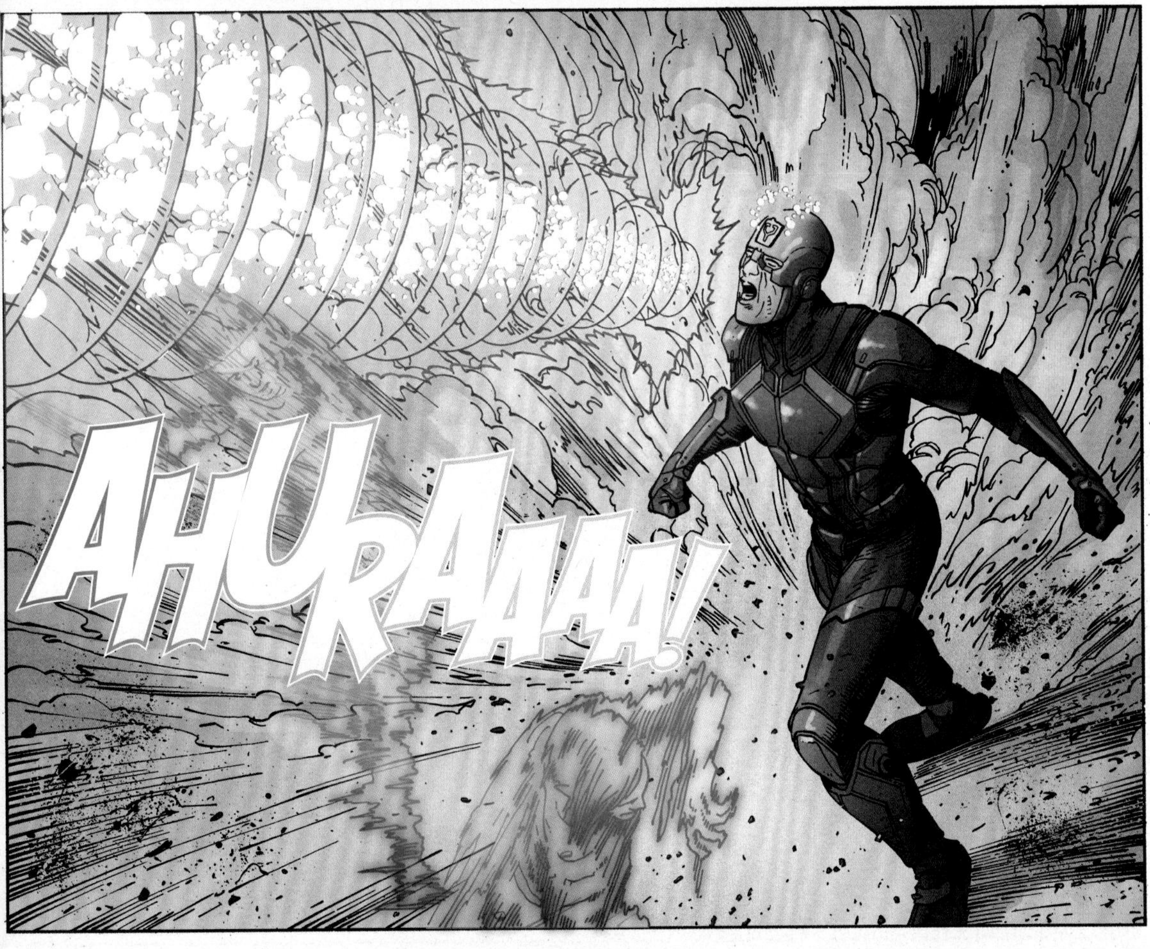
AHURAAAA!

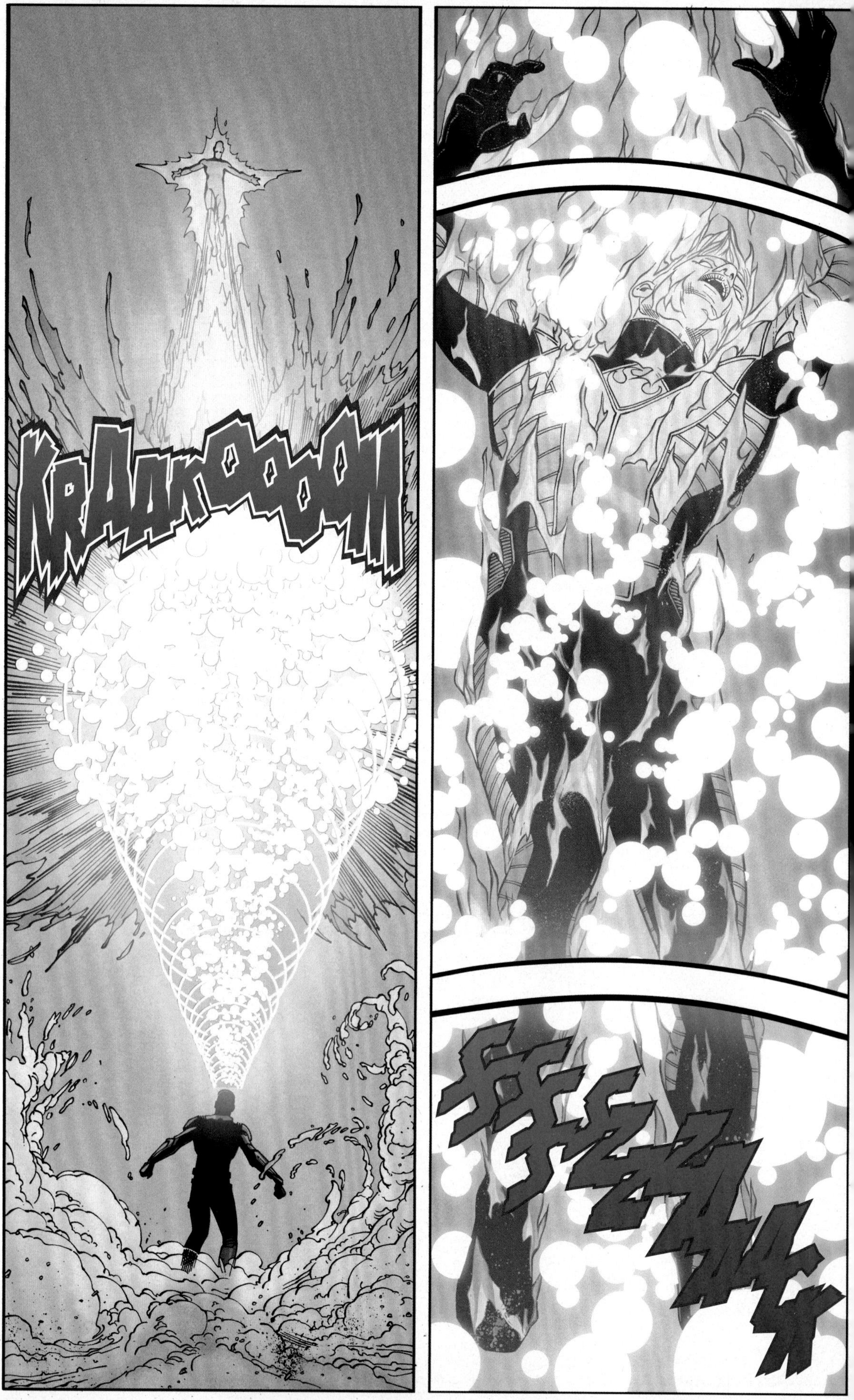
KRAAKOOOOM
SSSZZAAK

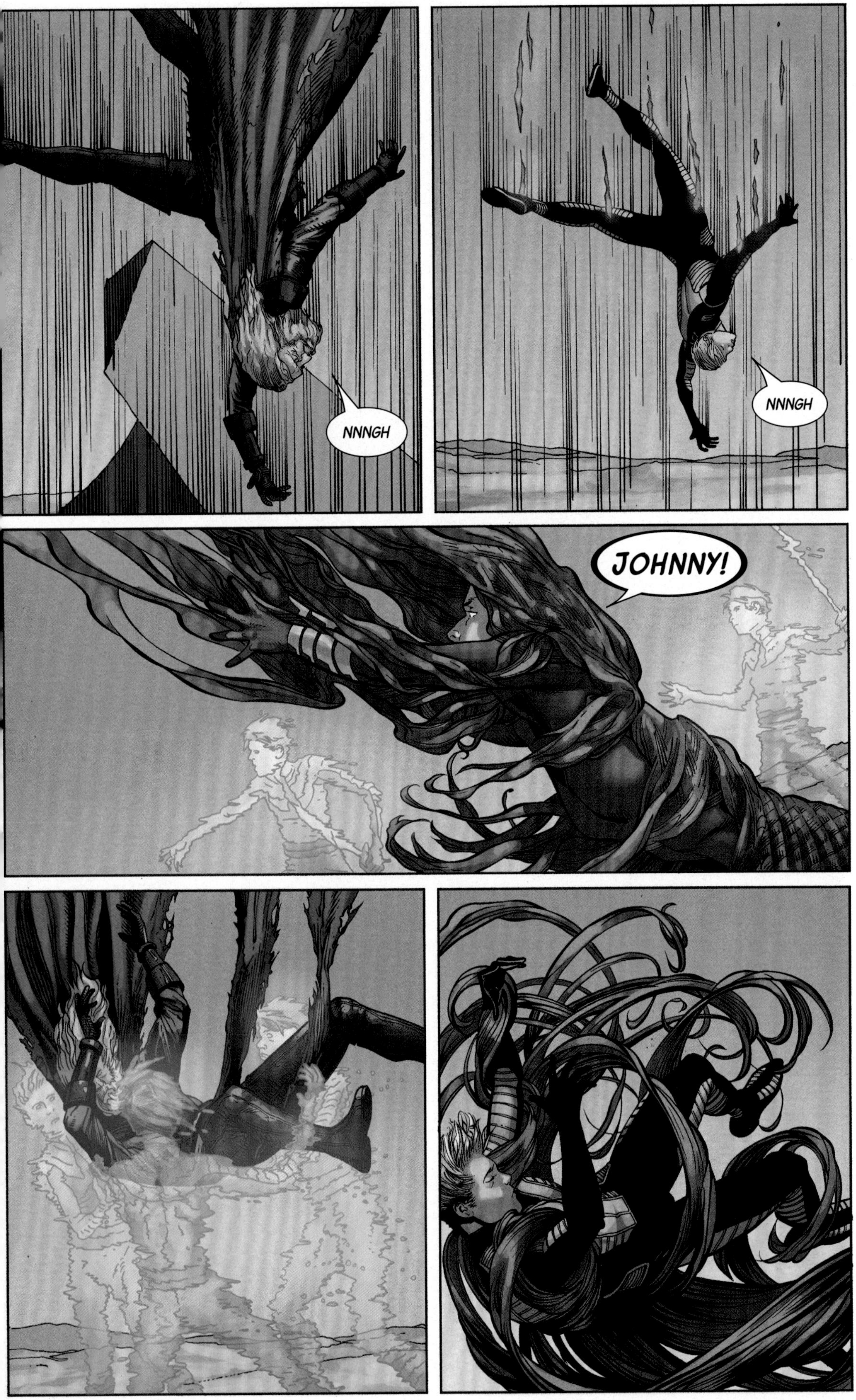
NNNGH
NNNGH
JOHNNY!

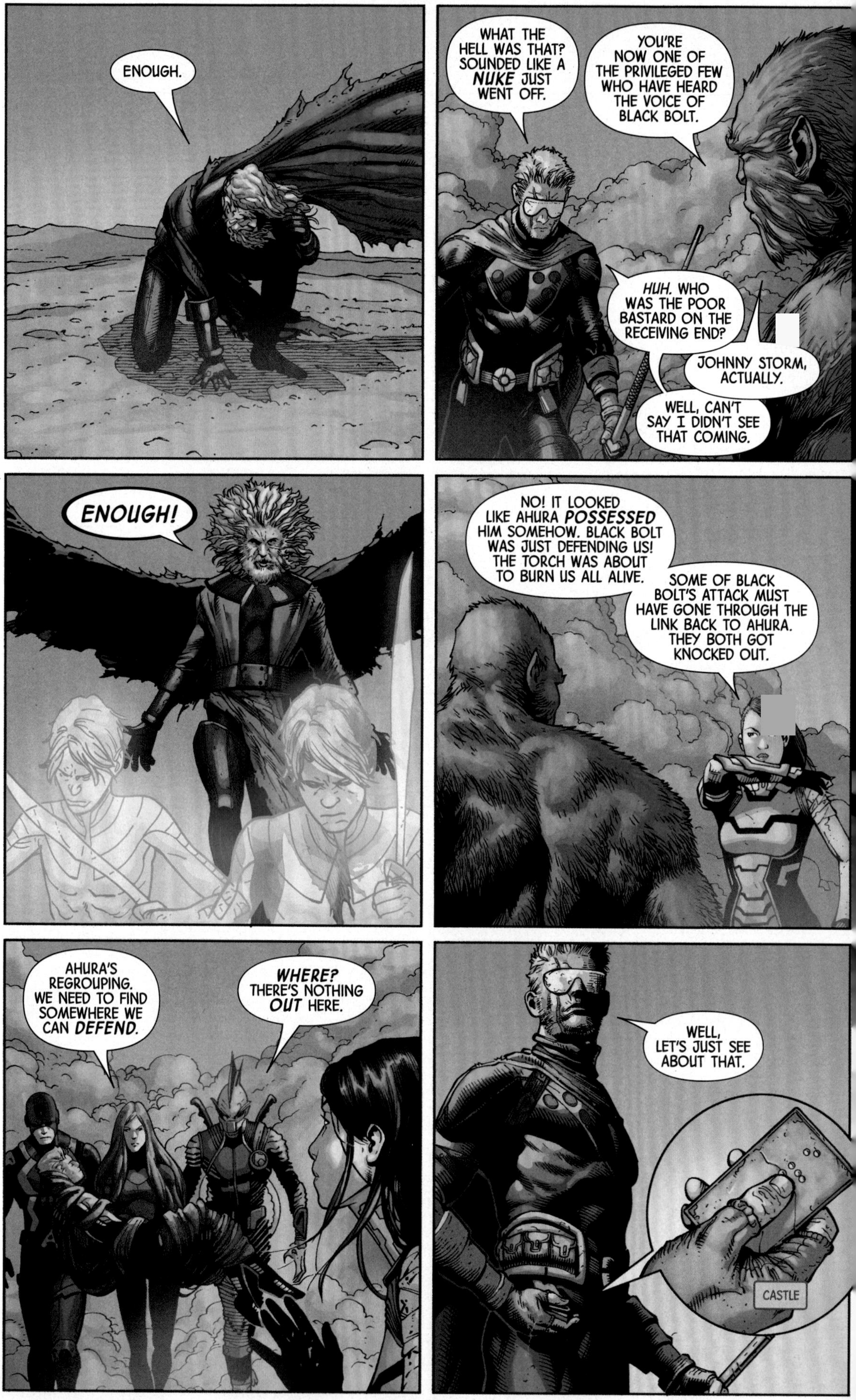
ENOUGH.
WHAT THE HELL WAS THAT? SOUNDED LIKE A NUKE JUST WENT OFF.
YOU'RE NOW ONE OF THE PRIVILEGED FEW WHO HAVE HEARD THE VOICE OF BLACK BOLT.
HUH. WHO WAS THE POOR BASTARD ON THE RECEIVING END?
JOHNNY STORM, ACTUALLY.
WELL, CAN'T SAY I DIDN'T SEE THAT COMING.
ENOUGH!
NO! IT LOOKED LIKE AHURA POSSESSED HIM SOMEHOW. BLACK BOLT WAS JUST DEFENDING US! THE TORCH WAS ABOUT TO BURN US ALL ALIVE.
SOME OF BLACK BOLT'S ATTACK MUST HAVE GONE THROUGH THE LINK BACK TO AHURA. THEY BOTH GOT KNOCKED OUT.
AHURA'S REGROUPING. WE NEED TO FIND SOMEWHERE WE CAN DEFEND.
WHERE? THERE'S NOTHING OUT HERE.
WELL, LET'S JUST SEE ABOUT THAT.
CASTLE

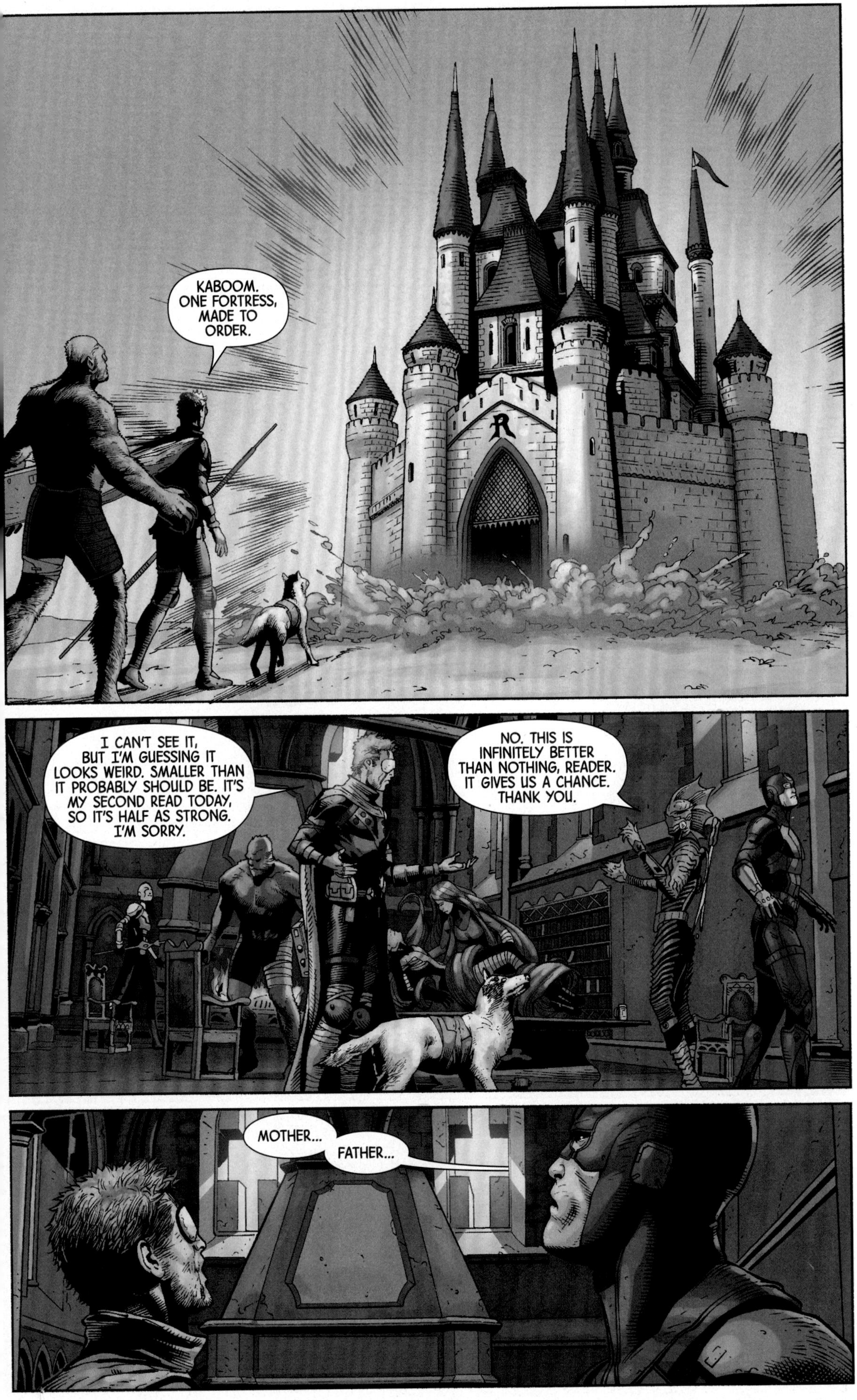
KABOOM. ONE FORTRESS, MADE TO ORDER.
I CAN'T SEE IT, BUT I'M GUESSING IT LOOKS WEIRD. SMALLER THAN IT PROBABLY SHOULD BE. IT'S MY SECOND READ TODAY, SO IT'S HALF AS STRONG. I'M SORRY.
NO. THIS IS INFINITELY BETTER THAN NOTHING, READER. IT GIVES US A CHANCE. THANK YOU.
MOTHER...
FATHER...

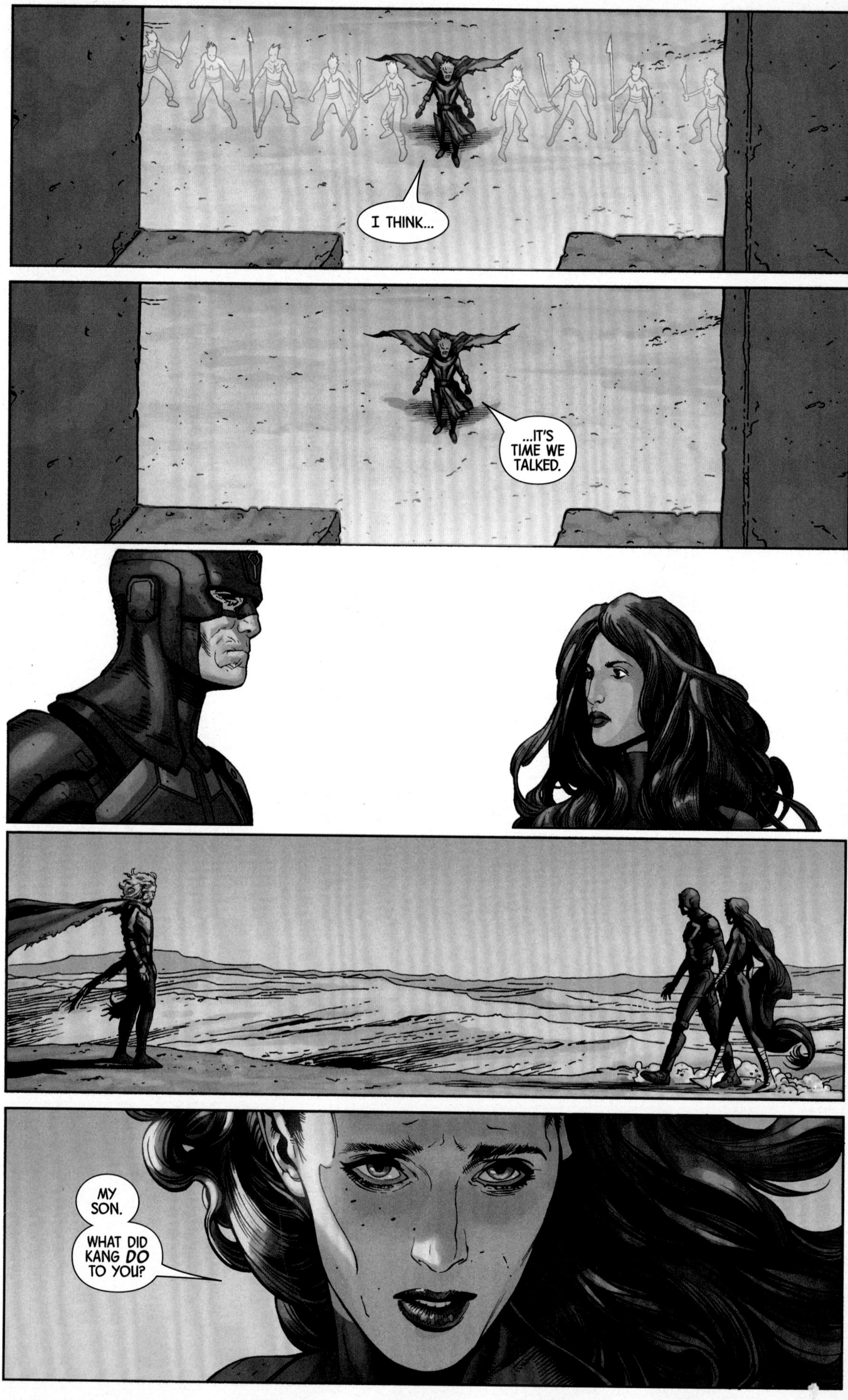
I THINK...
...IT'S TIME WE TALKED.
MY SON.
WHAT DID KANG *DO* TO YOU?

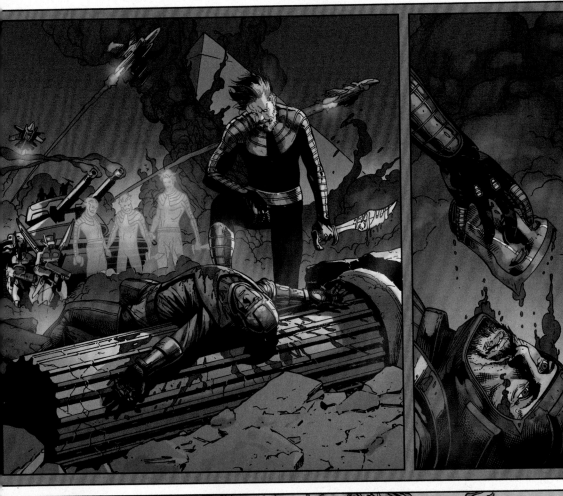

NOTHING, MOTHER.

I DID IT. I DID IT *ALL*.

KANG RAISED ME TO WAR. WE TRAVELED TOGETHER ACROSS THE TIMELINES, AND HE SET ME TASKS. BATTLES.

I DID AS HE ASKED. I WON THEM ALL. HE WAS MY GUARDIAN, AFTER ALL. MY TEACHER. MY *FATHER*.

I AM NO FOOL. I UNDERSTOOD SOON ENOUGH WHAT HE WAS DOING.

ERASING INHUMANS FROM THE TIMESTREAM.

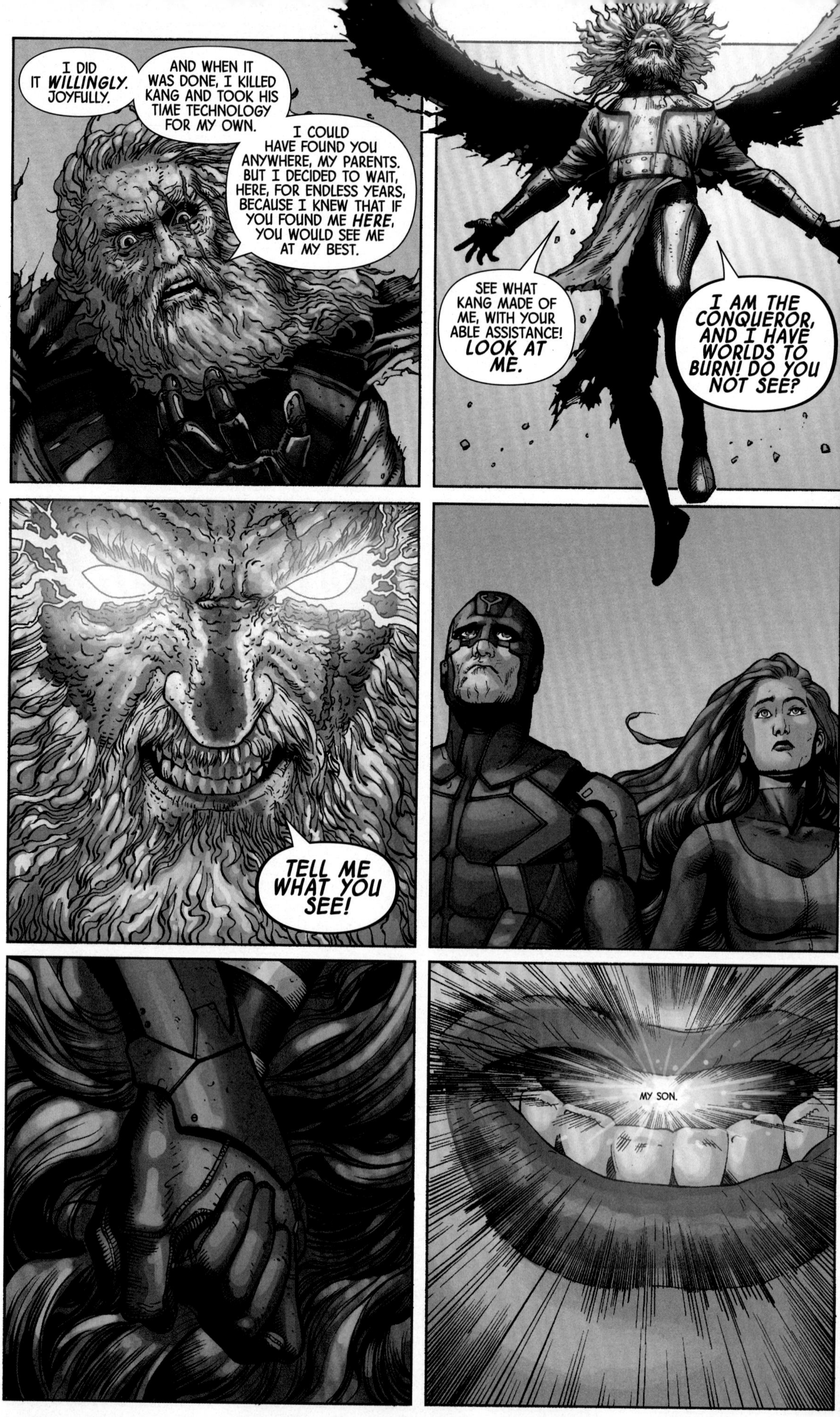
I DID IT *WILLINGLY.* JOYFULLY.
AND WHEN IT WAS DONE, I KILLED KANG AND TOOK HIS TIME TECHNOLOGY FOR MY OWN.
I COULD HAVE FOUND YOU ANYWHERE, MY PARENTS. BUT I DECIDED TO WAIT, HERE, FOR ENDLESS YEARS, BECAUSE I KNEW THAT IF YOU FOUND ME *HERE*, YOU WOULD SEE ME AT MY BEST.
SEE WHAT KANG MADE OF ME, WITH YOUR ABLE ASSISTANCE! *LOOK AT ME.*
I AM THE CONQUEROR, AND I HAVE WORLDS TO BURN! DO YOU NOT SEE?
TELL ME WHAT YOU SEE!
MY SON.

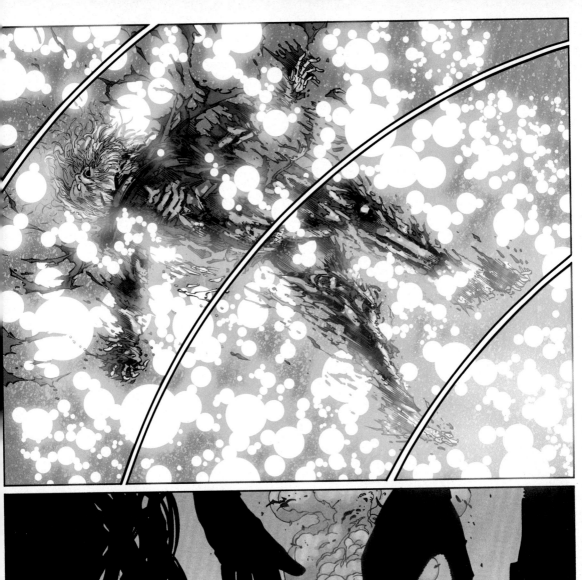

COME. ALL OF YOU.

WE NEED TO SAVE AHURA.

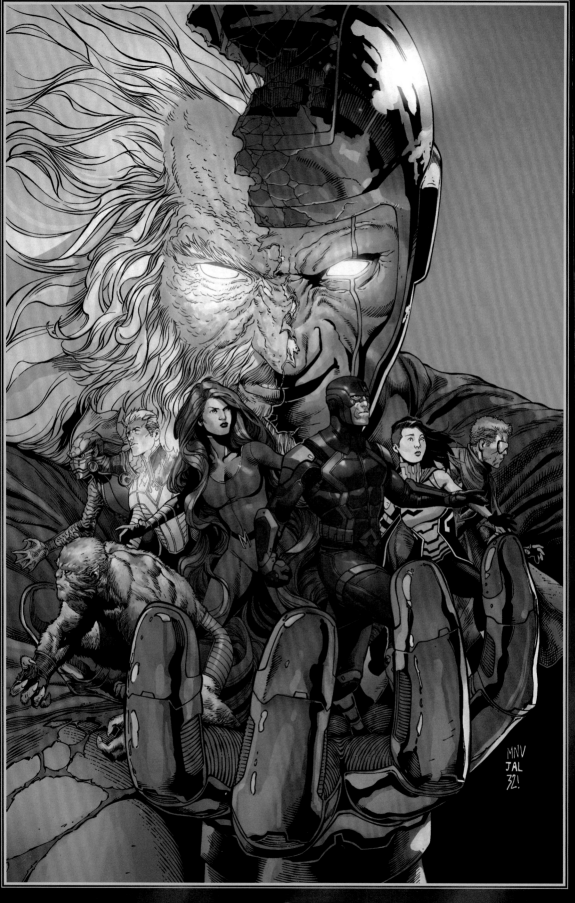

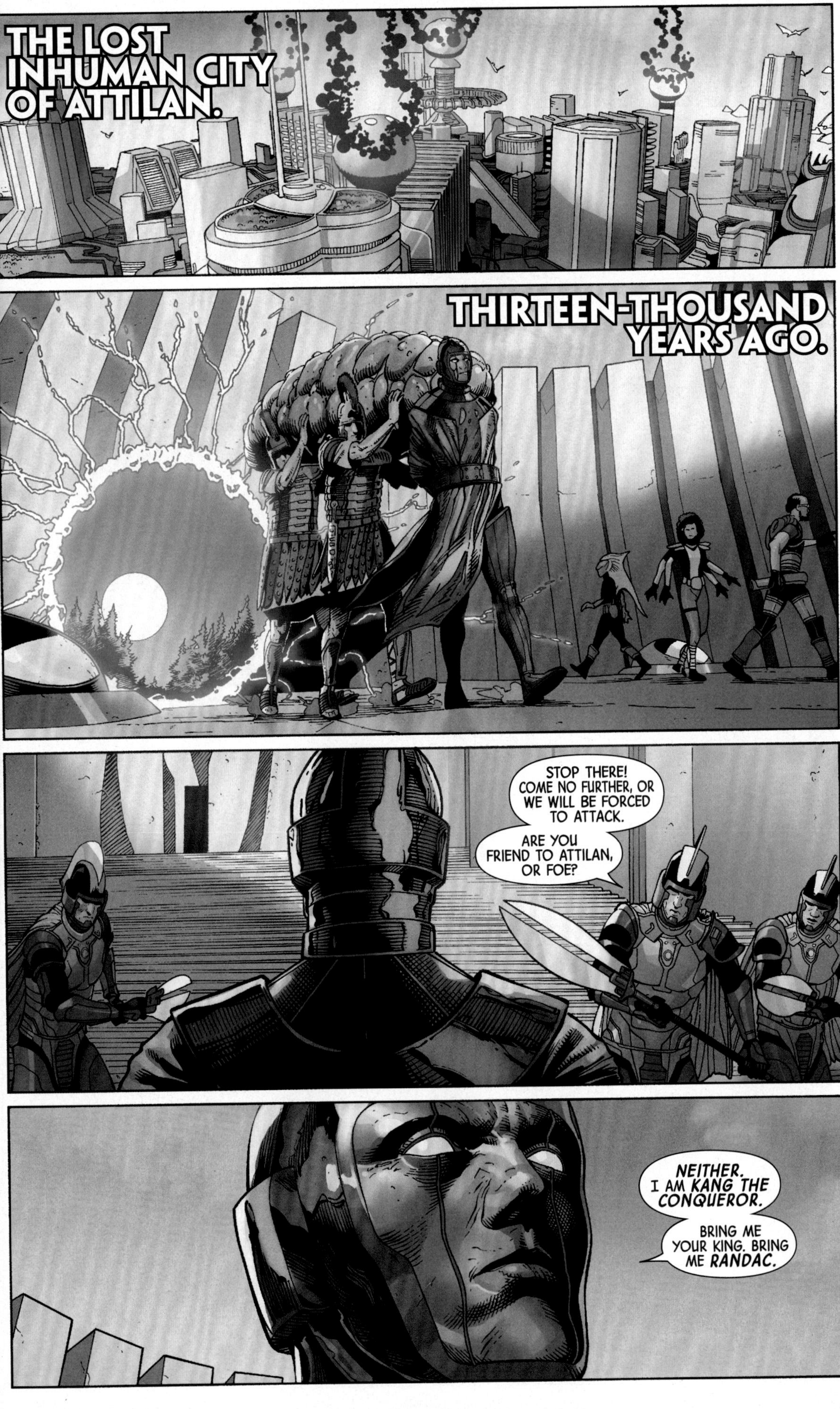
THE LOST INHUMAN CITY OF ATTILAN.
THIRTEEN-THOUSAND YEARS AGO.
STOP THERE! COME NO FURTHER, OR WE WILL BE FORCED TO ATTACK.
ARE YOU FRIEND TO ATTILAN, OR FOE?
NEITHER. I AM KANG THE CONQUEROR.
BRING ME YOUR KING. BRING ME RANDAC.

THIS IS NOT POSSIBLE.

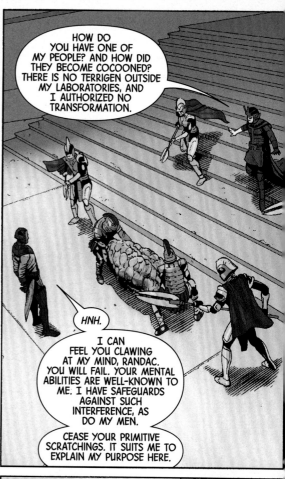

HOW DO YOU HAVE ONE OF MY PEOPLE? AND HOW DID THEY BECOME COCOONED? THERE IS NO TERRIGEN OUTSIDE MY LABORATORIES, AND I AUTHORIZED NO TRANSFORMATION.

HNH.

I CAN FEEL YOU CLAWING AT MY MIND, RANDAC. YOU WILL FAIL. YOUR MENTAL ABILITIES ARE WELL-KNOWN TO ME. I HAVE SAFEGUARDS AGAINST SUCH INTERFERENCE, AS DO MY MEN.

CEASE YOUR PRIMITIVE SCRATCHINGS. IT SUITS ME TO EXPLAIN MY PURPOSE HERE.

THIS IS AHURA, AN INHUMAN FROM FAR IN THE FUTURE. HE WAS GIVEN TO ME BY HIS FATHER, ANOTHER INHUMAN KING, BLACKAGAR BOLTAGON.

BLACK BOLT EXPOSED AHURA TO THE TERRIGEN MISTS, AND THEN ASKED ME TO USE MY TIME-SHIFTING TECHNOLOGY TO BRING HIM HERE, TO YOU.

I BELIEVE HE HOPED YOU MIGHT HELP WITH AHURA'S TRANSITION TO WHATEVER FORM HE WILL HOLD WHEN HE EMERGES FROM THE COCOON.

YES... MY EXPERIMENTS SUGGEST HE WILL POSSESS NEW ABILITIES, BUT THUS FAR TERRIGENESIS IS COMPLETELY UNPREDICTABLE. HE COULD BE ANYTHING. ANYTHING AT ALL.

I WILL HELP--NO MATTER WHAT TIME THIS CHILD COMES FROM, ALL INHUMANS ARE MY PEOPLE.

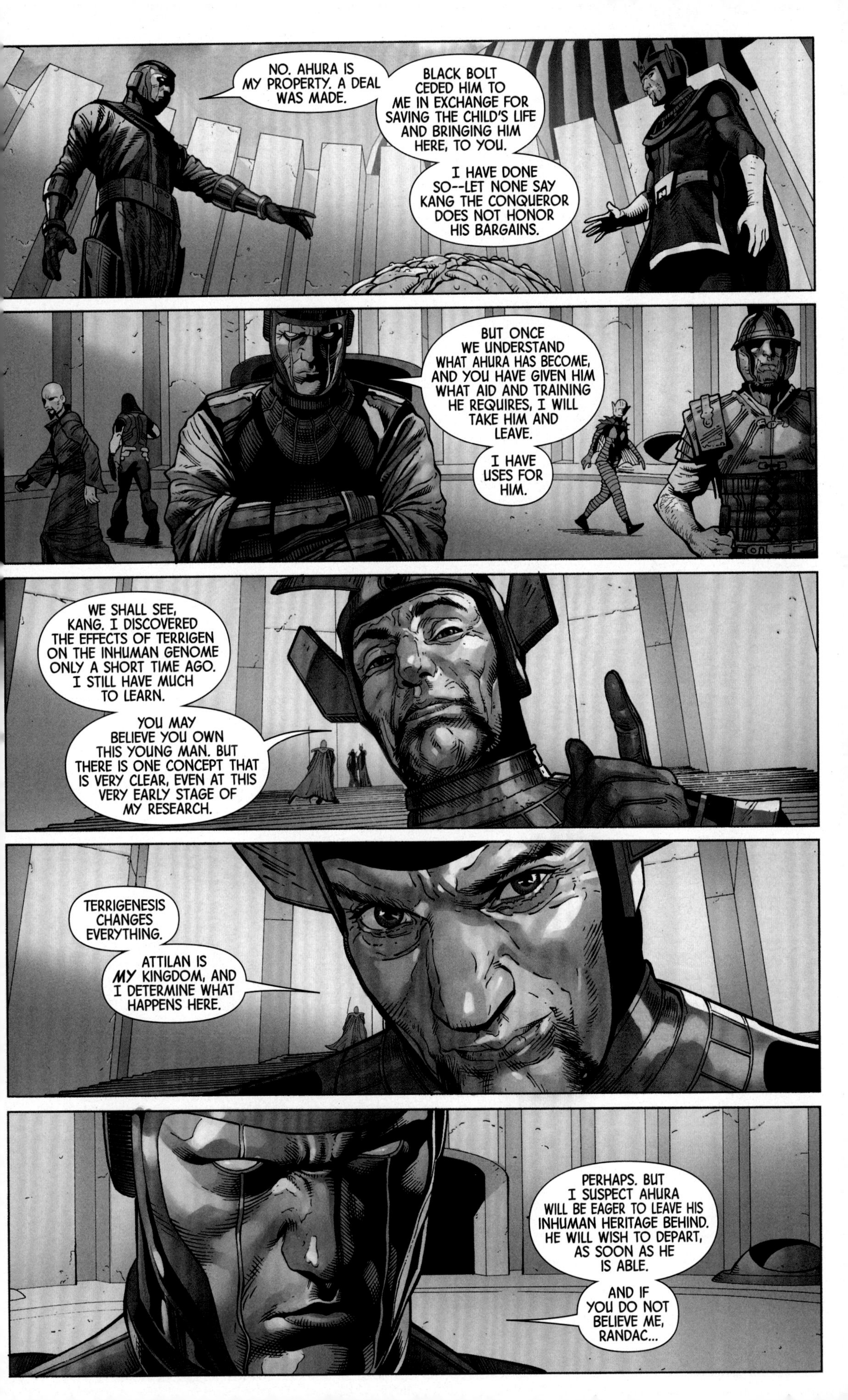
NO. AHURA IS MY PROPERTY. A DEAL WAS MADE.
BLACK BOLT CEDED HIM TO ME IN EXCHANGE FOR SAVING THE CHILD'S LIFE AND BRINGING HIM HERE, TO YOU.
I HAVE DONE SO--LET NONE SAY KANG THE CONQUEROR DOES NOT HONOR HIS BARGAINS.
BUT ONCE WE UNDERSTAND WHAT AHURA HAS BECOME, AND YOU HAVE GIVEN HIM WHAT AID AND TRAINING HE REQUIRES, I WILL TAKE HIM AND LEAVE.
I HAVE USES FOR HIM.
WE SHALL SEE, KANG. I DISCOVERED THE EFFECTS OF TERRIGEN ON THE INHUMAN GENOME ONLY A SHORT TIME AGO. I STILL HAVE MUCH TO LEARN.
YOU MAY BELIEVE YOU OWN THIS YOUNG MAN. BUT THERE IS ONE CONCEPT THAT IS VERY CLEAR, EVEN AT THIS VERY EARLY STAGE OF MY RESEARCH.
TERRIGENESIS CHANGES EVERYTHING.
ATTILAN IS *MY* KINGDOM, AND I DETERMINE WHAT HAPPENS HERE.
PERHAPS. BUT I SUSPECT AHURA WILL BE EAGER TO LEAVE HIS INHUMAN HERITAGE BEHIND. HE WILL WISH TO DEPART, AS SOON AS HE IS ABLE.
AND IF YOU DO NOT BELIEVE ME, RANDAC...

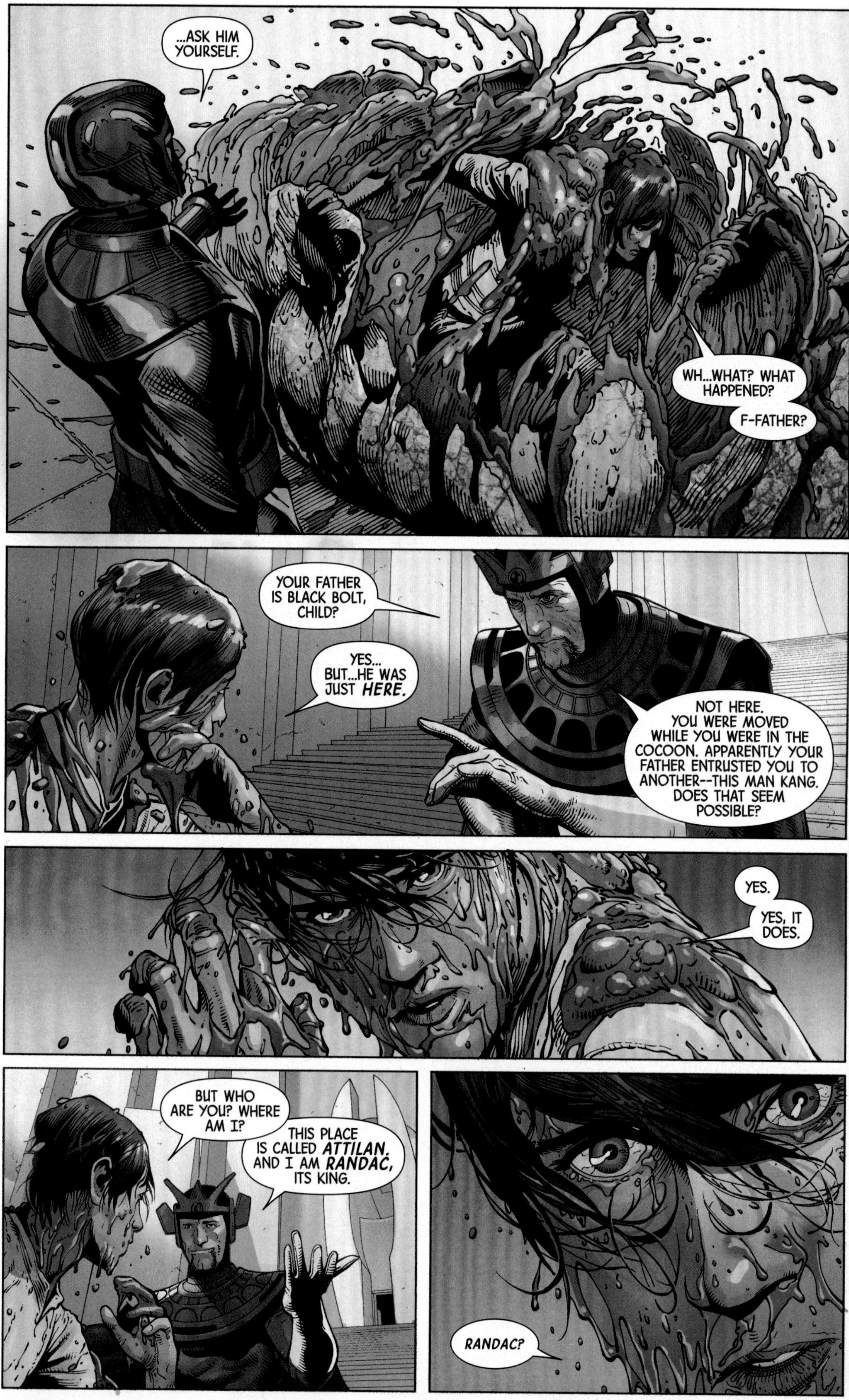
...ASK HIM YOURSELF.
WH...WHAT? WHAT HAPPENED?
F-FATHER?
YOUR FATHER IS BLACK BOLT, CHILD?
YES... BUT...HE WAS JUST *HERE.*
NOT HERE. YOU WERE MOVED WHILE YOU WERE IN THE COCOON. APPARENTLY YOUR FATHER ENTRUSTED YOU TO ANOTHER--THIS MAN KANG. DOES THAT SEEM POSSIBLE?
YES.
YES, IT DOES.
BUT WHO ARE YOU? WHERE AM I?
THIS PLACE IS CALLED *ATTILAN.* AND I AM *RANDAC,* ITS KING.
RANDAC?

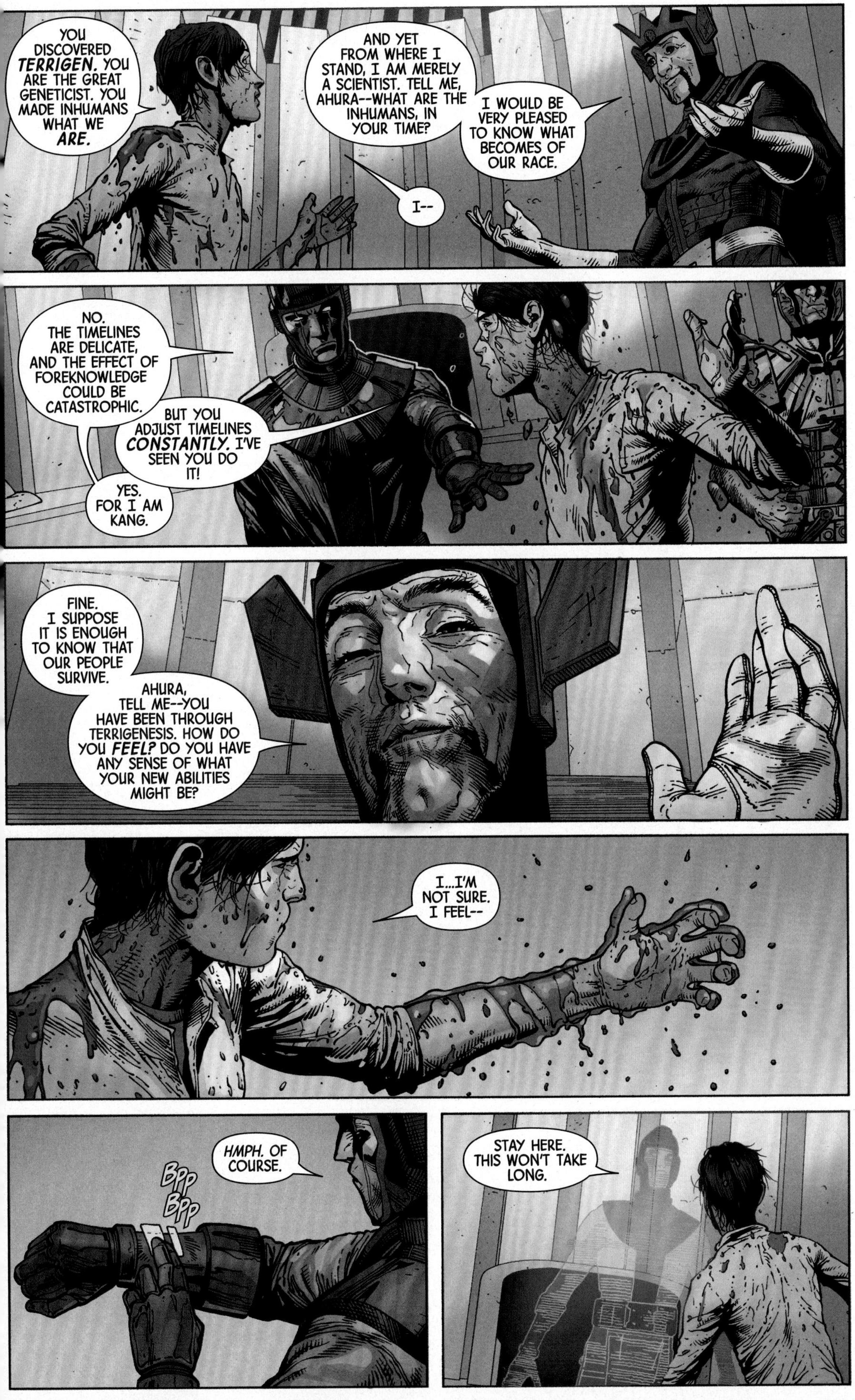
YOU DISCOVERED TERRIGEN. YOU ARE THE GREAT GENETICIST. YOU MADE INHUMANS WHAT WE ARE.
AND YET FROM WHERE I STAND, I AM MERELY A SCIENTIST. TELL ME, AHURA--WHAT ARE THE INHUMANS, IN YOUR TIME?
I WOULD BE VERY PLEASED TO KNOW WHAT BECOMES OF OUR RACE.
I--
NO. THE TIMELINES ARE DELICATE, AND THE EFFECT OF FOREKNOWLEDGE COULD BE CATASTROPHIC.
BUT YOU ADJUST TIMELINES CONSTANTLY. I'VE SEEN YOU DO IT!
YES. FOR I AM KANG.
FINE. I SUPPOSE IT IS ENOUGH TO KNOW THAT OUR PEOPLE SURVIVE.
AHURA, TELL ME--YOU HAVE BEEN THROUGH TERRIGENESIS. HOW DO YOU FEEL? DO YOU HAVE ANY SENSE OF WHAT YOUR NEW ABILITIES MIGHT BE?
I...I'M NOT SURE. I FEEL--
BPP BPP
HMPH. OF COURSE.
STAY HERE. THIS WON'T TAKE LONG.

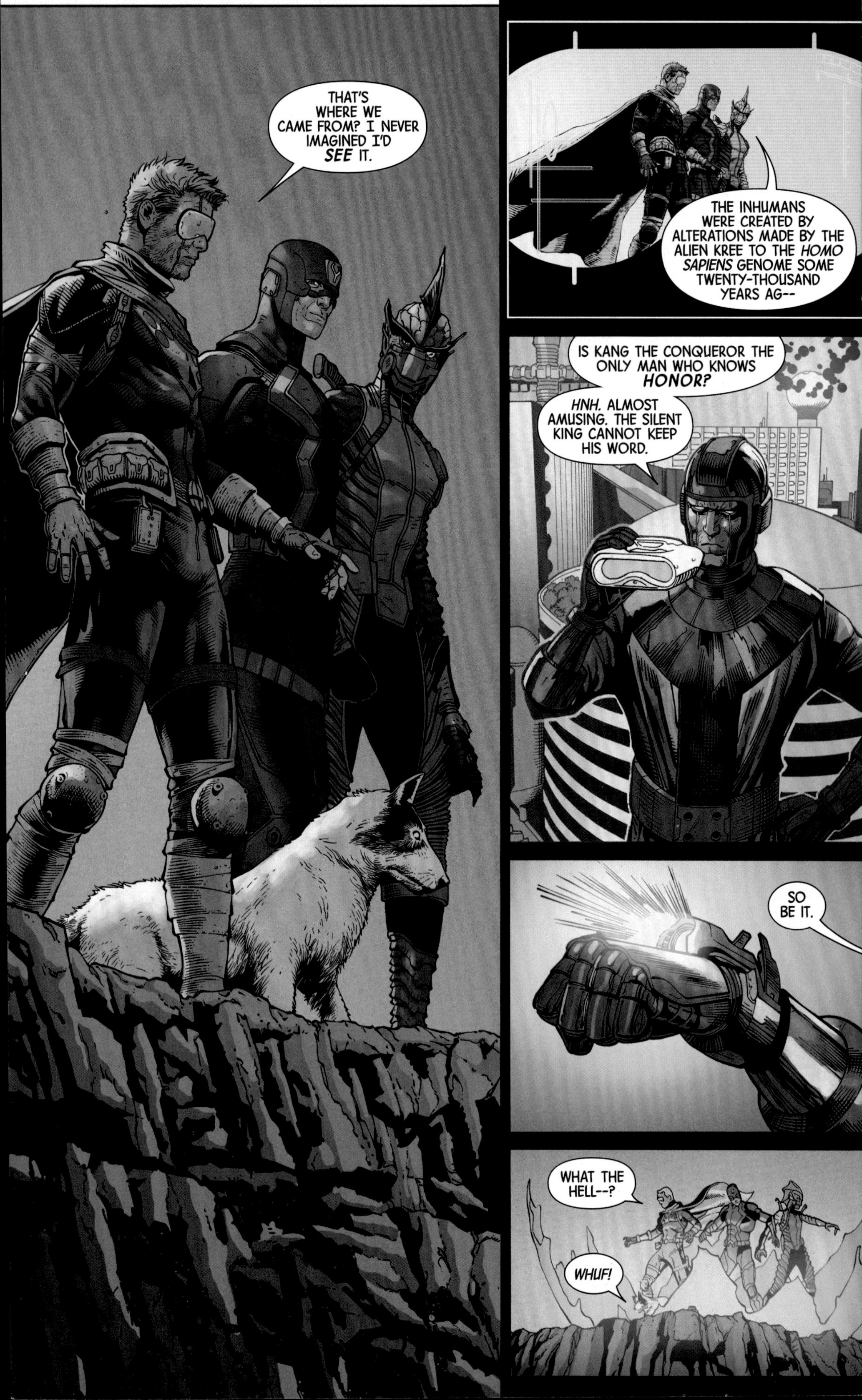
THAT'S WHERE WE CAME FROM? I NEVER IMAGINED I'D *SEE* IT.
THE INHUMANS WERE CREATED BY ALTERATIONS MADE BY THE ALIEN KREE TO THE *HOMO SAPIENS* GENOME SOME TWENTY-THOUSAND YEARS AG--
IS KANG THE CONQUEROR THE ONLY MAN WHO KNOWS *HONOR?*
HNH. ALMOST AMUSING. THE SILENT KING CANNOT KEEP HIS WORD.
SO BE IT.
WHAT THE HELL--?
WHUF!

AND OFF YOU WENT. SIMPLY BRILLIANT.

YOUR EARLIER TIME-JUMP TO THIS MOMENT MASKED OUR ARRIVAL NOW--KANG DOESN'T EVEN REALIZE WE'RE HERE.

DID YOU PLAN IT THIS WAY FROM THE START, BLACK BOLT? IF SO...THAT'S JUST INCREDIBLE.

ASK HIM IF KANG DAMN NEAR KILLING US BACK THEN WAS PART OF THE PLAN TOO, BEAST.

EITHER WAY, I WOULDN'T HOLD YOUR BREATH. BLACK BOLT'S NOT MUCH FOR EXPLAINING.

THIS GEAR'S FRIED.

MAYBE THAT OLD VERSION OF AHURA BOOBY-TRAPPED IT, OR MAYBE WE JUST DIDN'T USE IT RIGHT, READER, BUT NO MORE TIME TRAVEL FOR US. AT LEAST USING THIS.

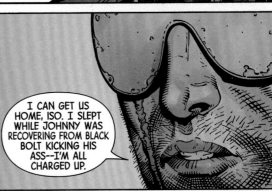

I CAN GET US HOME, ISO. I SLEPT WHILE JOHNNY WAS RECOVERING FROM BLACK BOLT KICKING HIS ASS--I'M ALL CHARGED UP.

KANG WON'T BE DISTRACTED FOR LONG. WE NEED TO FIND AHURA.

ANY IDEAS HOW WE'RE SUPPOSED TO DO THAT, MEDUSA?

YES, JOHNNY. WAIT HERE.

HELLO. MY NAME IS MEDUSA. THIRTEEN-THOUSAND YEARS FROM NOW, I AM QUEEN OF THE INHUMANS.

I HAVE TRAVELED BACK IN TIME TO PREVENT THE DOOM OF OUR RACE AT THE HANDS OF MY ONLY SON.

TAKE ME TO YOUR KING.

UH...

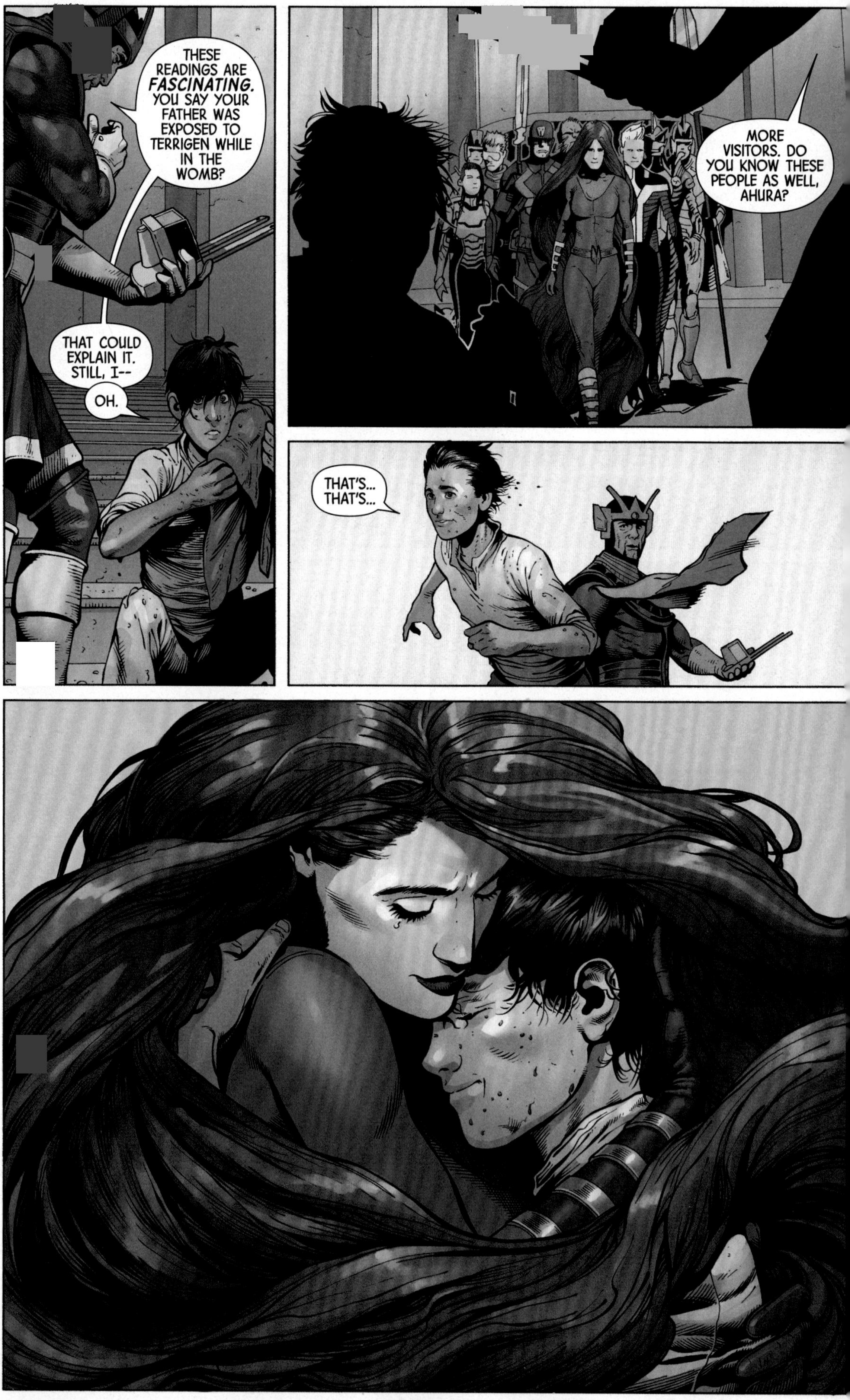
THESE READINGS ARE FASCINATING. YOU SAY YOUR FATHER WAS EXPOSED TO TERRIGEN WHILE IN THE WOMB?
THAT COULD EXPLAIN IT. STILL, I--
OH.
MORE VISITORS. DO YOU KNOW THESE PEOPLE AS WELL, AHURA?
THAT'S... THAT'S...

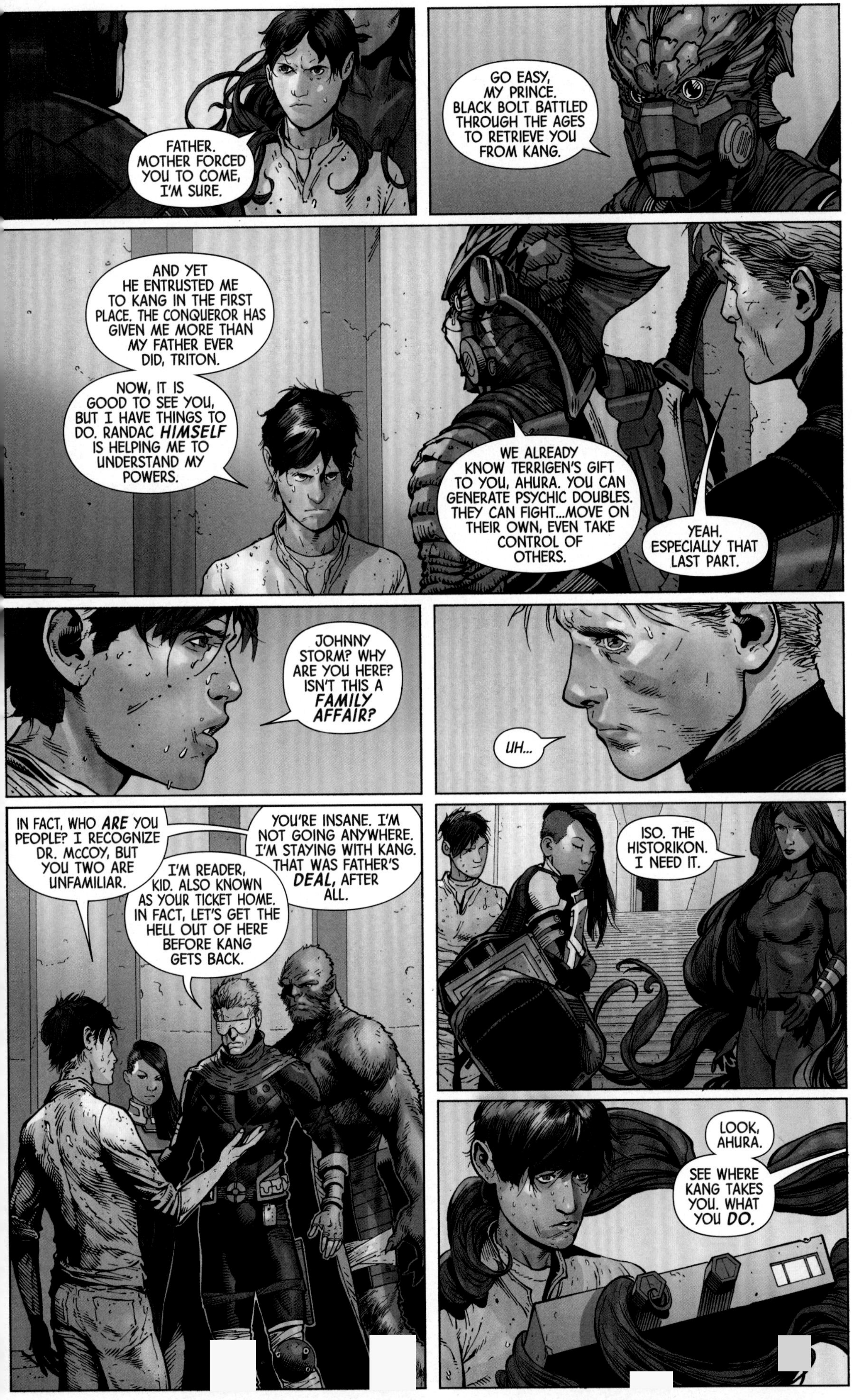
FATHER. MOTHER FORCED YOU TO COME, I'M SURE.
GO EASY, MY PRINCE. BLACK BOLT BATTLED THROUGH THE AGES TO RETRIEVE YOU FROM KANG.
AND YET HE ENTRUSTED ME TO KANG IN THE FIRST PLACE. THE CONQUEROR HAS GIVEN ME MORE THAN MY FATHER EVER DID, TRITON.
NOW, IT IS GOOD TO SEE YOU, BUT I HAVE THINGS TO DO. RANDAC *HIMSELF* IS HELPING ME TO UNDERSTAND MY POWERS.
WE ALREADY KNOW TERRIGEN'S GIFT TO YOU, AHURA. YOU CAN GENERATE PSYCHIC DOUBLES. THEY CAN FIGHT...MOVE ON THEIR OWN, EVEN TAKE CONTROL OF OTHERS.
YEAH. ESPECIALLY THAT LAST PART.
JOHNNY STORM? WHY ARE YOU HERE? ISN'T THIS A *FAMILY AFFAIR?*
UH...
IN FACT, WHO *ARE* YOU PEOPLE? I RECOGNIZE DR. McCOY, BUT YOU TWO ARE UNFAMILIAR.
I'M READER, KID. ALSO KNOWN AS YOUR TICKET HOME. IN FACT, LET'S GET THE HELL OUT OF HERE BEFORE KANG GETS BACK.
YOU'RE INSANE. I'M NOT GOING ANYWHERE. I'M STAYING WITH KANG. THAT WAS FATHER'S *DEAL,* AFTER ALL.
ISO. THE HISTORIKON. I NEED IT.
LOOK, AHURA.
SEE WHERE KANG TAKES YOU. WHAT YOU *DO.*

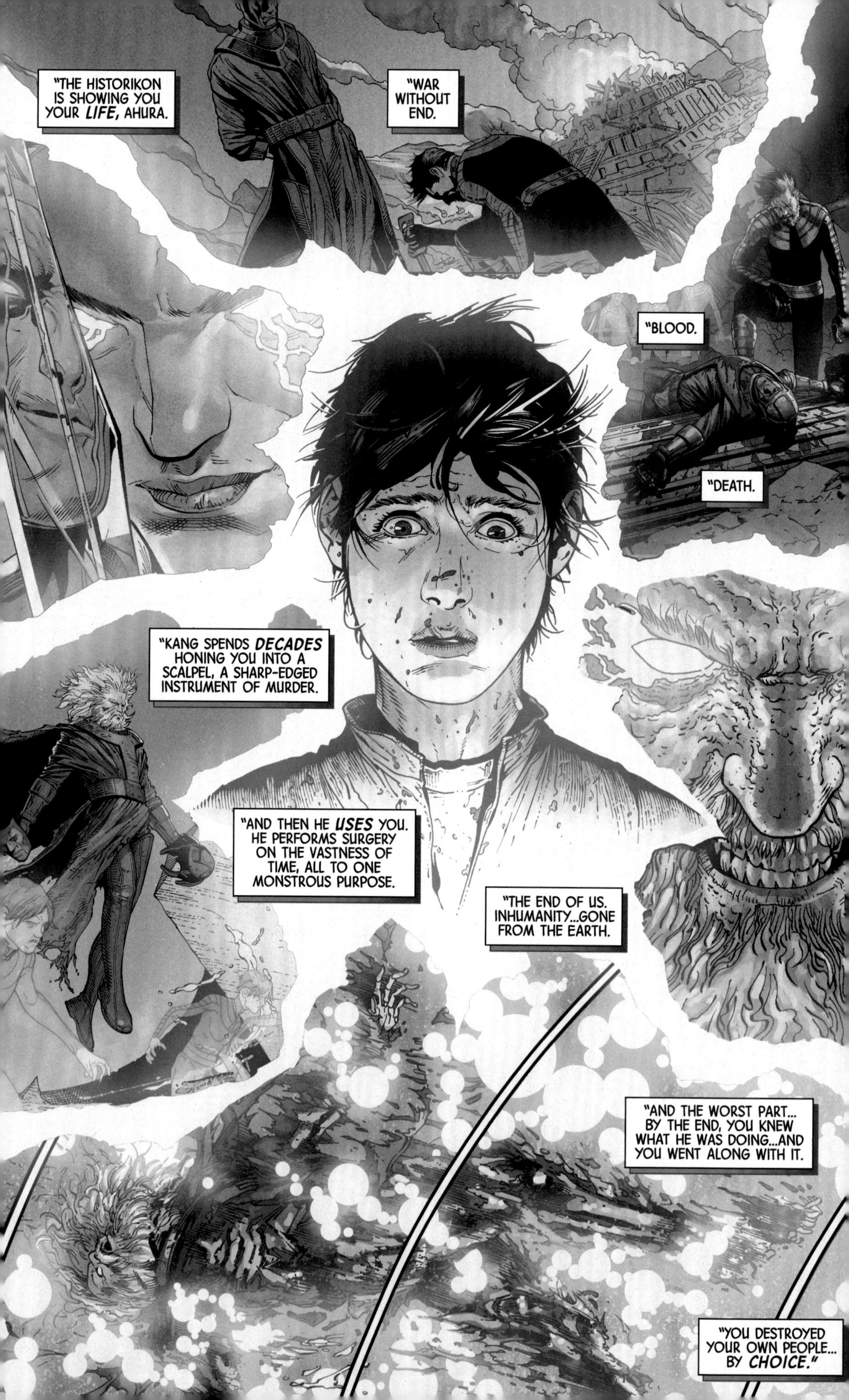
"THE HISTORIKON IS SHOWING YOU YOUR LIFE, AHURA.
"WAR WITHOUT END.
"BLOOD.
"DEATH.
"KANG SPENDS DECADES HONING YOU INTO A SCALPEL, A SHARP-EDGED INSTRUMENT OF MURDER.
"AND THEN HE USES YOU. HE PERFORMS SURGERY ON THE VASTNESS OF TIME, ALL TO ONE MONSTROUS PURPOSE.
"THE END OF US. INHUMANITY...GONE FROM THE EARTH.
"AND THE WORST PART... BY THE END, YOU KNEW WHAT HE WAS DOING...AND YOU WENT ALONG WITH IT.
"YOU DESTROYED YOUR OWN PEOPLE... BY CHOICE."

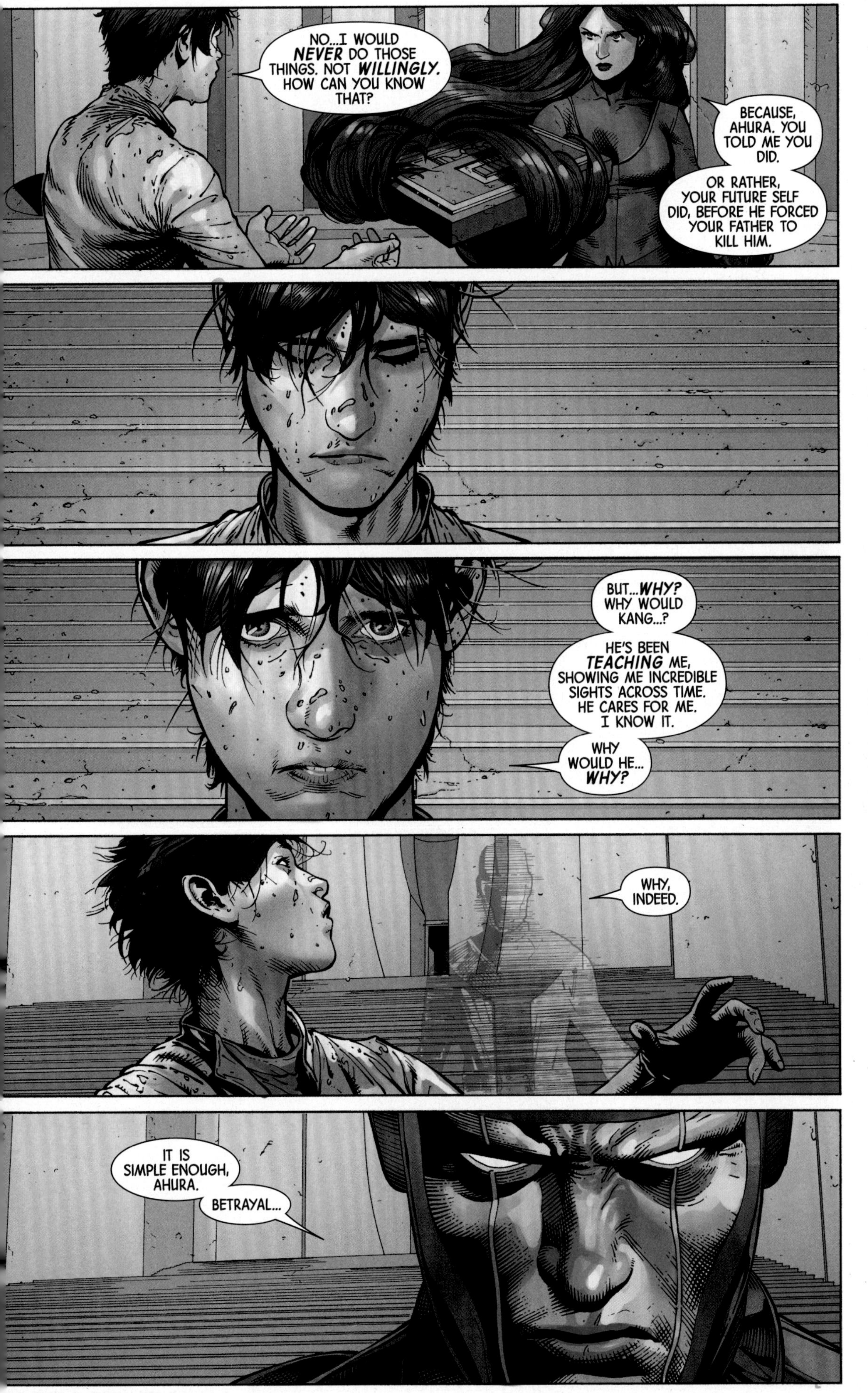
NO...I WOULD NEVER DO THOSE THINGS. NOT WILLINGLY. HOW CAN YOU KNOW THAT?
BECAUSE, AHURA. YOU TOLD ME YOU DID.
OR RATHER, YOUR FUTURE SELF DID, BEFORE HE FORCED YOUR FATHER TO KILL HIM.
BUT...WHY? WHY WOULD KANG...?
HE'S BEEN TEACHING ME, SHOWING ME INCREDIBLE SIGHTS ACROSS TIME. HE CARES FOR ME. I KNOW IT.
WHY WOULD HE... WHY?
WHY, INDEED.
IT IS SIMPLE ENOUGH, AHURA.
BETRAYAL...

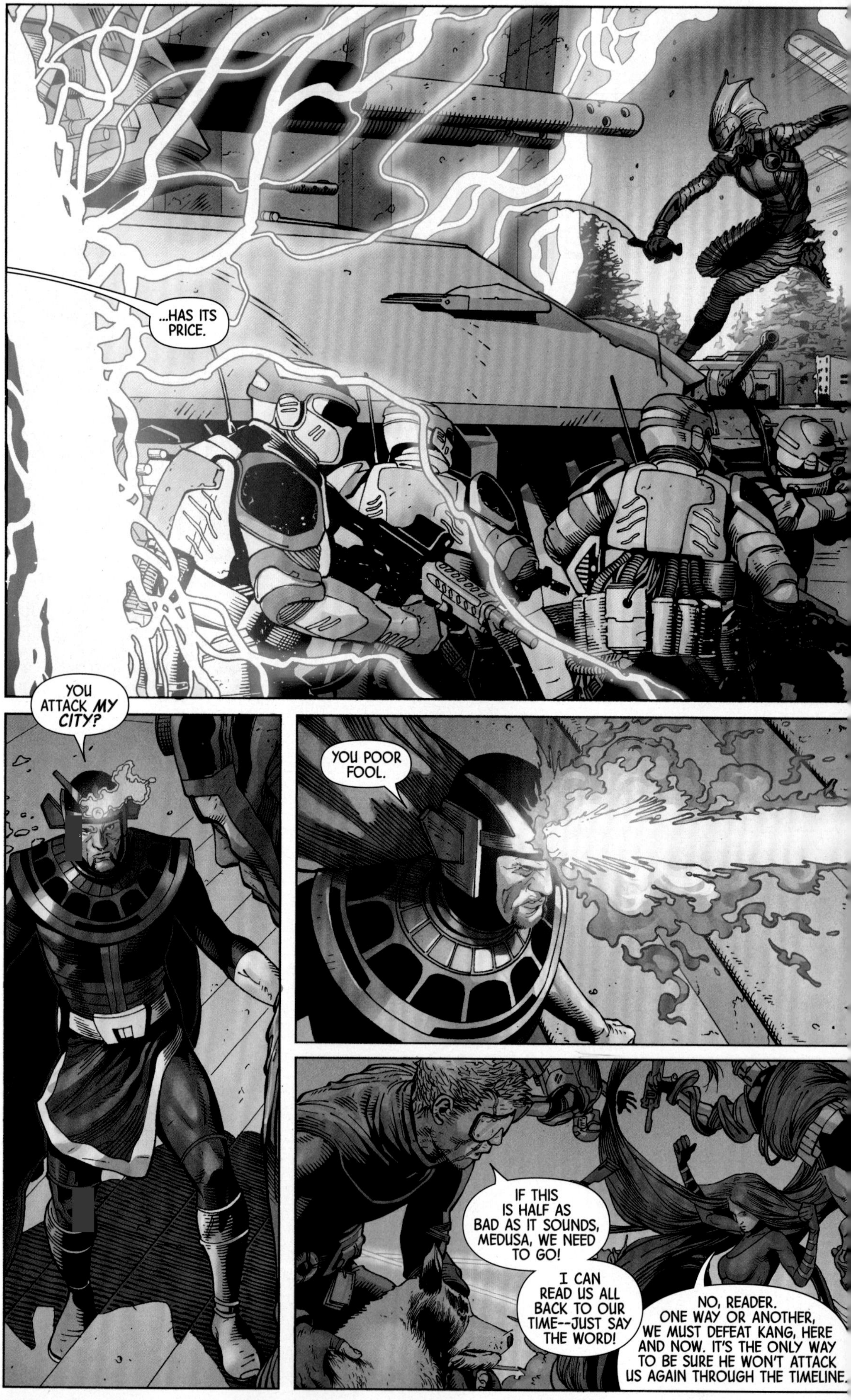
...HAS ITS PRICE.
YOU ATTACK MY CITY?
YOU POOR FOOL.
IF THIS IS HALF AS BAD AS IT SOUNDS, MEDUSA, WE NEED TO GO!
I CAN READ US ALL BACK TO OUR TIME--JUST SAY THE WORD!
NO, READER. ONE WAY OR ANOTHER, WE MUST DEFEAT KANG, HERE AND NOW. IT'S THE ONLY WAY TO BE SURE HE WON'T ATTACK US AGAIN THROUGH THE TIMELINE.

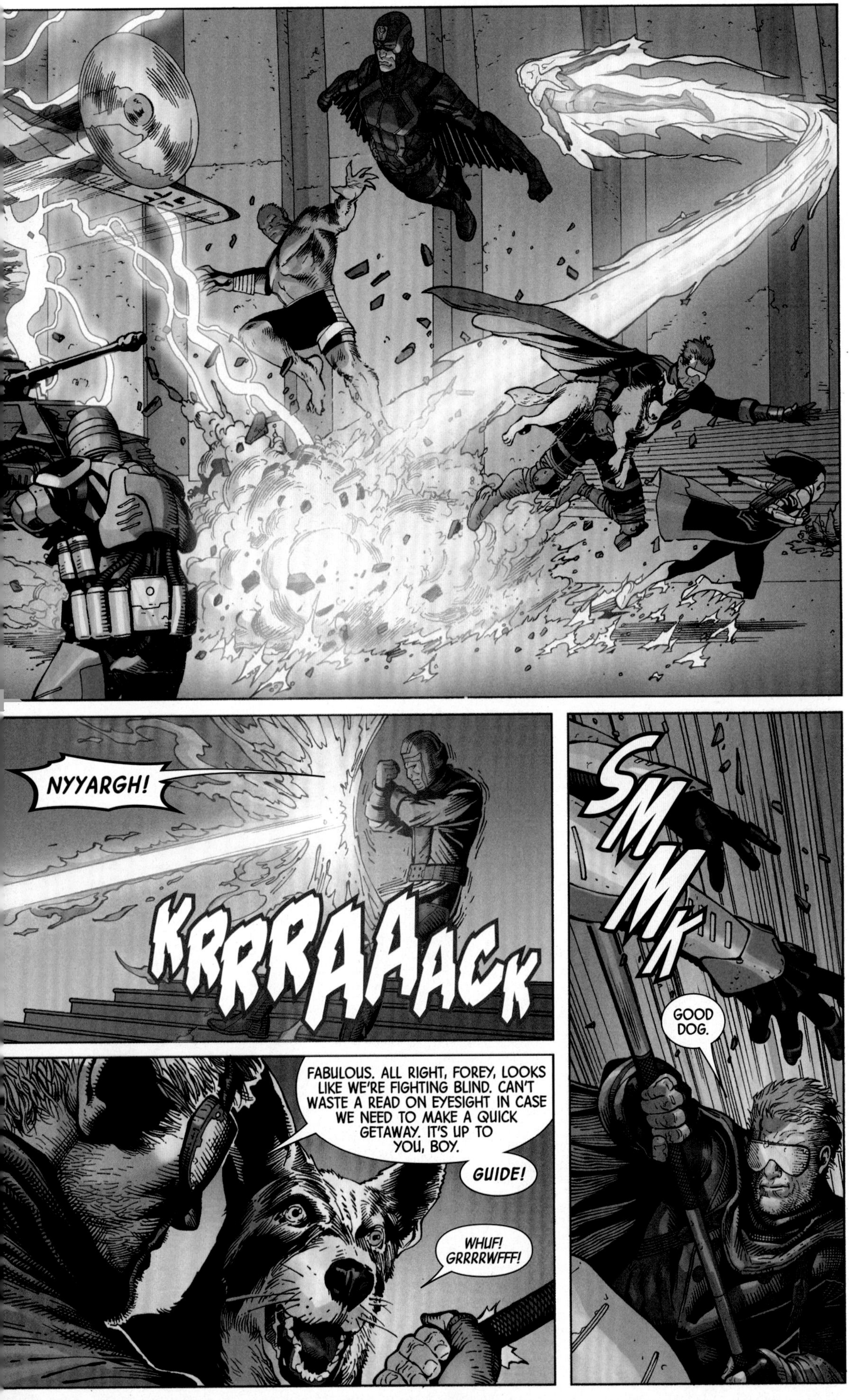
NYYARGH!
KRRRAAACK
SMMK
GOOD DOG.
FABULOUS. ALL RIGHT, FOREY, LOOKS LIKE WE'RE FIGHTING BLIND. CAN'T WASTE A READ ON EYESIGHT IN CASE WE NEED TO MAKE A QUICK GETAWAY. IT'S UP TO YOU, BOY.
GUIDE!
WHUF! GRRRRWFFF!

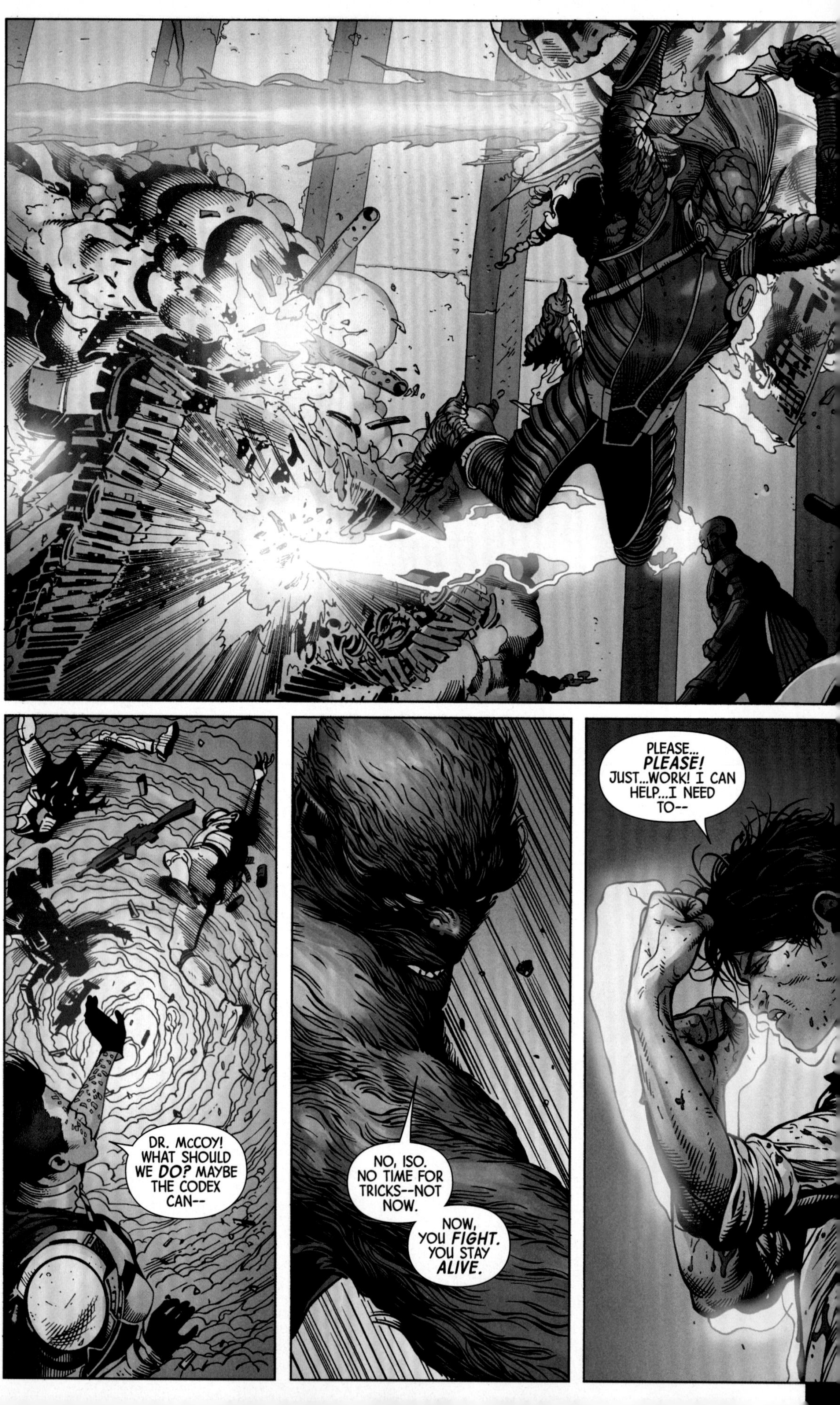
DR. McCOY! WHAT SHOULD WE DO? MAYBE THE CODEX CAN--
NO, ISO. NO TIME FOR TRICKS--NOT NOW.
NOW, YOU FIGHT. YOU STAY ALIVE.
PLEASE... PLEASE! JUST...WORK! I CAN HELP...I NEED TO--

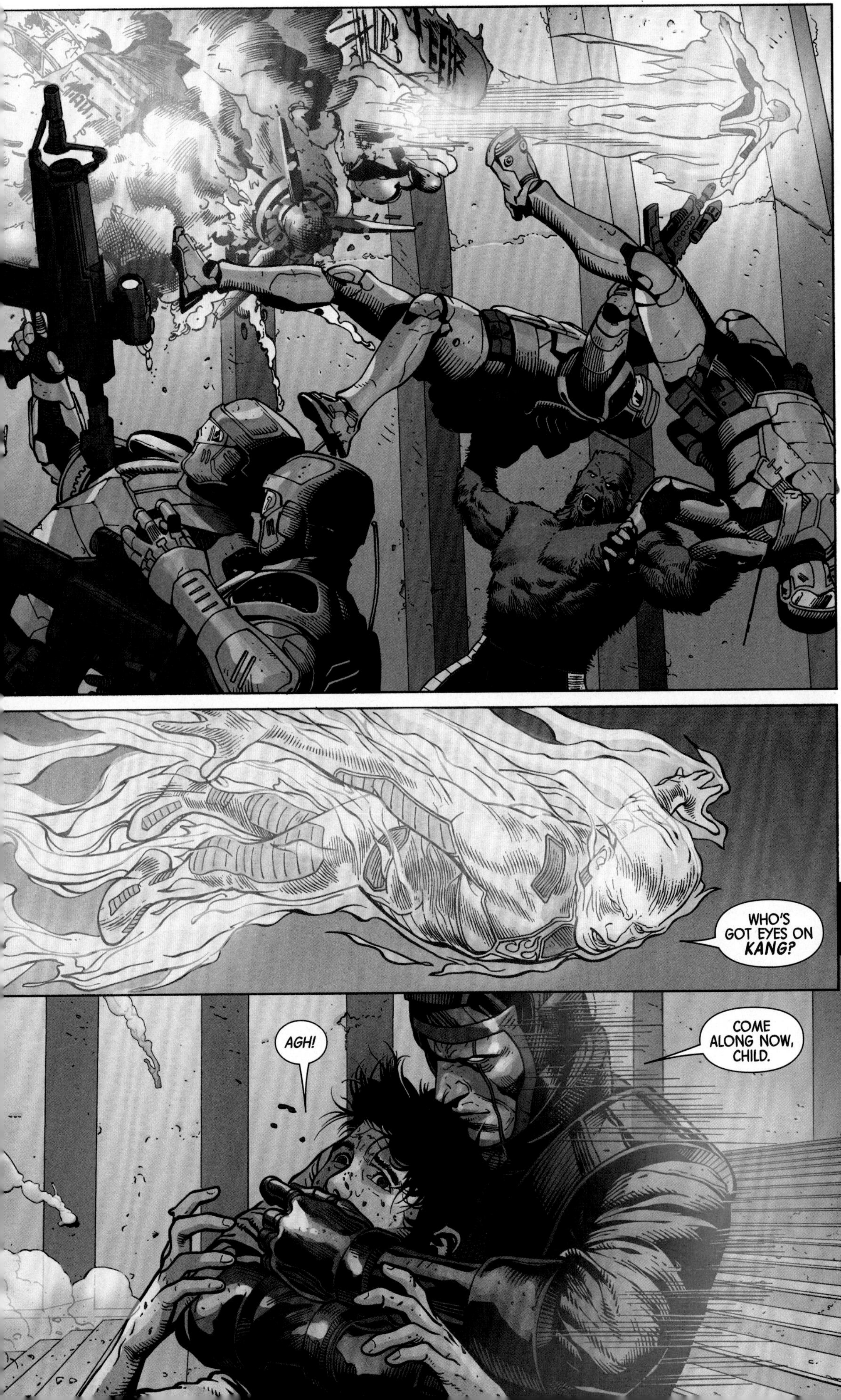
WHO'S GOT EYES ON *KANG?*
AGH!
COME ALONG NOW, CHILD.

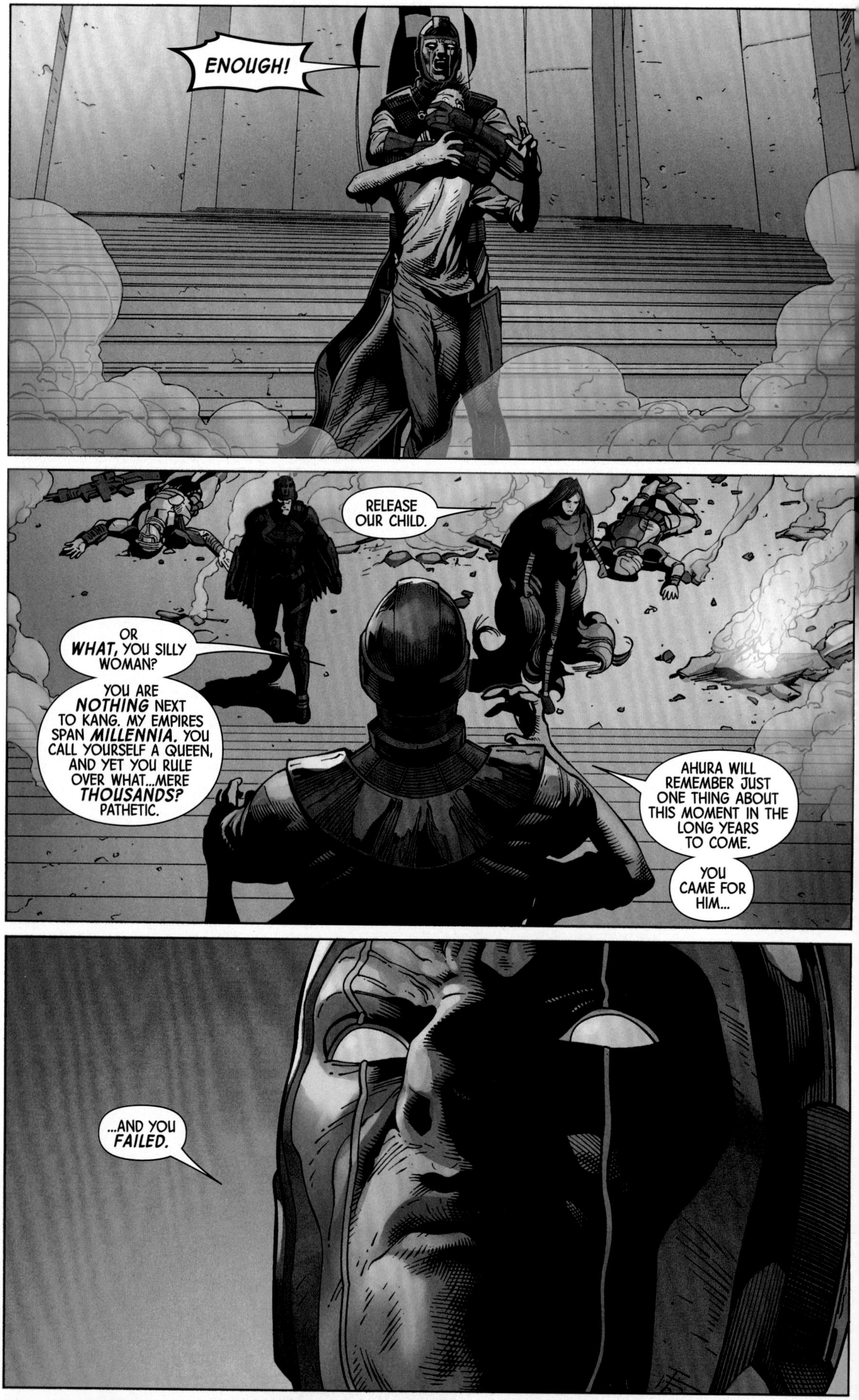
ENOUGH!
RELEASE OUR CHILD.
OR WHAT, YOU SILLY WOMAN?
YOU ARE NOTHING NEXT TO KANG. MY EMPIRES SPAN MILLENNIA. YOU CALL YOURSELF A QUEEN, AND YET YOU RULE OVER WHAT...MERE THOUSANDS? PATHETIC.
AHURA WILL REMEMBER JUST ONE THING ABOUT THIS MOMENT IN THE LONG YEARS TO COME.
YOU CAME FOR HIM...
...AND YOU FAILED.

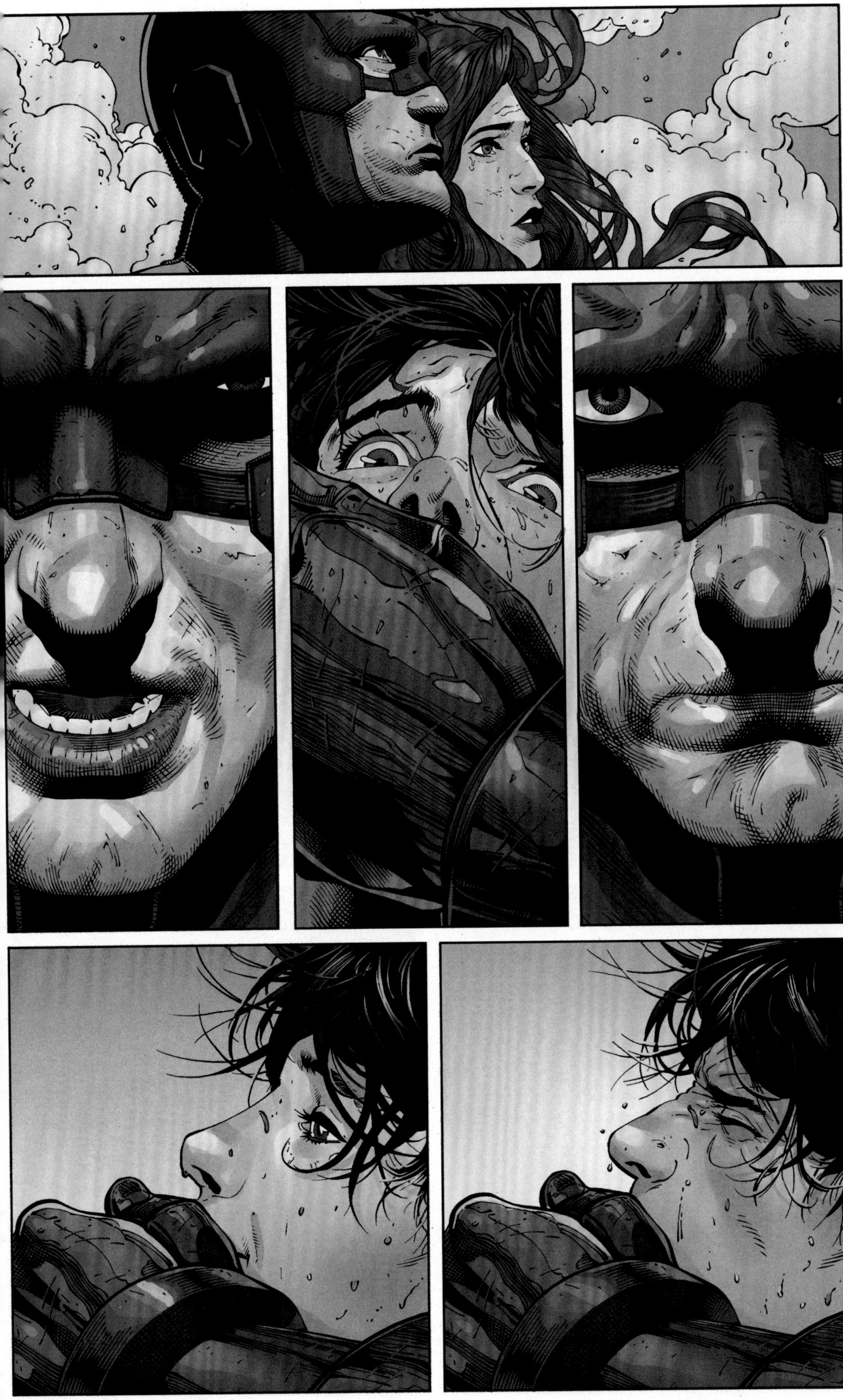

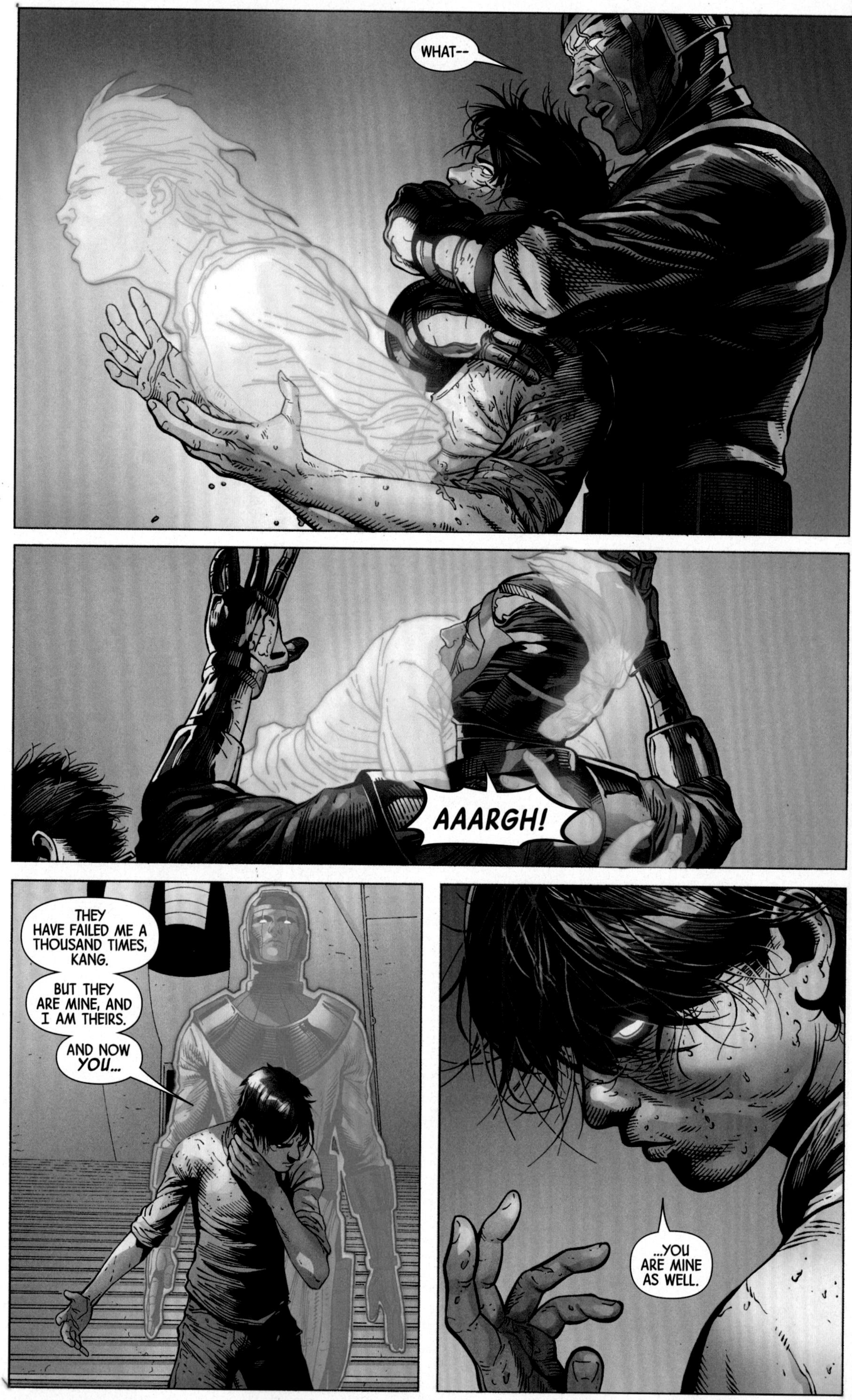
WHAT--
AAARGH!
THEY HAVE FAILED ME A THOUSAND TIMES, KANG.
BUT THEY ARE MINE, AND I AM THEIRS.
AND NOW *YOU*...
...YOU ARE MINE AS WELL.

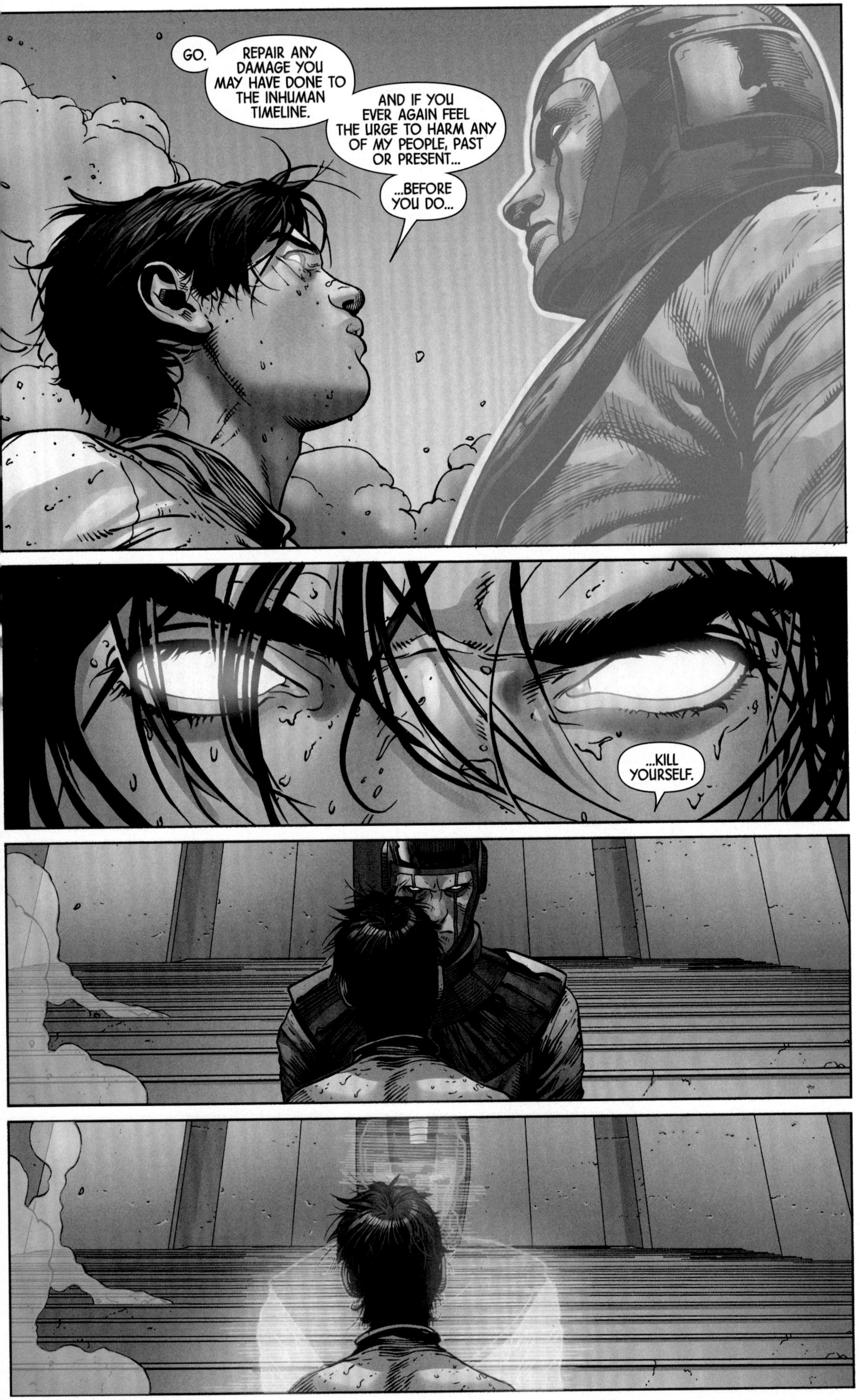
GO.
REPAIR ANY DAMAGE YOU MAY HAVE DONE TO THE INHUMAN TIMELINE.
AND IF YOU EVER AGAIN FEEL THE URGE TO HARM ANY OF MY PEOPLE, PAST OR PRESENT...
...BEFORE YOU DO...
...KILL YOURSELF.

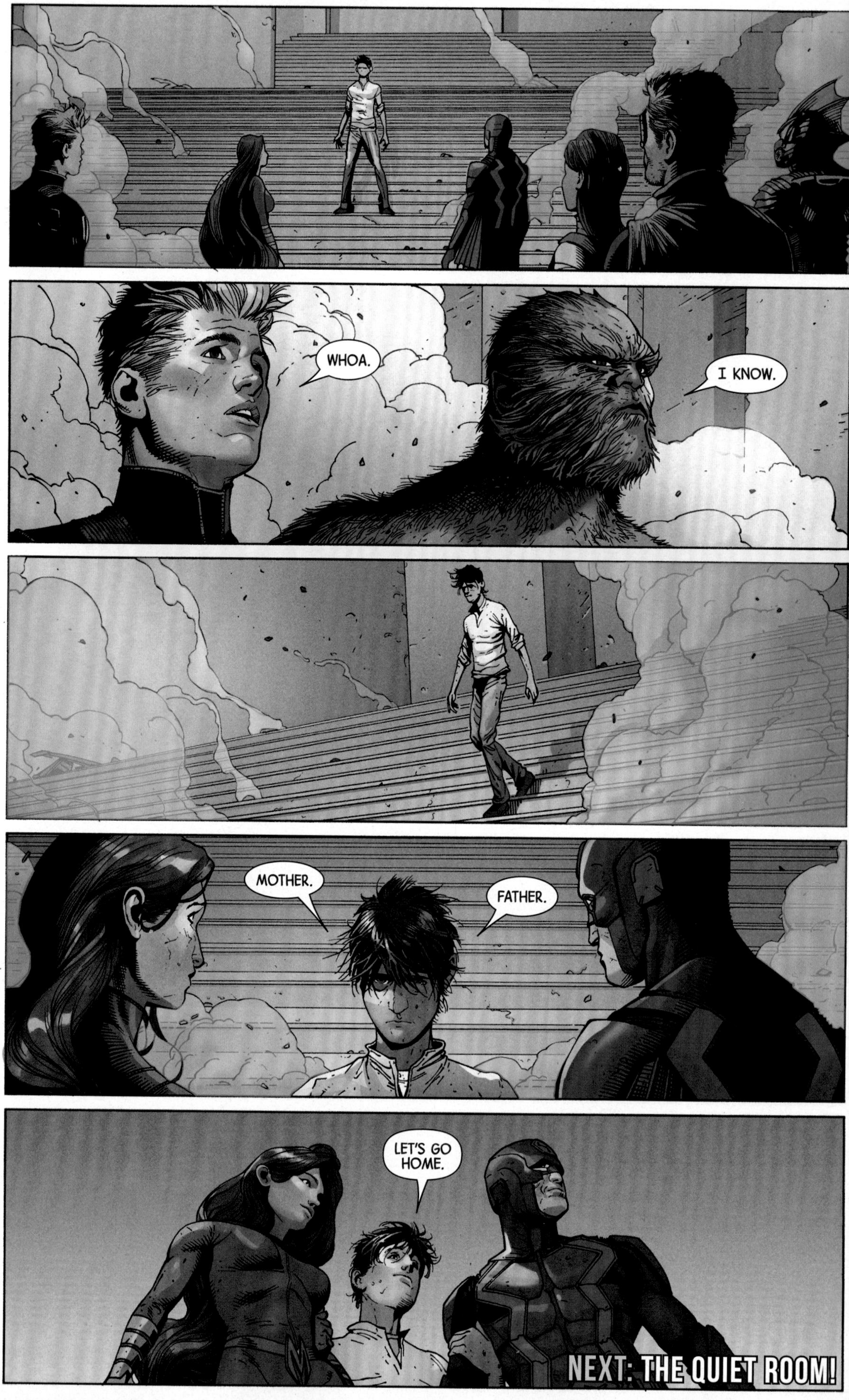
WHOA.
I KNOW.
MOTHER.
FATHER.
LET'S GO HOME.
NEXT: THE QUIET ROOM!

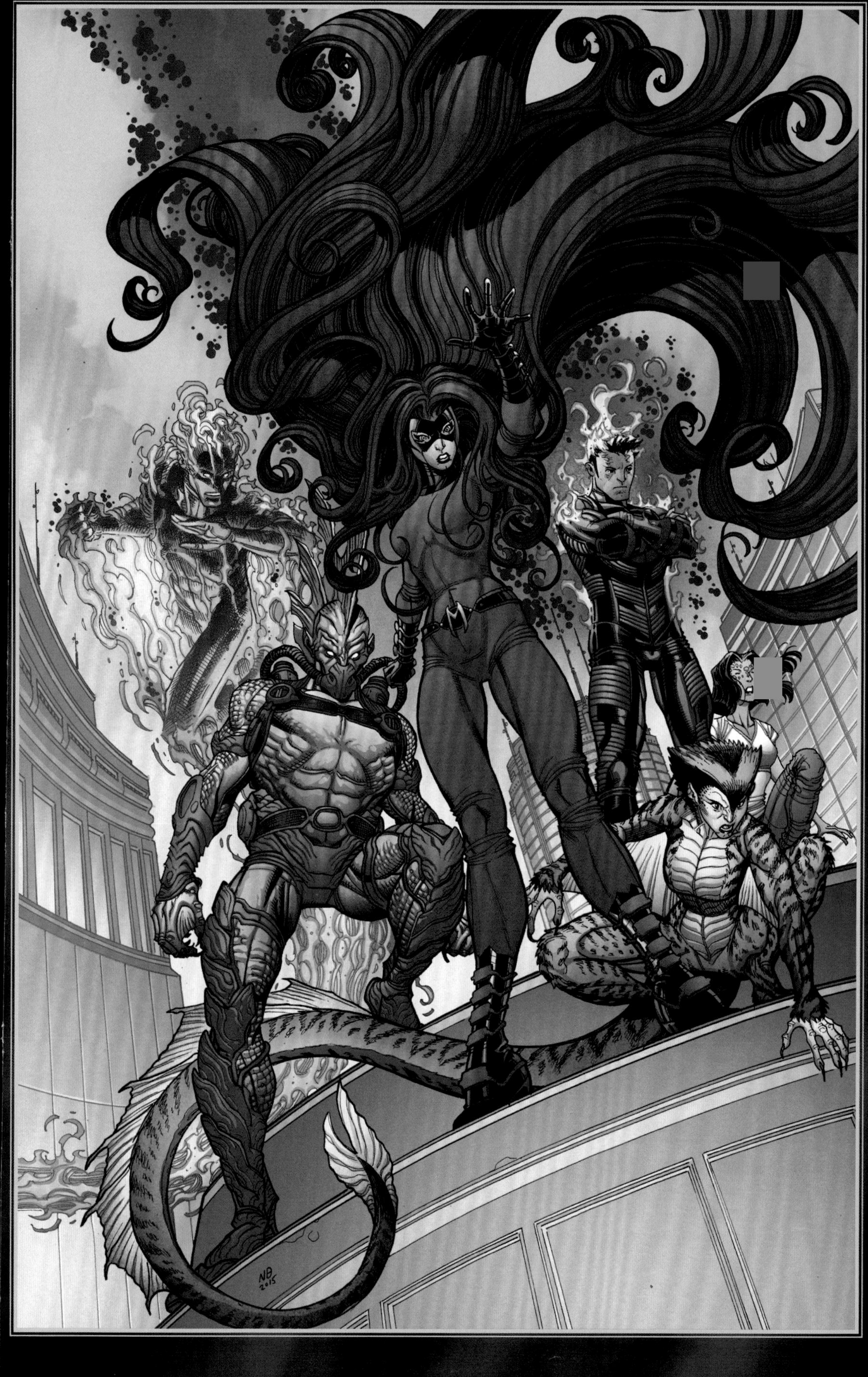
NB
2015

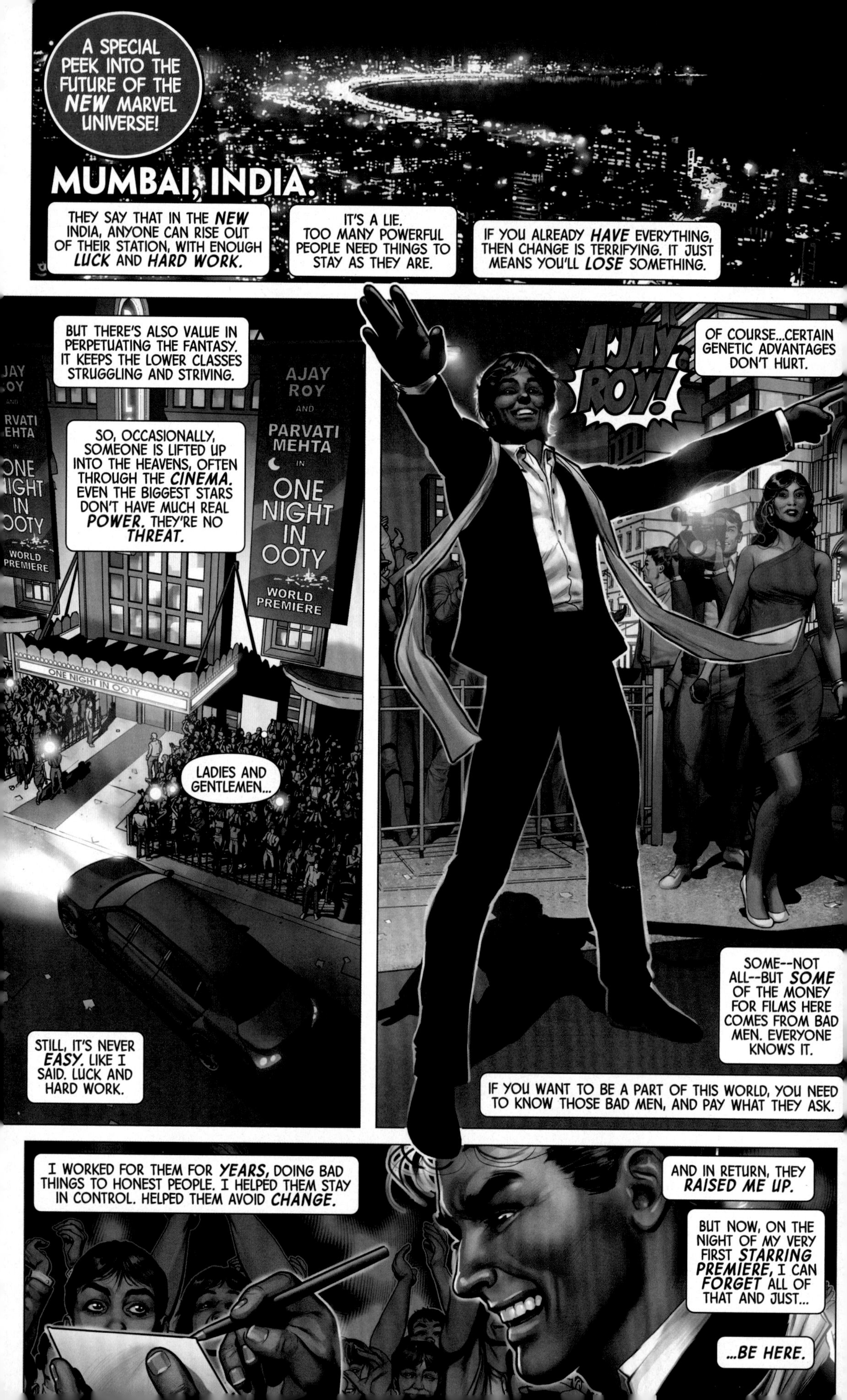

A SPECIAL PEEK INTO THE FUTURE OF THE NEW MARVEL UNIVERSE!
MUMBAI, INDIA.
THEY SAY THAT IN THE NEW INDIA, ANYONE CAN RISE OUT OF THEIR STATION, WITH ENOUGH LUCK AND HARD WORK.
IT'S A LIE. TOO MANY POWERFUL PEOPLE NEED THINGS TO STAY AS THEY ARE.
IF YOU ALREADY HAVE EVERYTHING, THEN CHANGE IS TERRIFYING. IT JUST MEANS YOU'LL LOSE SOMETHING.
BUT THERE'S ALSO VALUE IN PERPETUATING THE FANTASY. IT KEEPS THE LOWER CLASSES STRUGGLING AND STRIVING.
AJAY ROY AND PARVATI MEHTA IN ONE NIGHT IN OOTY WORLD PREMIERE
SO, OCCASIONALLY, SOMEONE IS LIFTED UP INTO THE HEAVENS, OFTEN THROUGH THE CINEMA. EVEN THE BIGGEST STARS DON'T HAVE MUCH REAL POWER. THEY'RE NO THREAT.
ONE NIGHT IN OOTY
LADIES AND GENTLEMEN...
STILL, IT'S NEVER EASY. LIKE I SAID. LUCK AND HARD WORK.
AJAY ROY!
OF COURSE...CERTAIN GENETIC ADVANTAGES DON'T HURT.
SOME--NOT ALL--BUT SOME OF THE MONEY FOR FILMS HERE COMES FROM BAD MEN. EVERYONE KNOWS IT.
IF YOU WANT TO BE A PART OF THIS WORLD, YOU NEED TO KNOW THOSE BAD MEN, AND PAY WHAT THEY ASK.
I WORKED FOR THEM FOR YEARS, DOING BAD THINGS TO HONEST PEOPLE. I HELPED THEM STAY IN CONTROL. HELPED THEM AVOID CHANGE.
AND IN RETURN, THEY RAISED ME UP.
BUT NOW, ON THE NIGHT OF MY VERY FIRST STARRING PREMIERE, I CAN FORGET ALL OF THAT AND JUST...
...BE HERE.

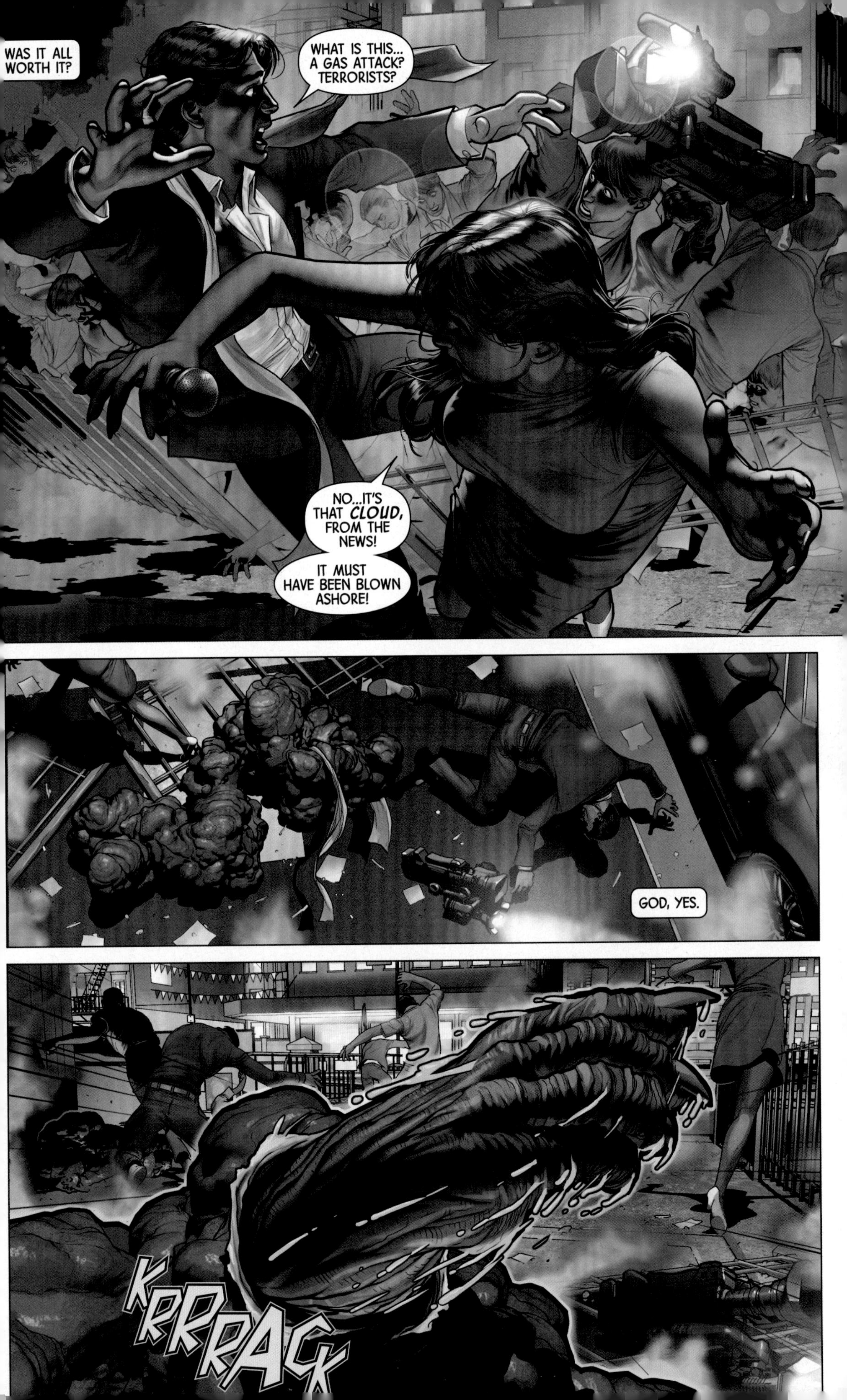
WAS IT ALL WORTH IT?
WHAT IS THIS... A GAS ATTACK? TERRORISTS?
NO...IT'S THAT CLOUD, FROM THE NEWS!
IT MUST HAVE BEEN BLOWN ASHORE!
GOD, YES.
KRRRACK

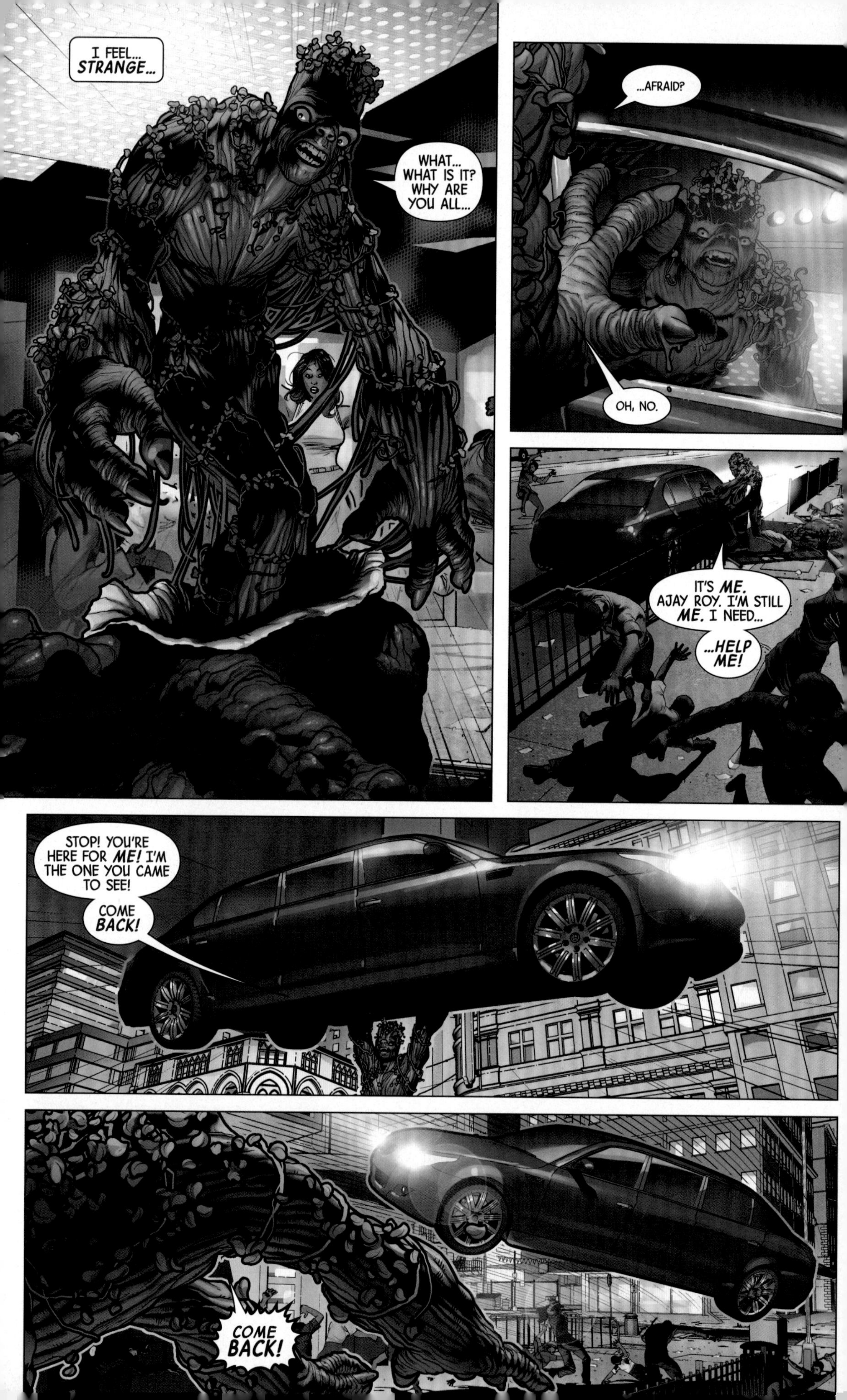

I FEEL... STRANGE...
WHAT... WHAT IS IT? WHY ARE YOU ALL...
...AFRAID?
OH, NO.
IT'S ME. AJAY ROY. I'M STILL ME. I NEED...
...HELP ME!
STOP! YOU'RE HERE FOR ME! I'M THE ONE YOU CAME TO SEE!
COME BACK!
COME BACK!

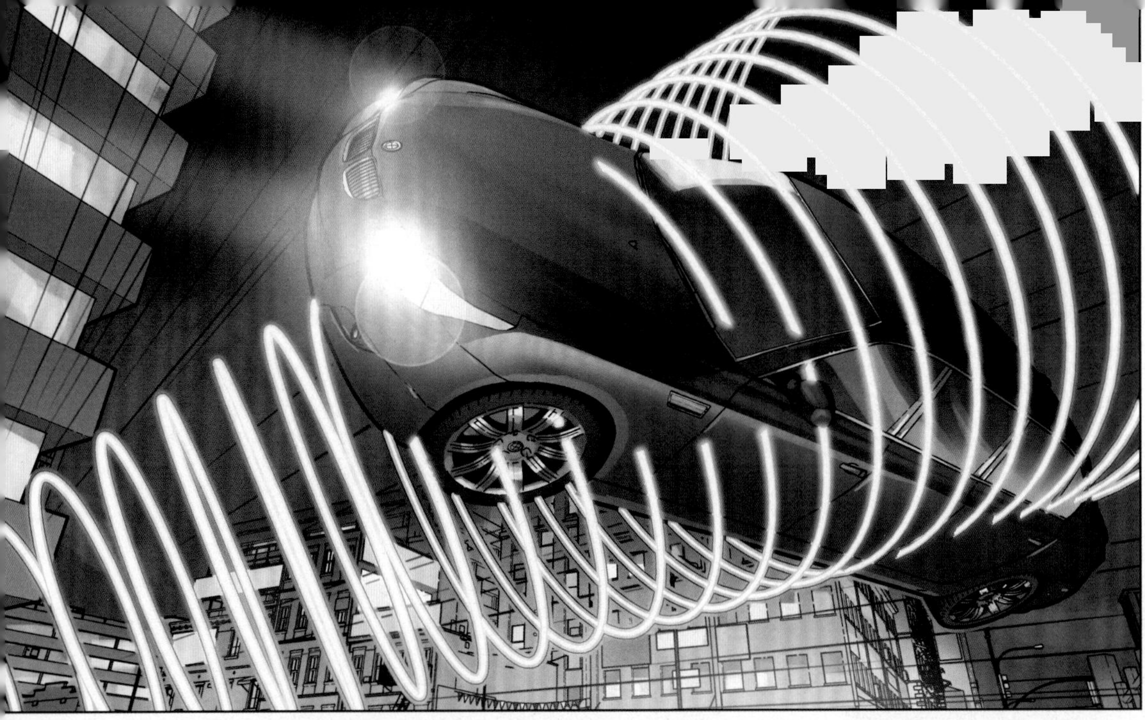

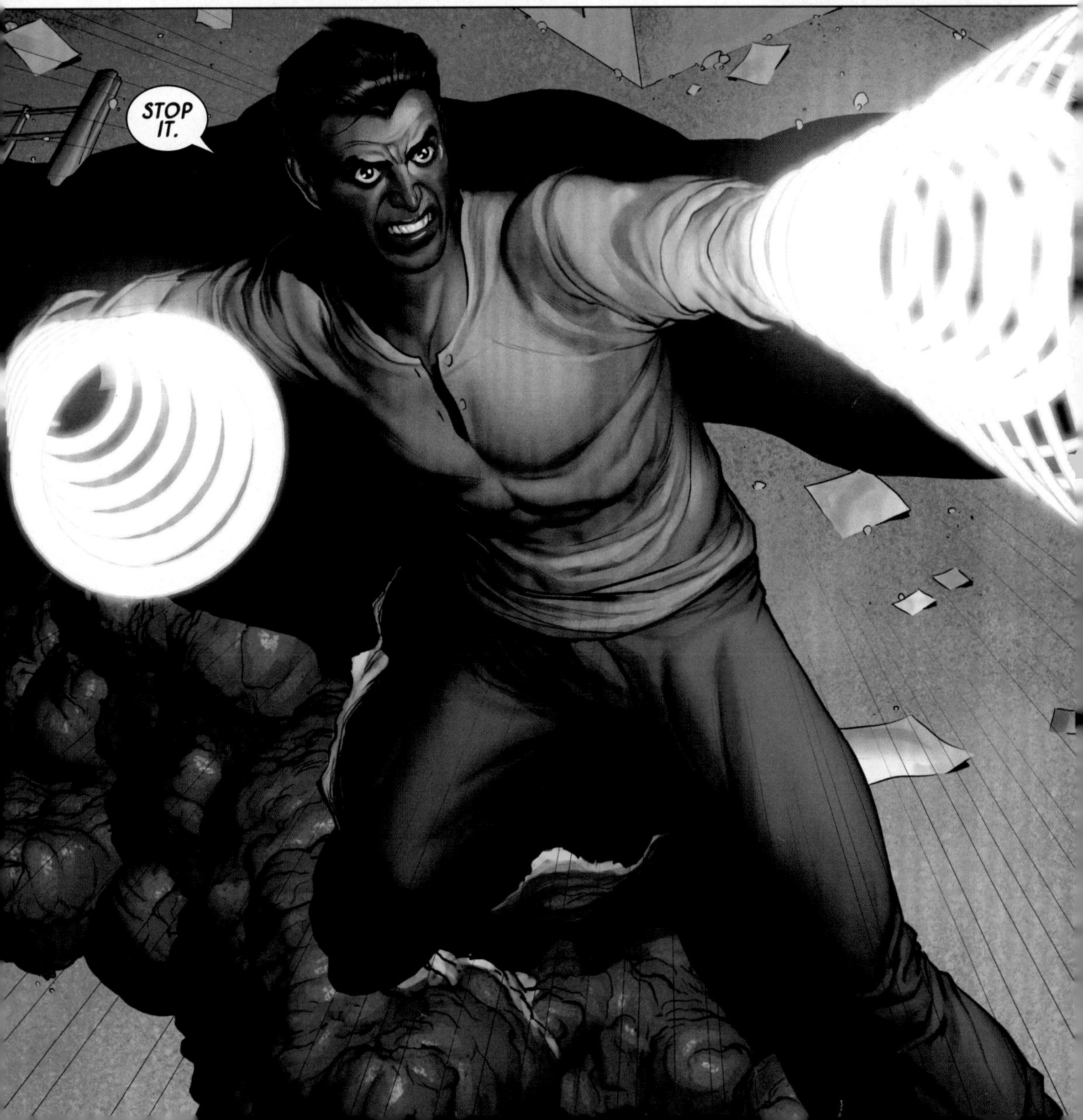
STOP IT.

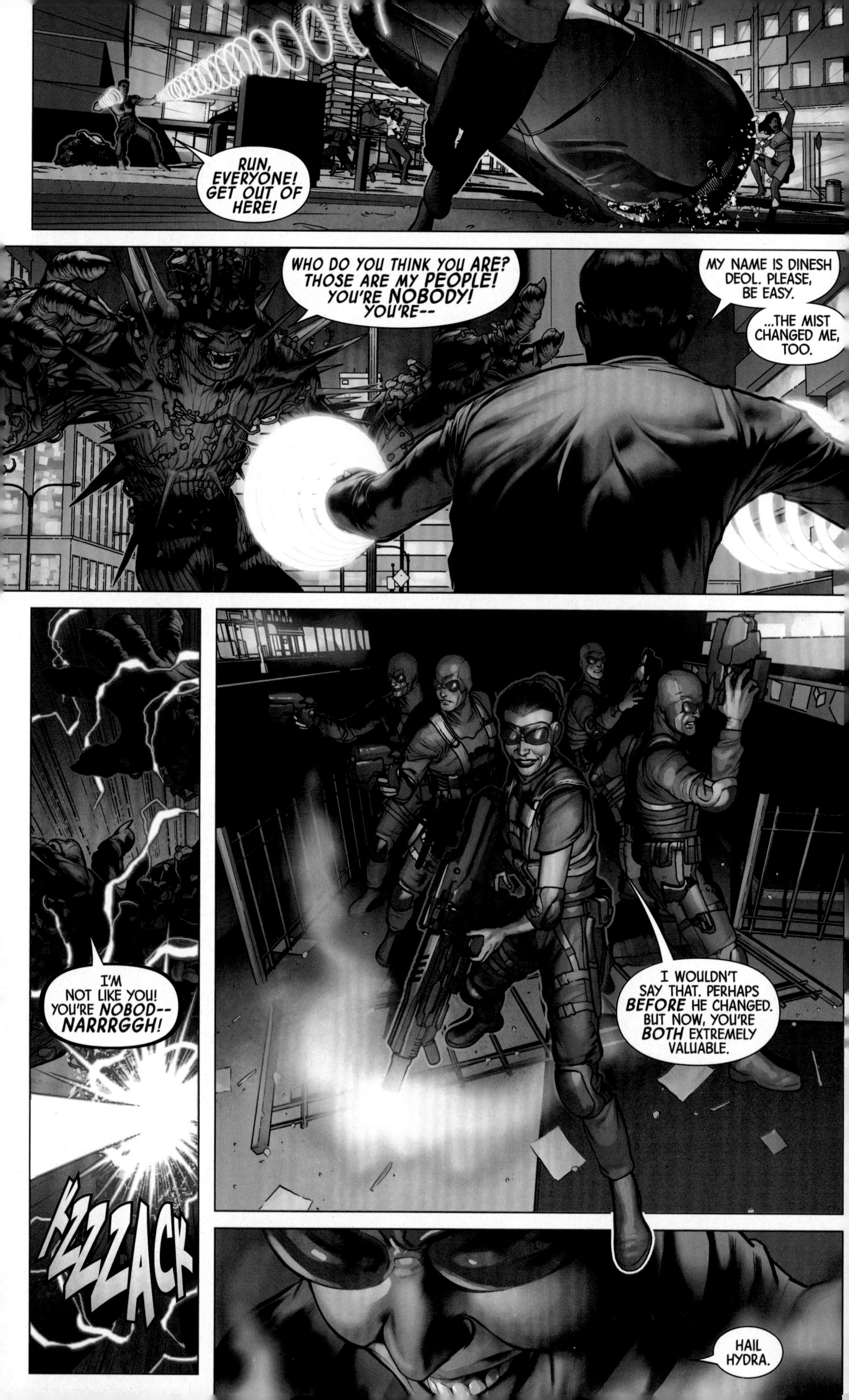
RUN, EVERYONE! GET OUT OF HERE!
WHO DO YOU THINK YOU ARE? THOSE ARE MY PEOPLE! YOU'RE NOBODY! YOU'RE--
MY NAME IS DINESH DEOL. PLEASE, BE EASY.
...THE MIST CHANGED ME, TOO.
I'M NOT LIKE YOU! YOU'RE NOBOD-- NARRRGGH!
KZZZACK
I WOULDN'T SAY THAT. PERHAPS BEFORE HE CHANGED. BUT NOW, YOU'RE BOTH EXTREMELY VALUABLE.
HAIL HYDRA.

GRRRRAGH!
YOU FOUR--AFTER HIM. HE'S HEADED FOR THE SLUMS. BURN THEM DOWN IF YOU MUST, BUT BRING HIM TO ME.
YES, MISTRESS.
HE'S STILL UP, EVEN AFTER THE STUN BLAST. GOOD. HE'S STRONG. HE WILL MAKE A MARVELOUS TOOL.
I'LL GET THIS ONE. HE LOOKS WEAK.
ONE SHOT SHOULD PUT HIM DOWN.
WAIT, DON'T--
ZZZACK

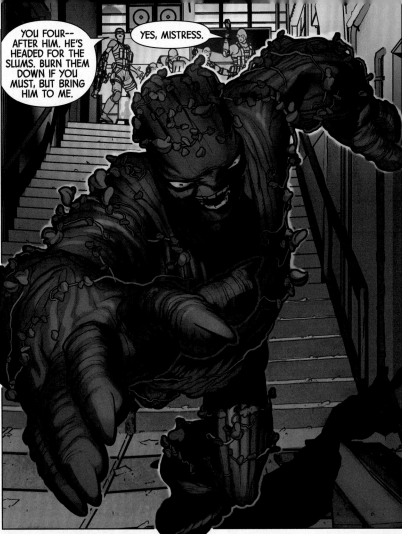

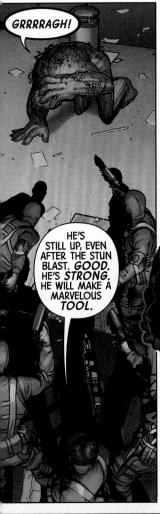

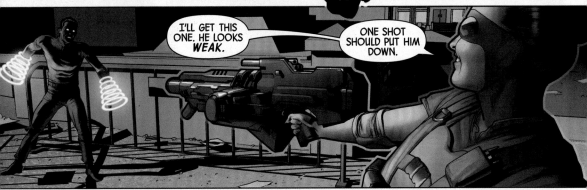

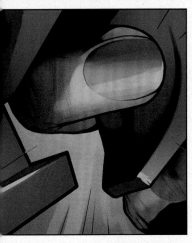

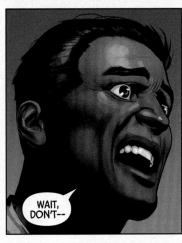

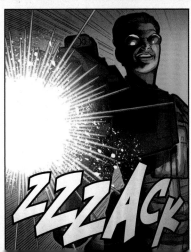

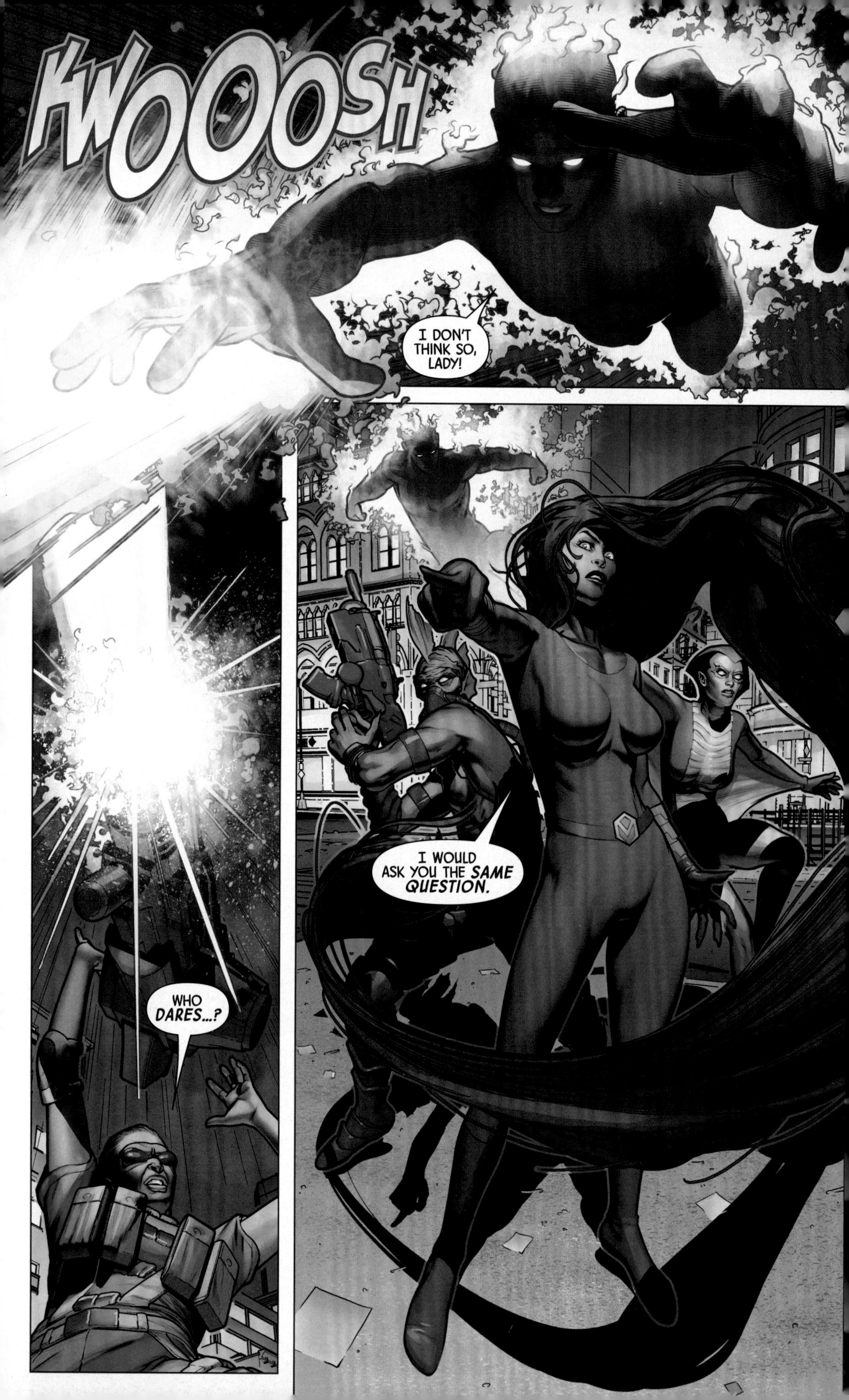
KWOOOSH
I DON'T THINK SO, LADY!
WHO DARES...?
I WOULD ASK YOU THE SAME QUESTION.

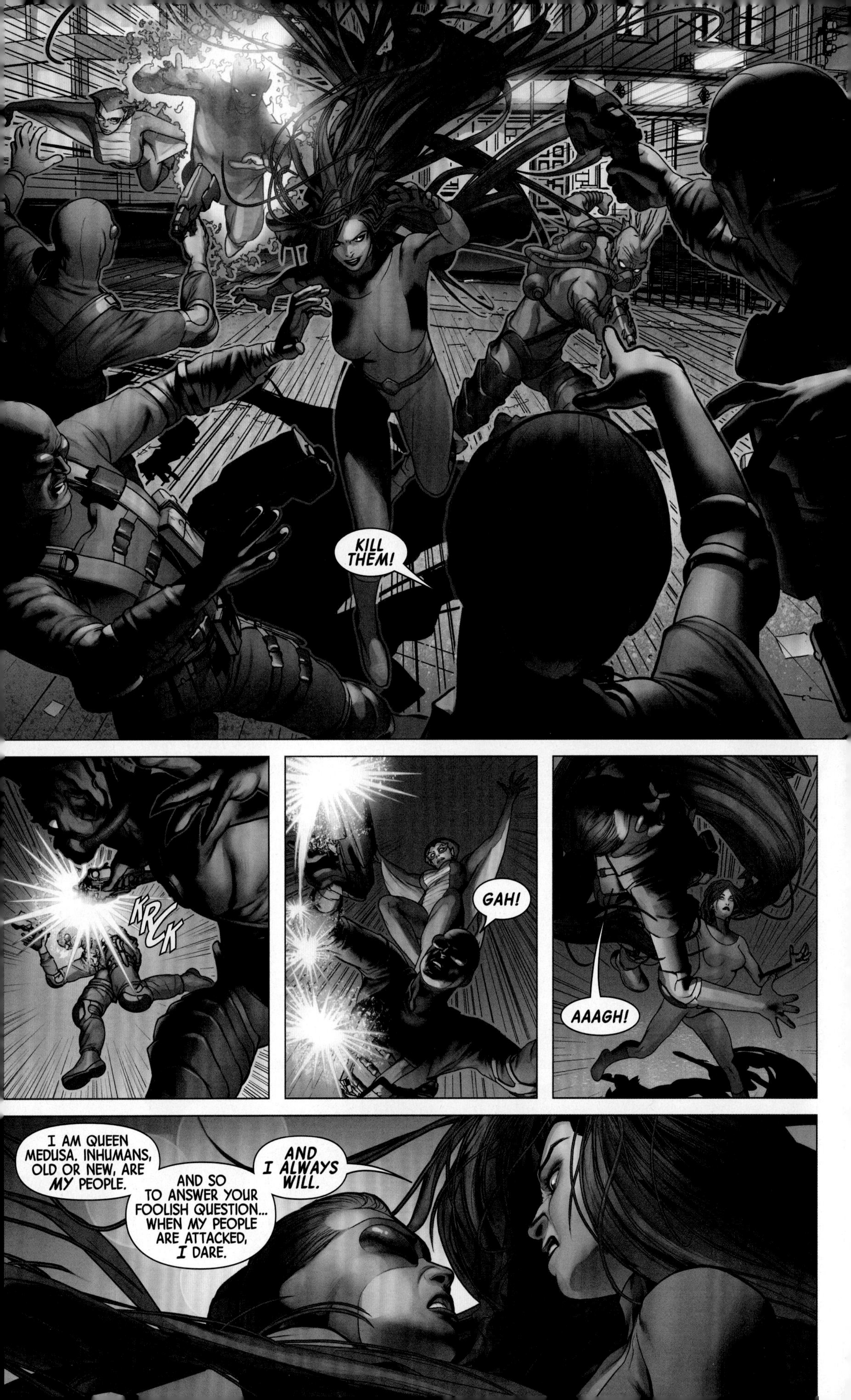
KILL THEM!
KRAK
GAH!
AAAGH!
I AM QUEEN MEDUSA. INHUMANS, OLD OR NEW, ARE MY PEOPLE.
AND SO TO ANSWER YOUR FOOLISH QUESTION... WHEN MY PEOPLE ARE ATTACKED, I DARE.
AND I ALWAYS WILL.

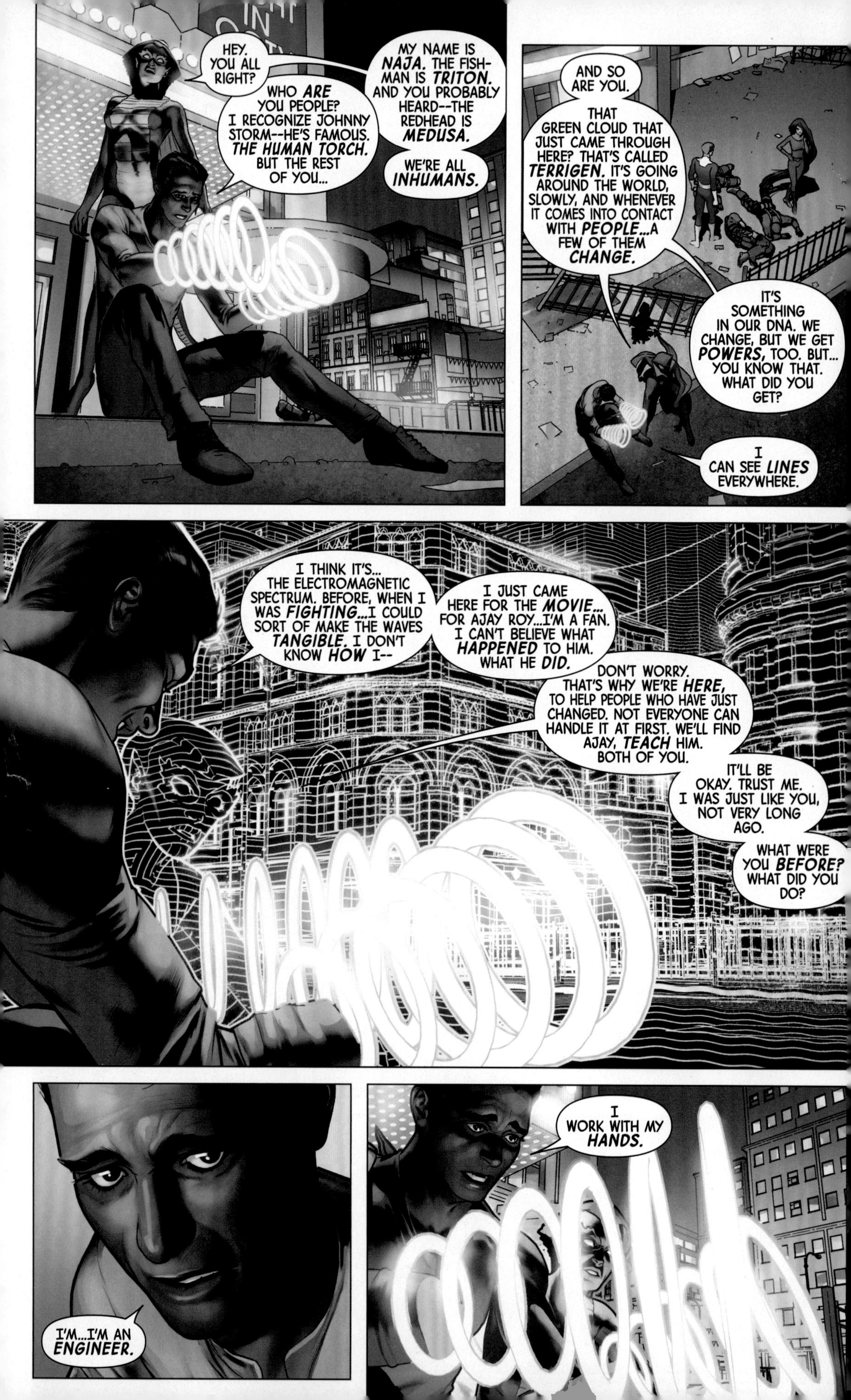
HEY. YOU ALL RIGHT?
WHO ARE YOU PEOPLE? I RECOGNIZE JOHNNY STORM--HE'S FAMOUS. THE HUMAN TORCH. BUT THE REST OF YOU...
MY NAME IS NAJA. THE FISH-MAN IS TRITON. AND YOU PROBABLY HEARD--THE REDHEAD IS MEDUSA.
WE'RE ALL INHUMANS.
AND SO ARE YOU.
THAT GREEN CLOUD THAT JUST CAME THROUGH HERE? THAT'S CALLED TERRIGEN. IT'S GOING AROUND THE WORLD, SLOWLY, AND WHENEVER IT COMES INTO CONTACT WITH PEOPLE...A FEW OF THEM CHANGE.
IT'S SOMETHING IN OUR DNA. WE CHANGE, BUT WE GET POWERS, TOO. BUT... YOU KNOW THAT. WHAT DID YOU GET?
I CAN SEE LINES EVERYWHERE.
I THINK IT'S... THE ELECTROMAGNETIC SPECTRUM. BEFORE, WHEN I WAS FIGHTING...I COULD SORT OF MAKE THE WAVES TANGIBLE. I DON'T KNOW HOW I--
I JUST CAME HERE FOR THE MOVIE... FOR AJAY ROY...I'M A FAN. I CAN'T BELIEVE WHAT HAPPENED TO HIM. WHAT HE DID.
DON'T WORRY. THAT'S WHY WE'RE HERE, TO HELP PEOPLE WHO HAVE JUST CHANGED. NOT EVERYONE CAN HANDLE IT AT FIRST. WE'LL FIND AJAY, TEACH HIM. BOTH OF YOU.
IT'LL BE OKAY. TRUST ME. I WAS JUST LIKE YOU, NOT VERY LONG AGO.
WHAT WERE YOU BEFORE? WHAT DID YOU DO?
I'M...I'M AN ENGINEER.
I WORK WITH MY HANDS.

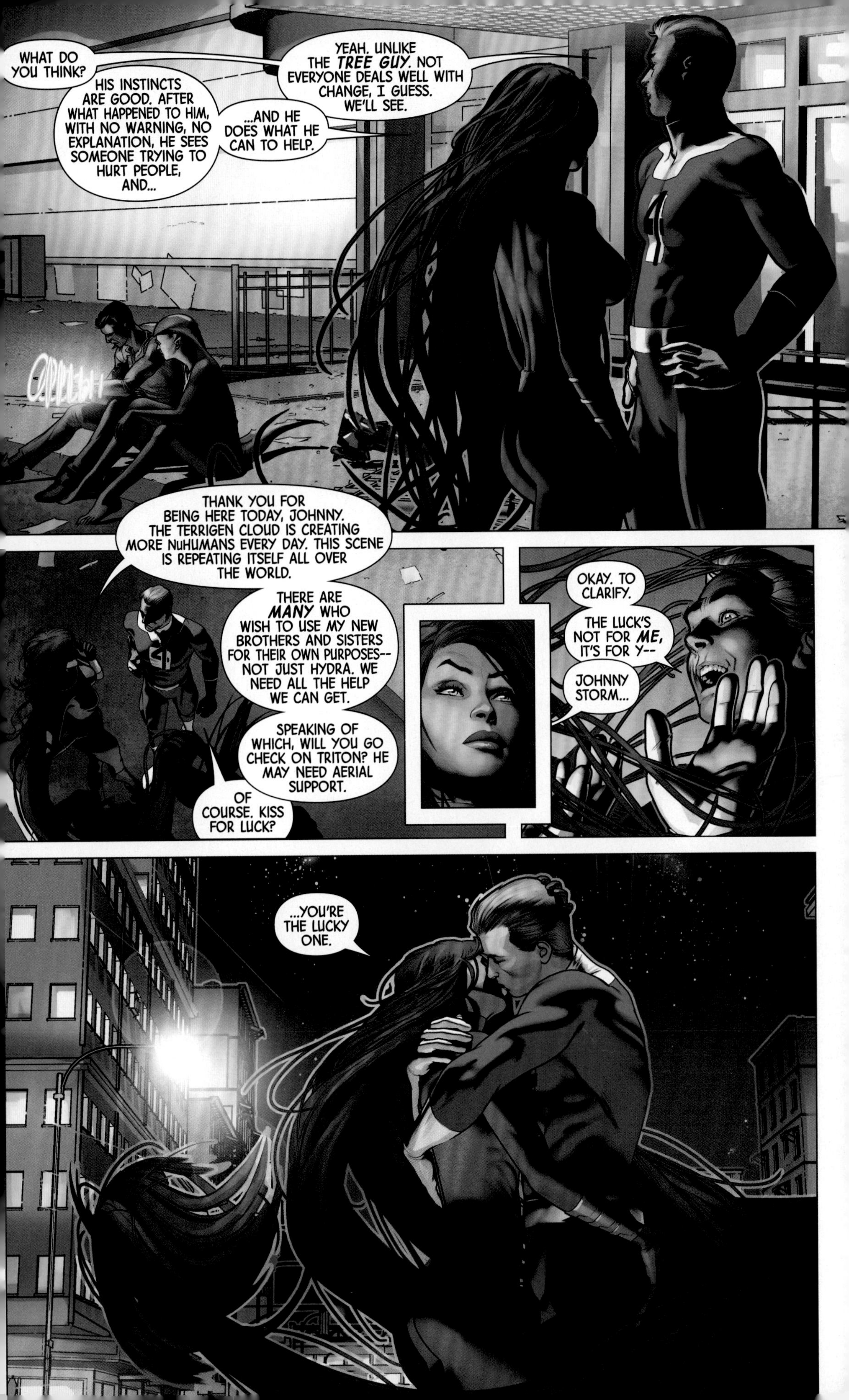
WHAT DO YOU THINK?
HIS INSTINCTS ARE GOOD. AFTER WHAT HAPPENED TO HIM, WITH NO WARNING, NO EXPLANATION, HE SEES SOMEONE TRYING TO HURT PEOPLE, AND...
...AND HE DOES WHAT HE CAN TO HELP.
YEAH. UNLIKE THE TREE GUY. NOT EVERYONE DEALS WELL WITH CHANGE, I GUESS. WE'LL SEE.
THANK YOU FOR BEING HERE TODAY, JOHNNY. THE TERRIGEN CLOUD IS CREATING MORE NuHUMANS EVERY DAY. THIS SCENE IS REPEATING ITSELF ALL OVER THE WORLD.
THERE ARE MANY WHO WISH TO USE MY NEW BROTHERS AND SISTERS FOR THEIR OWN PURPOSES-- NOT JUST HYDRA. WE NEED ALL THE HELP WE CAN GET.
SPEAKING OF WHICH, WILL YOU GO CHECK ON TRITON? HE MAY NEED AERIAL SUPPORT.
OF COURSE. KISS FOR LUCK?
OKAY. TO CLARIFY.
THE LUCK'S NOT FOR ME, IT'S FOR Y--
JOHNNY STORM...
...YOU'RE THE LUCKY ONE.

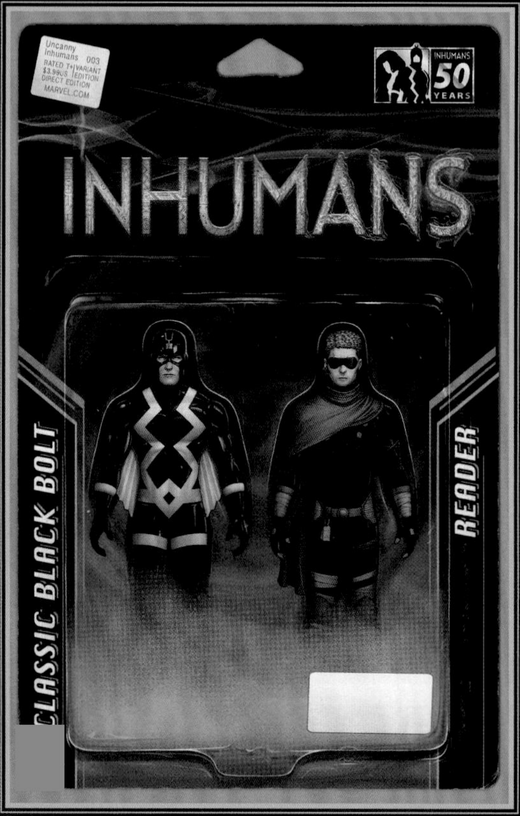
INHUMANS
50
YEARS
INHUMANS
CLASSIC BLACK BOLT
READER

#3 ACTION FIGURE VARIANT
BY JOHN TYLER CHRISTOPHER

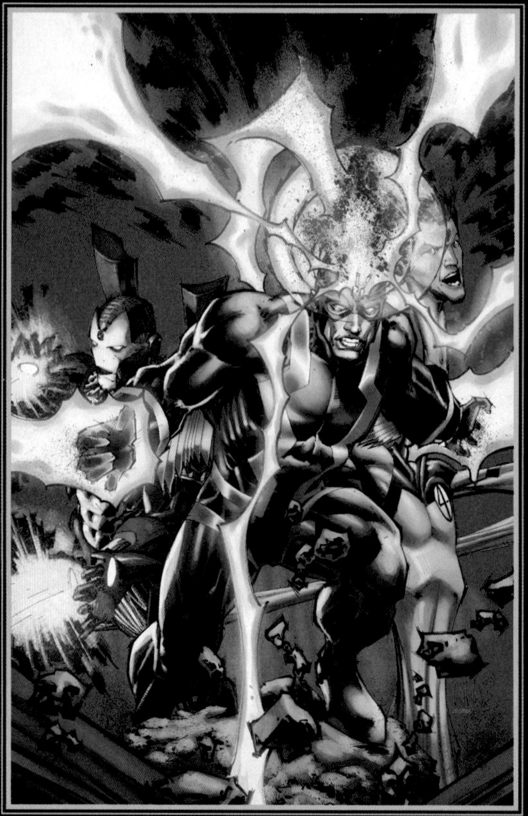

#3 MARVEL '92 VARIANT
BY WHILCE PORTACIO & CHRIS SOTOMAYOR

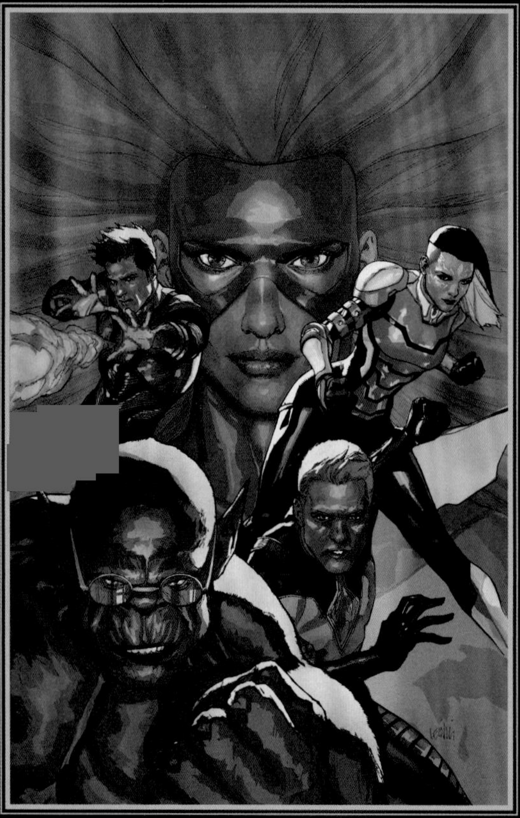

#3 VARIANT
BY LEINIL FRANCIS YU

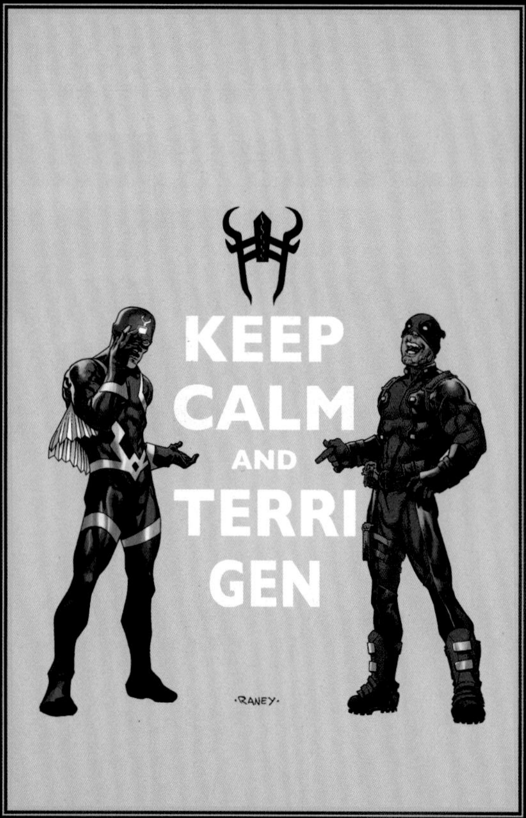
KEEP
CALM
AND
TERRI
GEN
RANEY

#4 DEADPOOL VARIANT
BY TOM RANEY & FRANK MARTIN

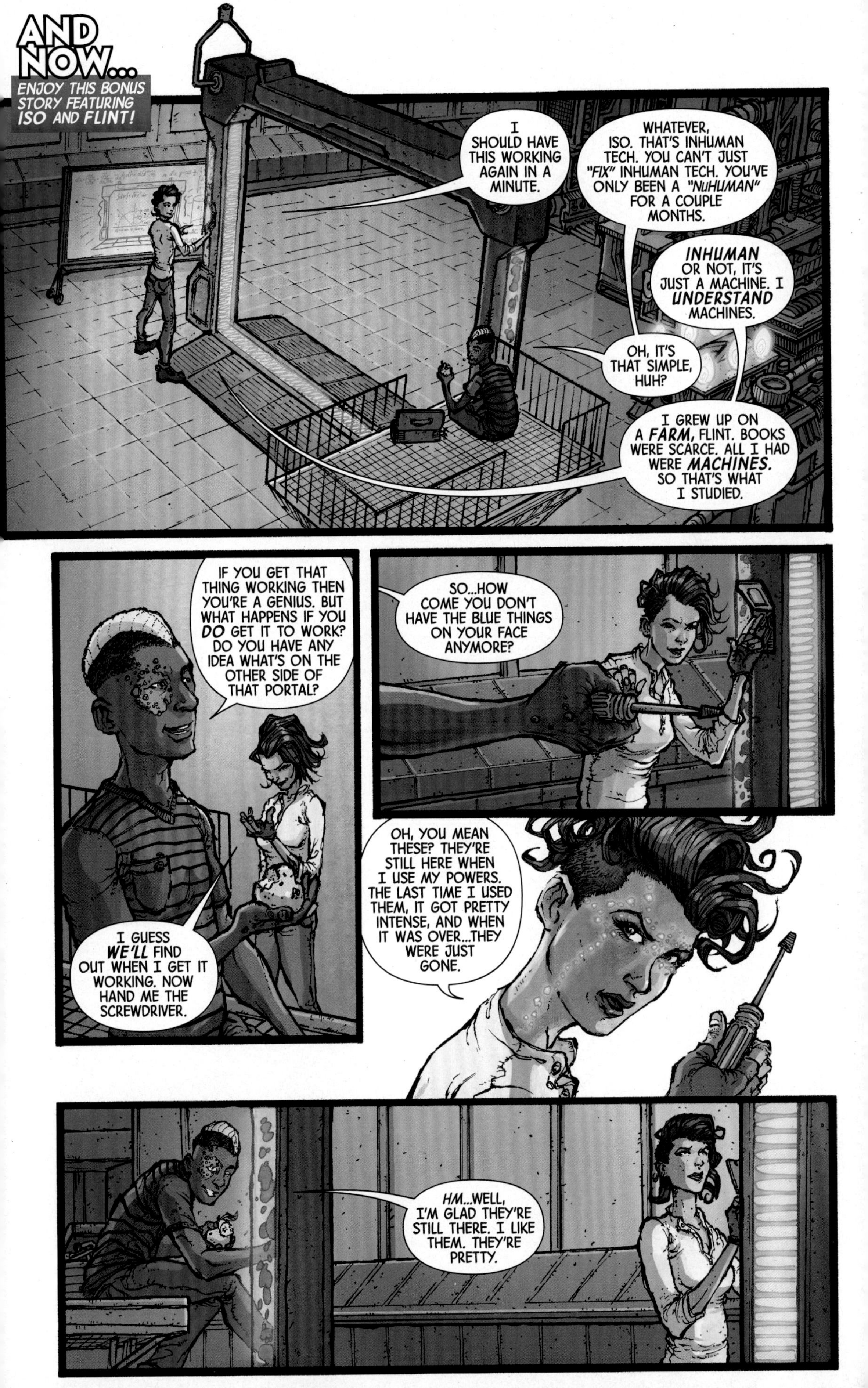
AND NOW...
ENJOY THIS BONUS STORY FEATURING ISO AND FLINT!
I SHOULD HAVE THIS WORKING AGAIN IN A MINUTE.
WHATEVER, ISO. THAT'S INHUMAN TECH. YOU CAN'T JUST "FIX" INHUMAN TECH. YOU'VE ONLY BEEN A "NUHUMAN" FOR A COUPLE MONTHS.
INHUMAN OR NOT, IT'S JUST A MACHINE. I UNDERSTAND MACHINES.
OH, IT'S THAT SIMPLE, HUH?
I GREW UP ON A FARM, FLINT. BOOKS WERE SCARCE. ALL I HAD WERE MACHINES. SO THAT'S WHAT I STUDIED.
IF YOU GET THAT THING WORKING THEN YOU'RE A GENIUS. BUT WHAT HAPPENS IF YOU DO GET IT TO WORK? DO YOU HAVE ANY IDEA WHAT'S ON THE OTHER SIDE OF THAT PORTAL?
I GUESS WE'LL FIND OUT WHEN I GET IT WORKING. NOW HAND ME THE SCREWDRIVER.
SO...HOW COME YOU DON'T HAVE THE BLUE THINGS ON YOUR FACE ANYMORE?
OH, YOU MEAN THESE? THEY'RE STILL HERE WHEN I USE MY POWERS. THE LAST TIME I USED THEM, IT GOT PRETTY INTENSE, AND WHEN IT WAS OVER...THEY WERE JUST GONE.
HM...WELL, I'M GLAD THEY'RE STILL THERE. I LIKE THEM. THEY'RE PRETTY.

I WISH THESE ROCKS WERE GONE FROM MY FACE SO I COULD FIT IN WITH THE REAL WORLD AGAIN.

MAYBE YOU CAN. YOUR WHOLE DEAL IS THAT YOU CAN CONTROL ROCKS, RIGHT? WHY WOULDN'T YOU BE ABLE TO CONTROL THE ONES ON YOUR FACE?

TRY IT. JUST FOCUS LIKE WHEN YOU USE YOUR POWERS.

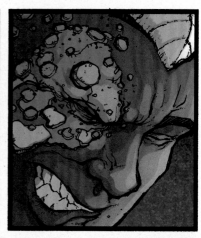

NOPE.

MAYBE YOU'RE OVERTHINKING IT? MINE HAPPENED WITHOUT ME REALIZING IT.

WOULD YOU PULL THAT LEVER?

HERE GOES--

WHA--

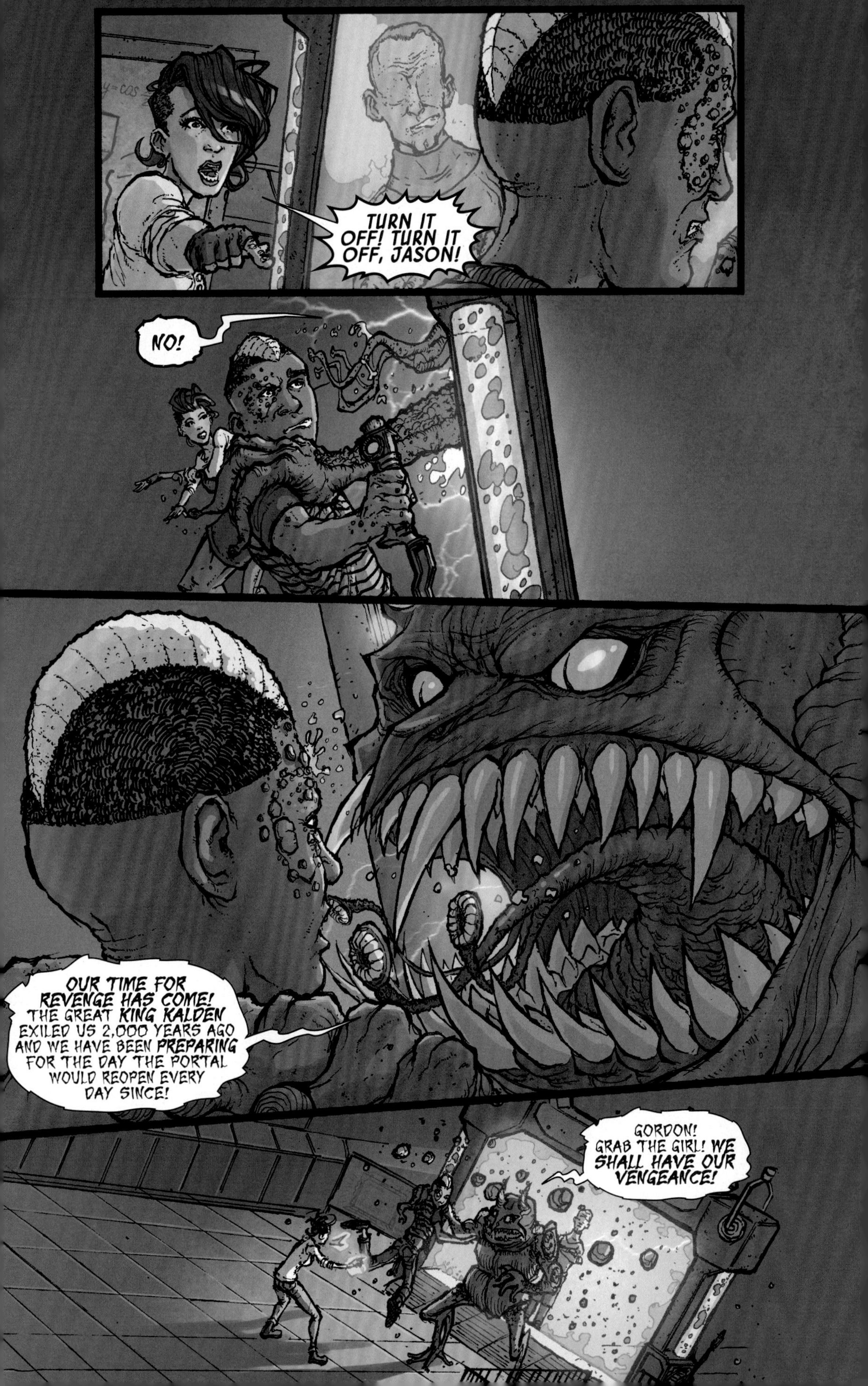
TURN IT OFF! TURN IT OFF, JASON!
NO!
OUR TIME FOR REVENGE HAS COME! THE GREAT KING KALDEN EXILED US 2,000 YEARS AGO AND WE HAVE BEEN PREPARING FOR THE DAY THE PORTAL WOULD REOPEN EVERY DAY SINCE!
GORDON! GRAB THE GIRL! WE SHALL HAVE OUR VENGEANCE!

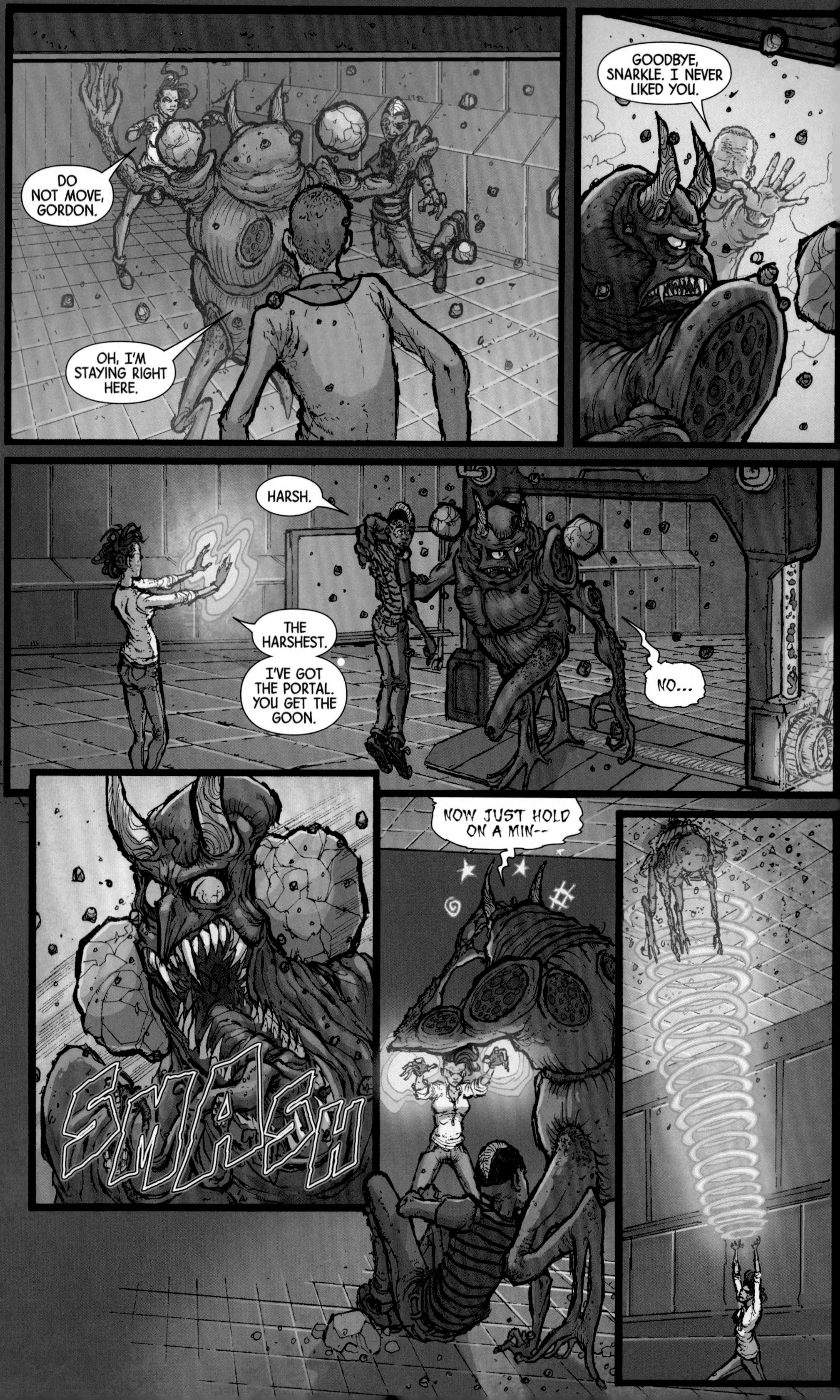
DO NOT MOVE, GORDON.
OH, I'M STAYING RIGHT HERE.
GOODBYE, SNARKLE. I NEVER LIKED YOU.
HARSH.
THE HARSHEST.
I'VE GOT THE PORTAL. YOU GET THE GOON.
NO...
SMASH
NOW JUST HOLD ON A MIN--

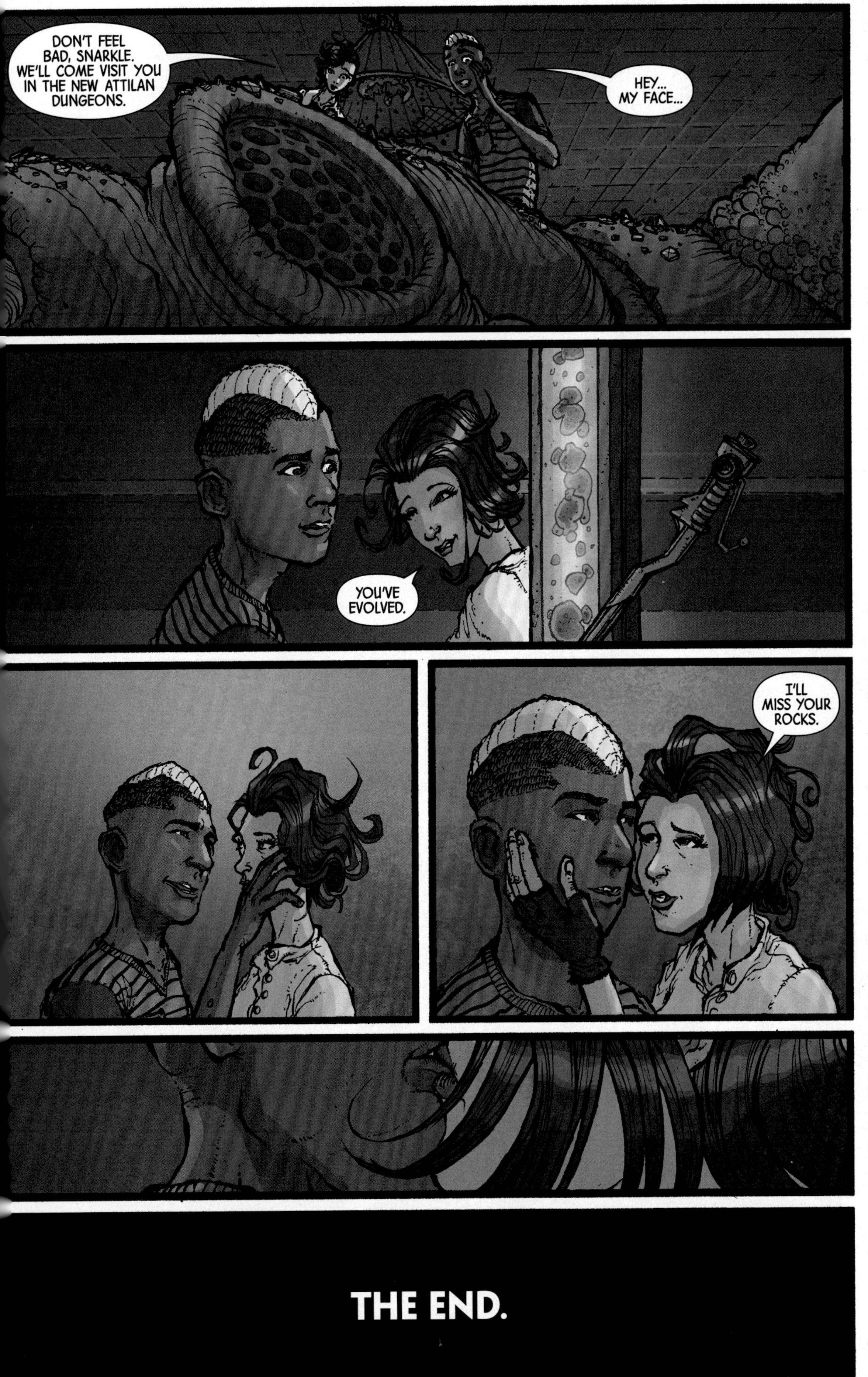
DON'T FEEL BAD, SNARKLE. WE'LL COME VISIT YOU IN THE NEW ATTILAN DUNGEONS.
HEY... MY FACE...
YOU'VE EVOLVED.
I'LL MISS YOUR ROCKS.
THE END.

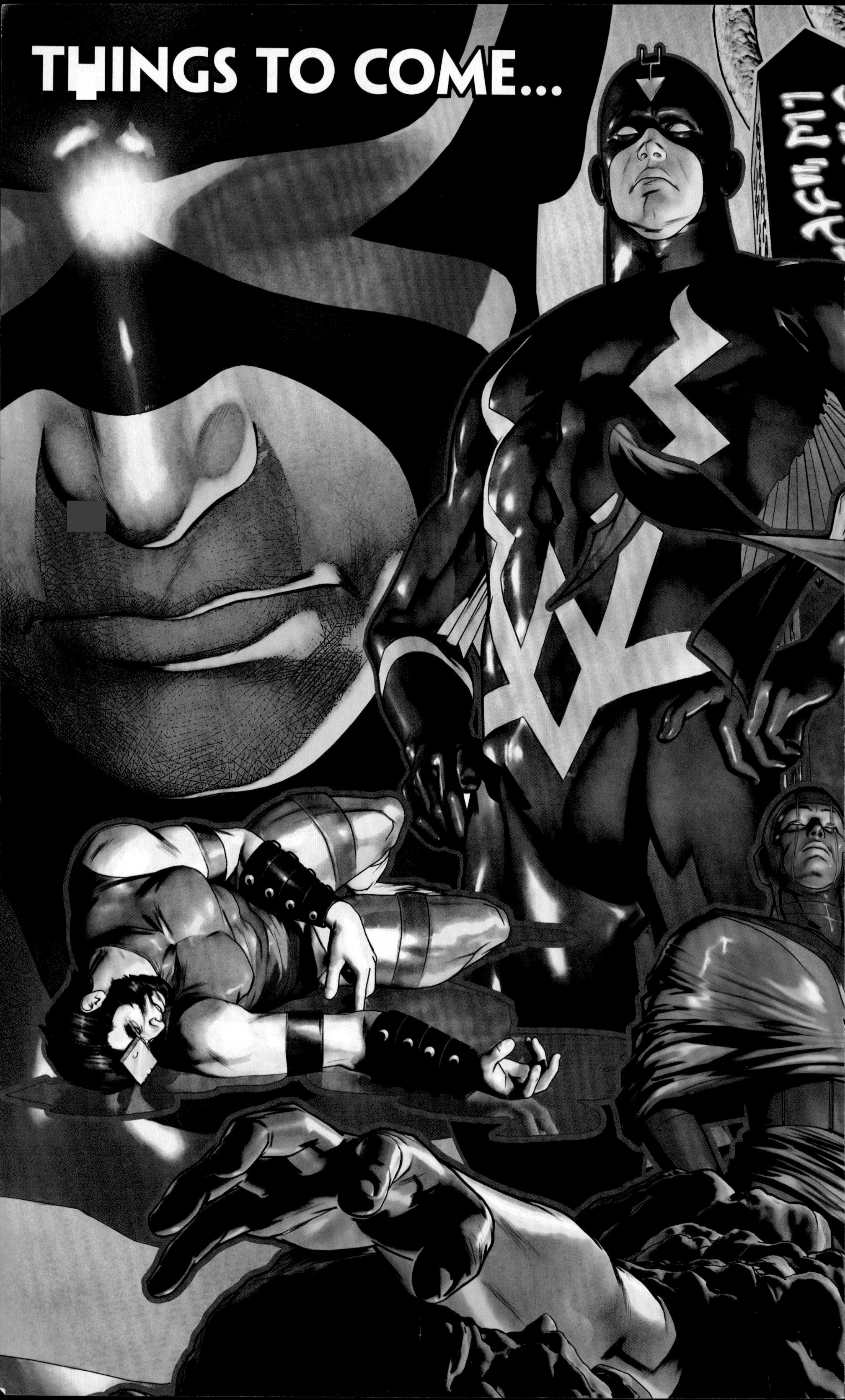
THINGS TO COME...

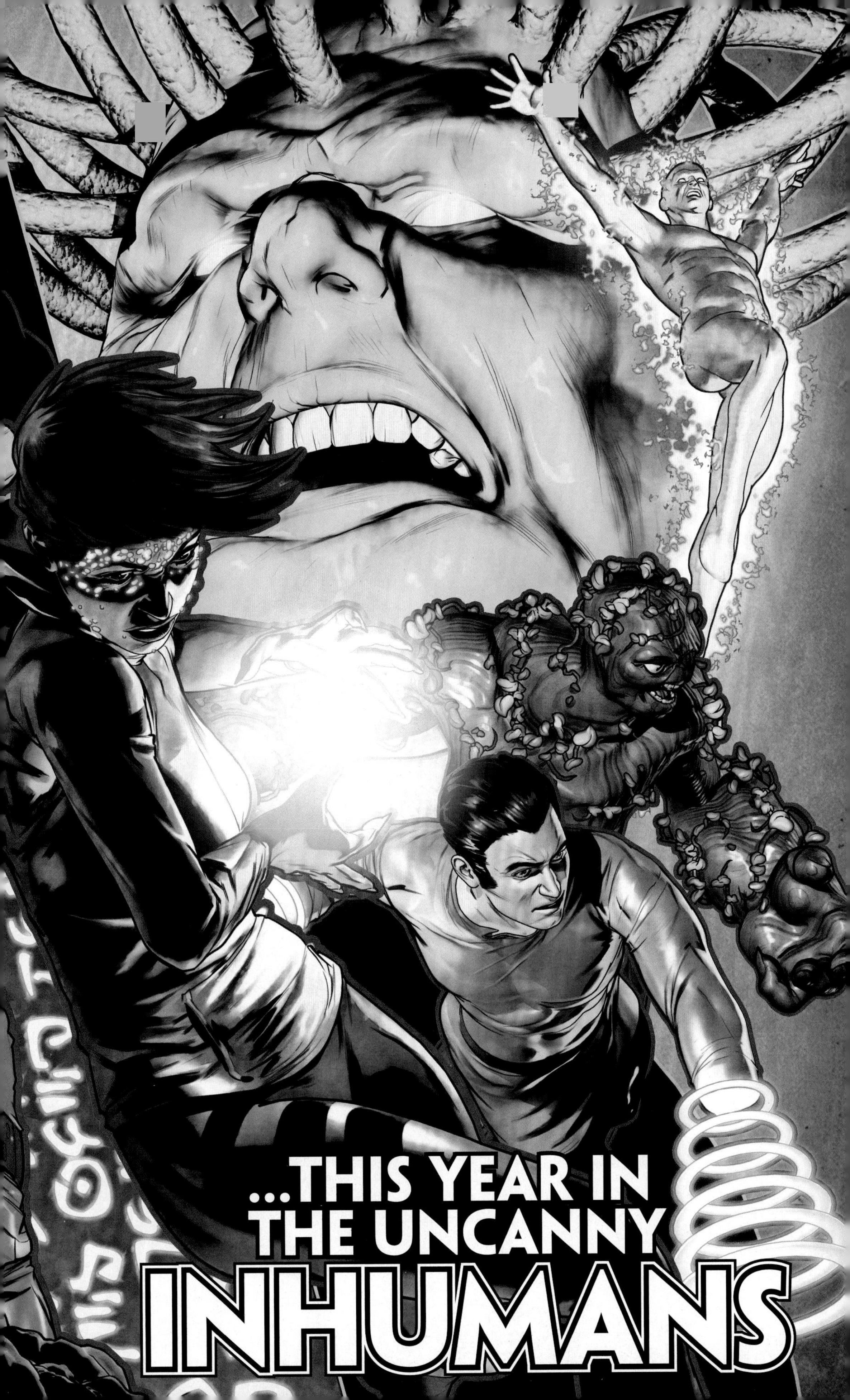
...THIS YEAR IN
THE UNCANNY
INHUMANS

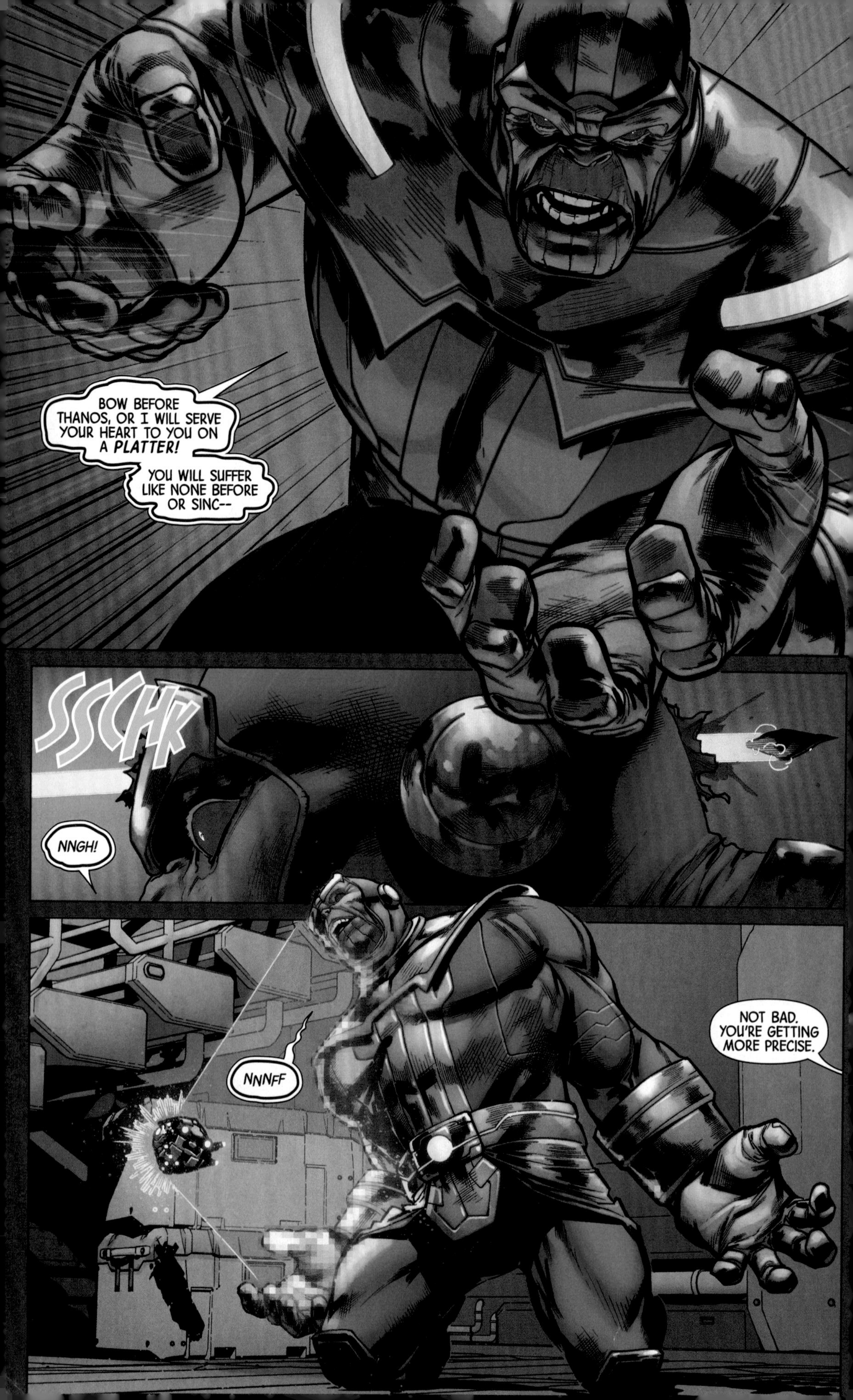
BOW BEFORE THANOS, OR I WILL SERVE YOUR HEART TO YOU ON A *PLATTER!*
YOU WILL SUFFER LIKE NONE BEFORE OR SINC--
SSCHK
NNGH!
NNNFF
NOT BAD. YOU'RE GETTING MORE PRECISE.

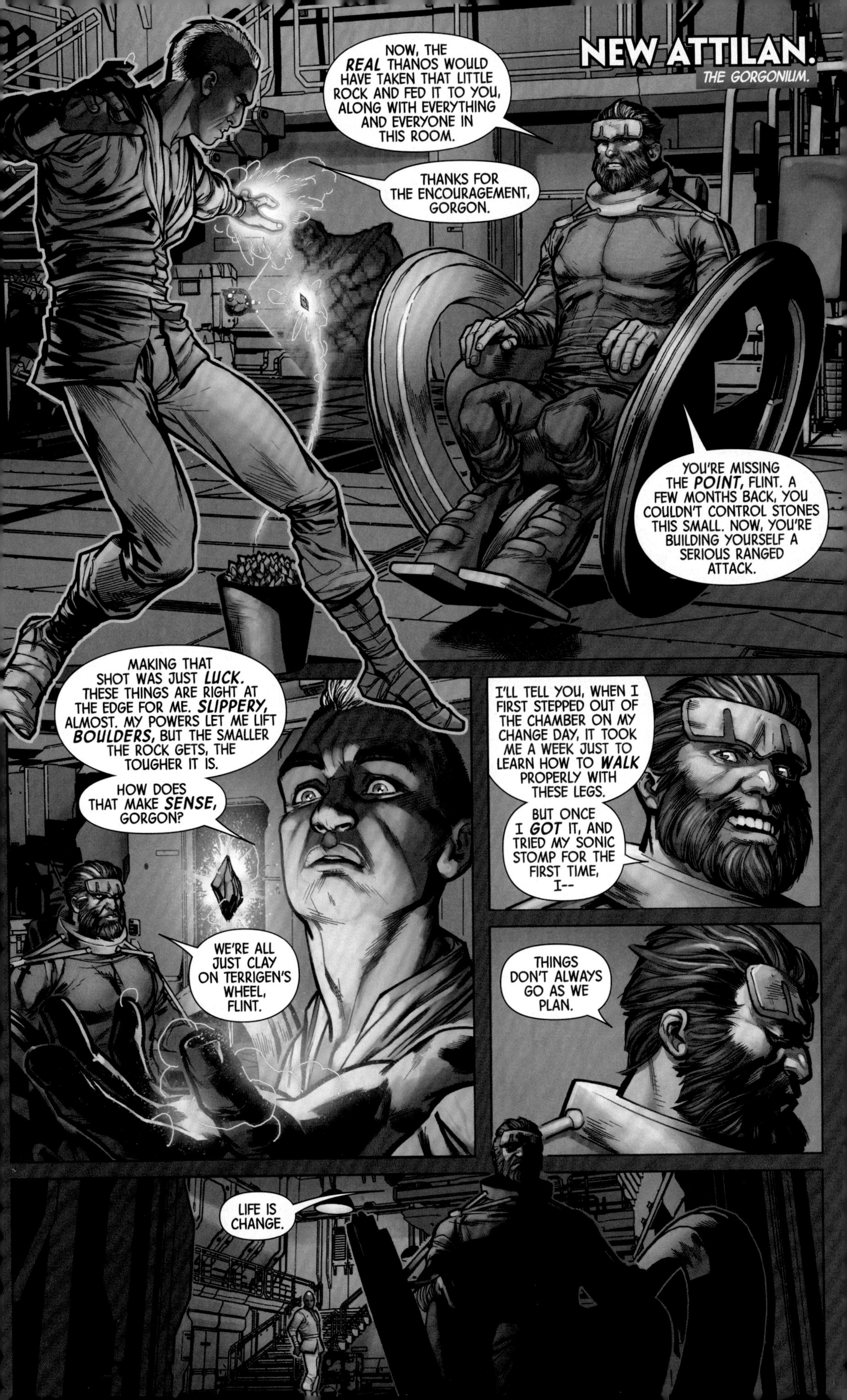
NEW ATTILAN.
THE GORGONIUM.
NOW, THE REAL THANOS WOULD HAVE TAKEN THAT LITTLE ROCK AND FED IT TO YOU, ALONG WITH EVERYTHING AND EVERYONE IN THIS ROOM.
THANKS FOR THE ENCOURAGEMENT, GORGON.
YOU'RE MISSING THE POINT, FLINT. A FEW MONTHS BACK, YOU COULDN'T CONTROL STONES THIS SMALL. NOW, YOU'RE BUILDING YOURSELF A SERIOUS RANGED ATTACK.
MAKING THAT SHOT WAS JUST LUCK. THESE THINGS ARE RIGHT AT THE EDGE FOR ME. SLIPPERY, ALMOST. MY POWERS LET ME LIFT BOULDERS, BUT THE SMALLER THE ROCK GETS, THE TOUGHER IT IS.
HOW DOES THAT MAKE SENSE, GORGON?
WE'RE ALL JUST CLAY ON TERRIGEN'S WHEEL, FLINT.
I'LL TELL YOU, WHEN I FIRST STEPPED OUT OF THE CHAMBER ON MY CHANGE DAY, IT TOOK ME A WEEK JUST TO LEARN HOW TO WALK PROPERLY WITH THESE LEGS.
BUT ONCE I GOT IT, AND TRIED MY SONIC STOMP FOR THE FIRST TIME, I--
THINGS DON'T ALWAYS GO AS WE PLAN.
LIFE IS CHANGE.

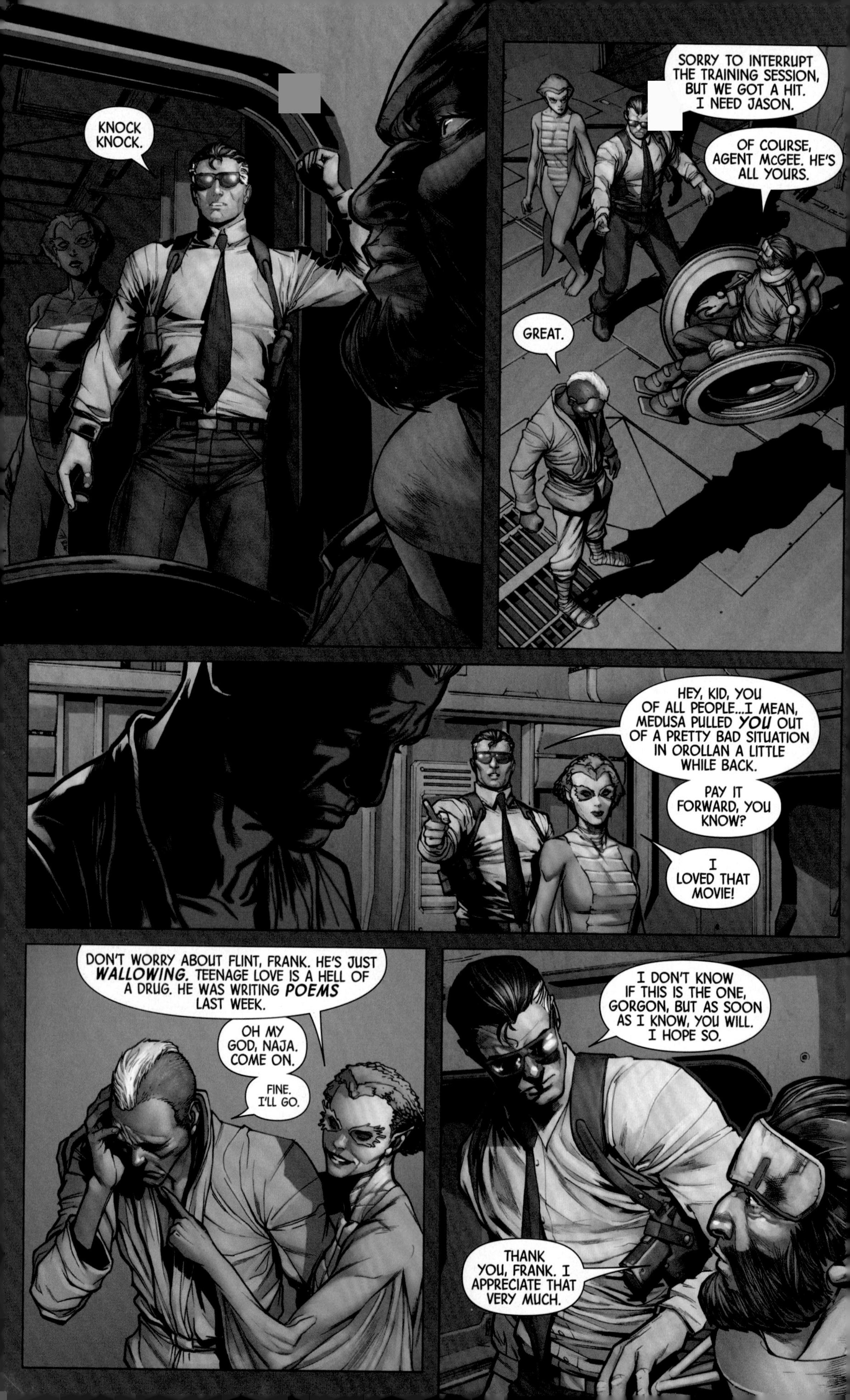
KNOCK KNOCK.
SORRY TO INTERRUPT THE TRAINING SESSION, BUT WE GOT A HIT. I NEED JASON.
OF COURSE, AGENT McGEE. HE'S ALL YOURS.
GREAT.
HEY, KID, YOU OF ALL PEOPLE...I MEAN, MEDUSA PULLED YOU OUT OF A PRETTY BAD SITUATION IN OROLLAN A LITTLE WHILE BACK.
PAY IT FORWARD, YOU KNOW?
I LOVED THAT MOVIE!
DON'T WORRY ABOUT FLINT, FRANK. HE'S JUST WALLOWING. TEENAGE LOVE IS A HELL OF A DRUG. HE WAS WRITING POEMS LAST WEEK.
OH MY GOD, NAJA. COME ON.
FINE. I'LL GO.
I DON'T KNOW IF THIS IS THE ONE, GORGON, BUT AS SOON AS I KNOW, YOU WILL. I HOPE SO.
THANK YOU, FRANK. I APPRECIATE THAT VERY MUCH.

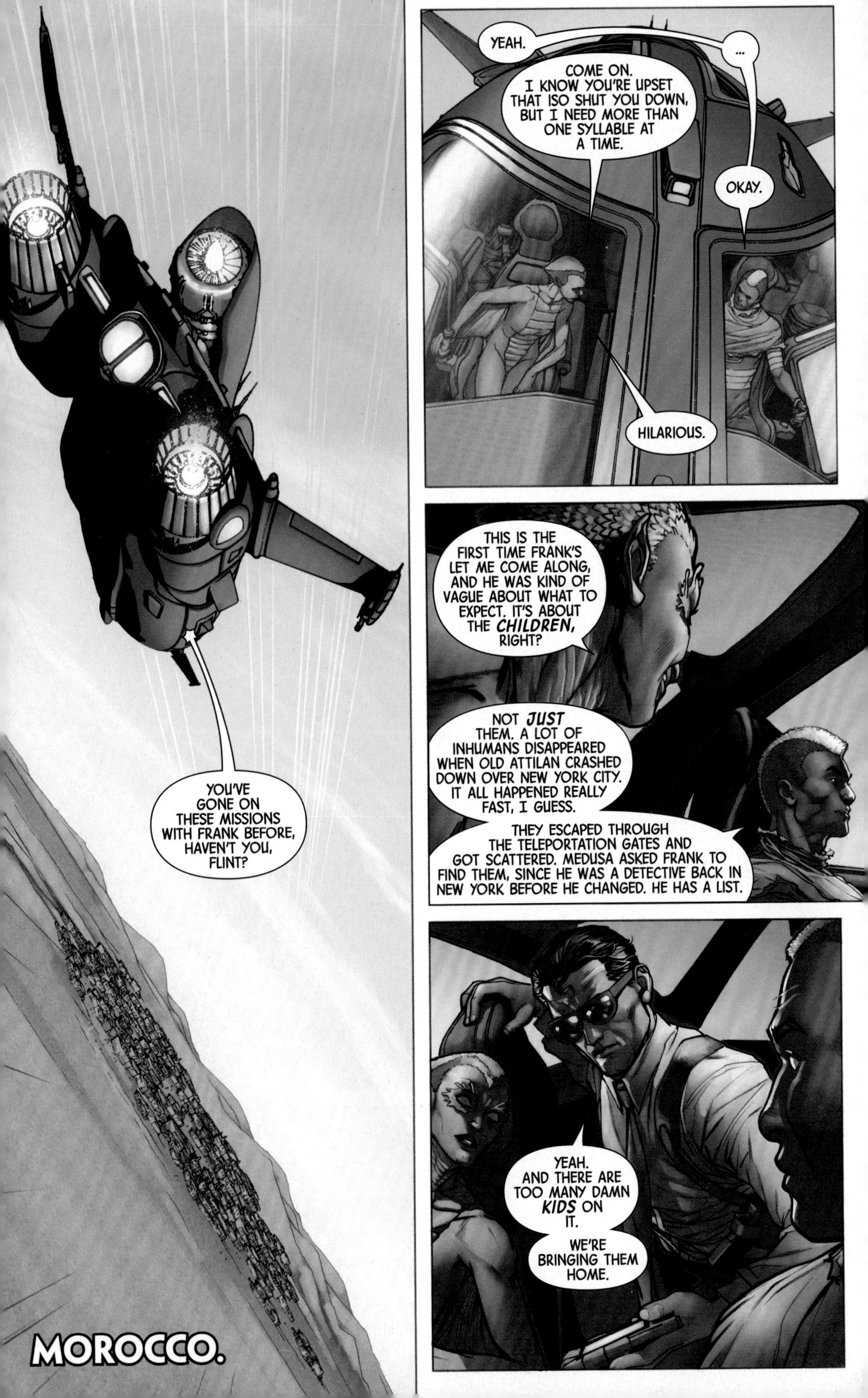
YOU'VE GONE ON THESE MISSIONS WITH FRANK BEFORE, HAVEN'T YOU, FLINT?
MOROCCO.
YEAH.
...
COME ON. I KNOW YOU'RE UPSET THAT ISO SHUT YOU DOWN, BUT I NEED MORE THAN ONE SYLLABLE AT A TIME.
OKAY.
HILARIOUS.
THIS IS THE FIRST TIME FRANK'S LET ME COME ALONG, AND HE WAS KIND OF VAGUE ABOUT WHAT TO EXPECT. IT'S ABOUT THE CHILDREN, RIGHT?
NOT JUST THEM. A LOT OF INHUMANS DISAPPEARED WHEN OLD ATTILAN CRASHED DOWN OVER NEW YORK CITY. IT ALL HAPPENED REALLY FAST, I GUESS.
THEY ESCAPED THROUGH THE TELEPORTATION GATES AND GOT SCATTERED. MEDUSA ASKED FRANK TO FIND THEM, SINCE HE WAS A DETECTIVE BACK IN NEW YORK BEFORE HE CHANGED. HE HAS A LIST.
YEAH. AND THERE ARE TOO MANY DAMN KIDS ON IT.
WE'RE BRINGING THEM HOME.

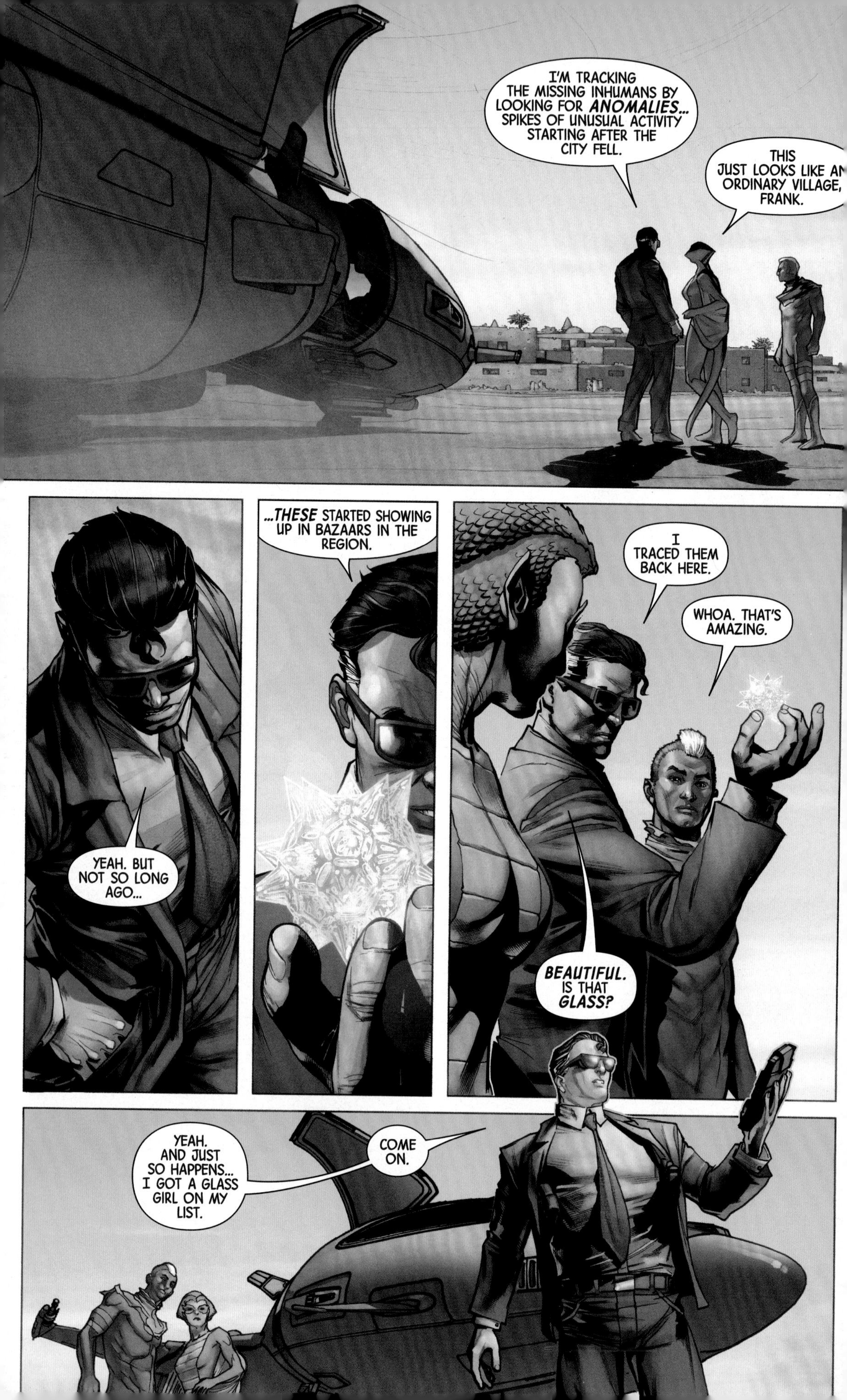
I'M TRACKING THE MISSING INHUMANS BY LOOKING FOR ANOMALIES... SPIKES OF UNUSUAL ACTIVITY STARTING AFTER THE CITY FELL.
THIS JUST LOOKS LIKE AN ORDINARY VILLAGE, FRANK.
YEAH. BUT NOT SO LONG AGO...
...THESE STARTED SHOWING UP IN BAZAARS IN THE REGION.
I TRACED THEM BACK HERE.
WHOA. THAT'S AMAZING.
BEAUTIFUL. IS THAT GLASS?
YEAH. AND JUST SO HAPPENS... I GOT A GLASS GIRL ON MY LIST.
COME ON.

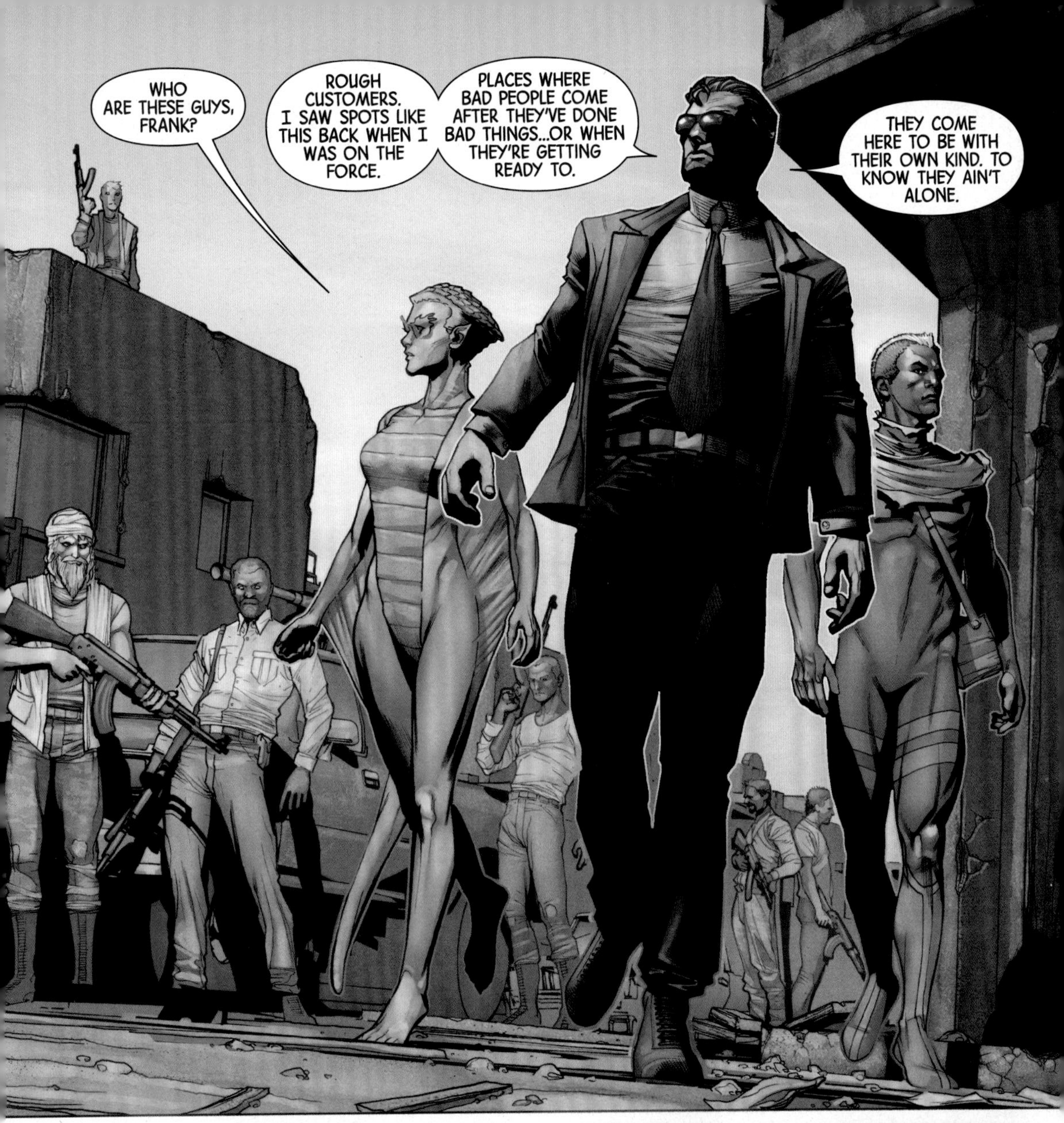
WHO ARE THESE GUYS, FRANK?
ROUGH CUSTOMERS. I SAW SPOTS LIKE THIS BACK WHEN I WAS ON THE FORCE.
PLACES WHERE BAD PEOPLE COME AFTER THEY'VE DONE BAD THINGS...OR WHEN THEY'RE GETTING READY TO.
THEY COME HERE TO BE WITH THEIR OWN KIND. TO KNOW THEY AIN'T ALONE.

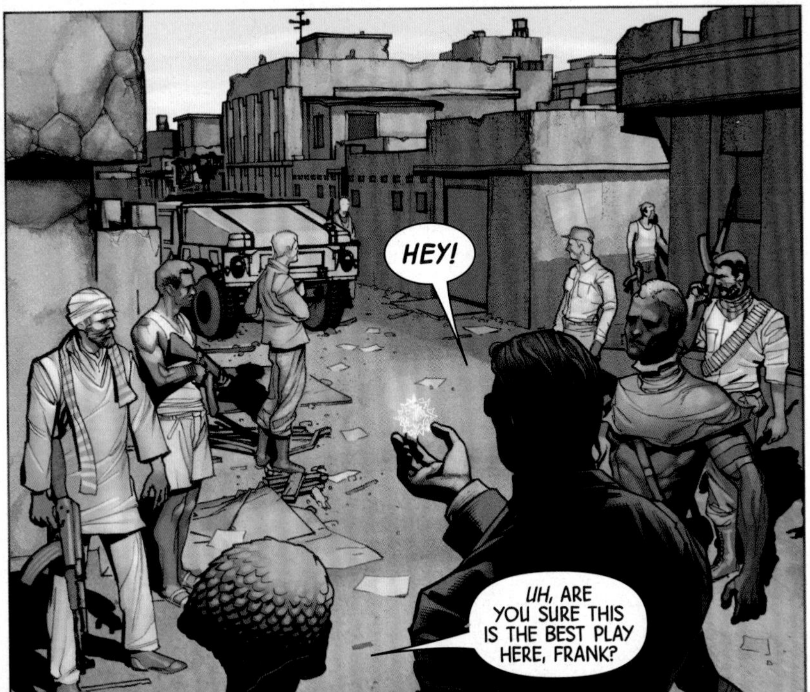
HEY!
UH, ARE YOU SURE THIS IS THE BEST PLAY HERE, FRANK?

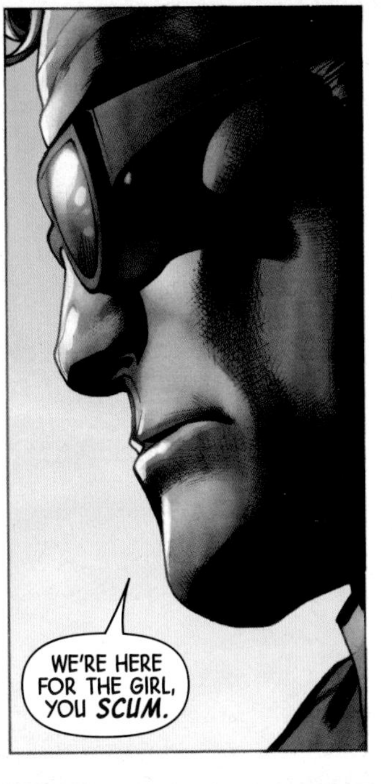
WE'RE HERE FOR THE GIRL, YOU SCUM.

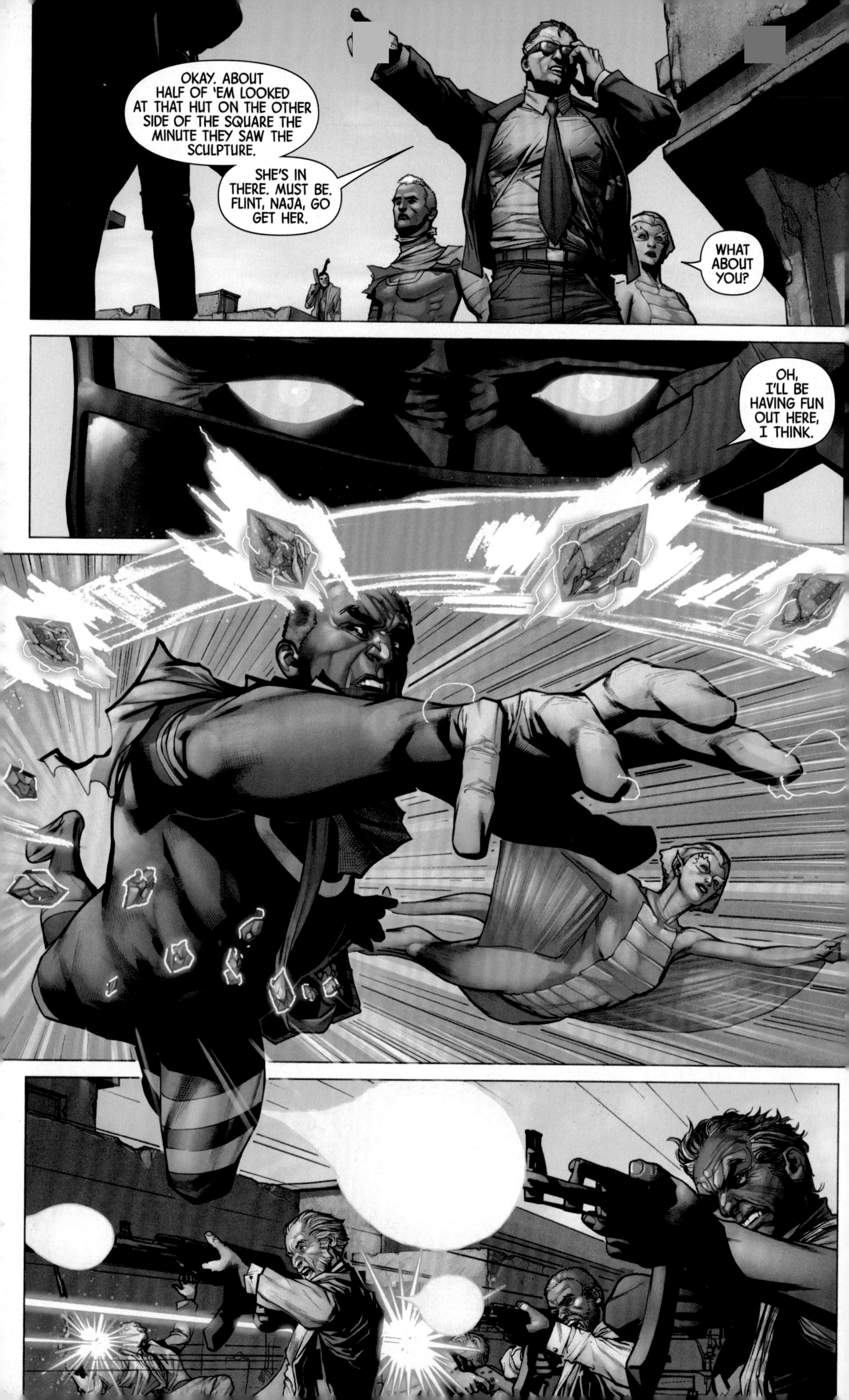
OKAY. ABOUT HALF OF 'EM LOOKED AT THAT HUT ON THE OTHER SIDE OF THE SQUARE THE MINUTE THEY SAW THE SCULPTURE.
SHE'S IN THERE. MUST BE. FLINT, NAJA, GO GET HER.
WHAT ABOUT YOU?
OH, I'LL BE HAVING FUN OUT HERE, I THINK.

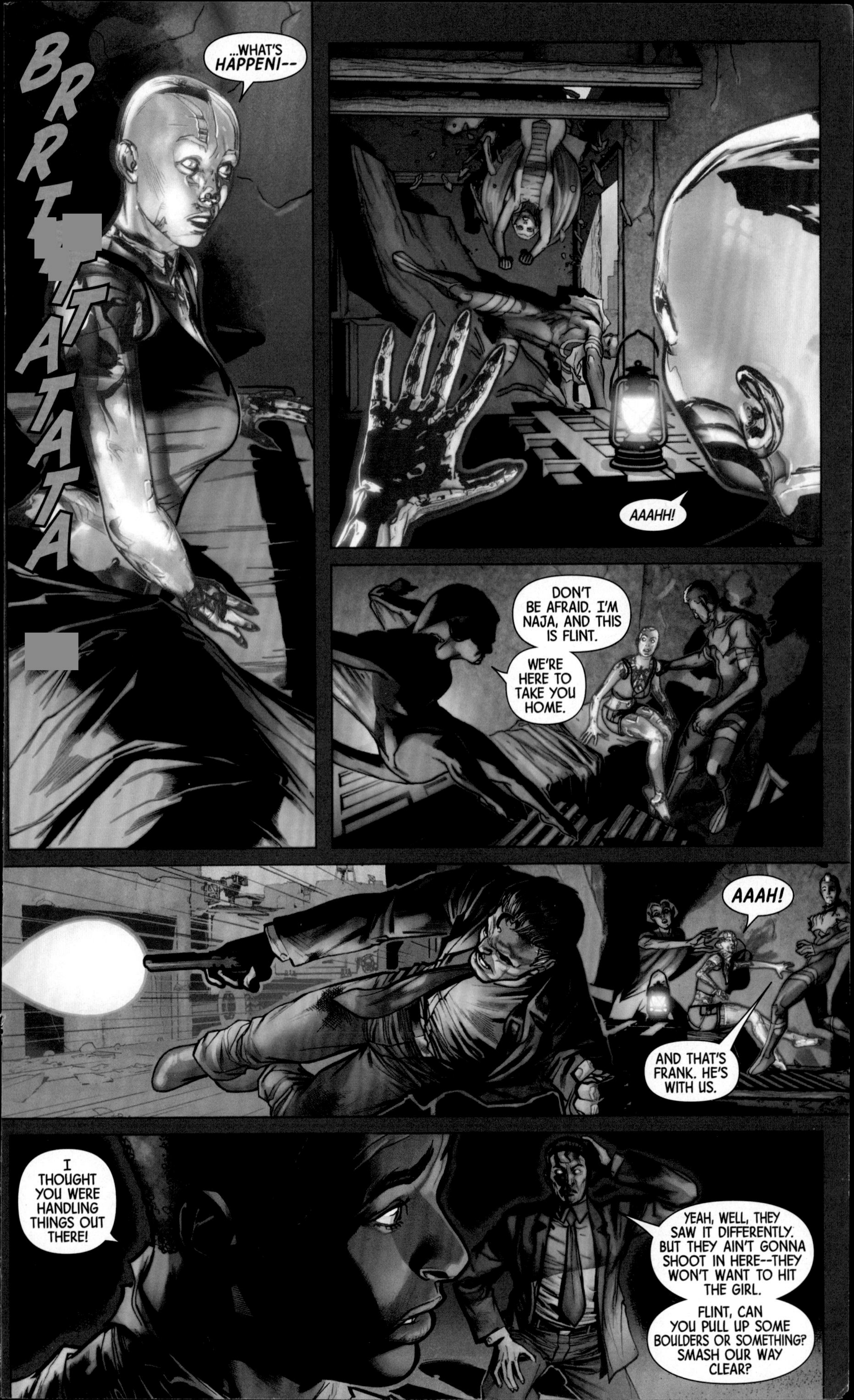
BRR
TATATA
...WHAT'S HAPPENI--
AAAHH!
DON'T BE AFRAID. I'M NAJA, AND THIS IS FLINT.
WE'RE HERE TO TAKE YOU HOME.
AAAH!
AND THAT'S FRANK. HE'S WITH US.
I THOUGHT YOU WERE HANDLING THINGS OUT THERE!
YEAH, WELL, THEY SAW IT DIFFERENTLY. BUT THEY AIN'T GONNA SHOOT IN HERE--THEY WON'T WANT TO HIT THE GIRL.
FLINT, CAN YOU PULL UP SOME BOULDERS OR SOMETHING? SMASH OUR WAY CLEAR?

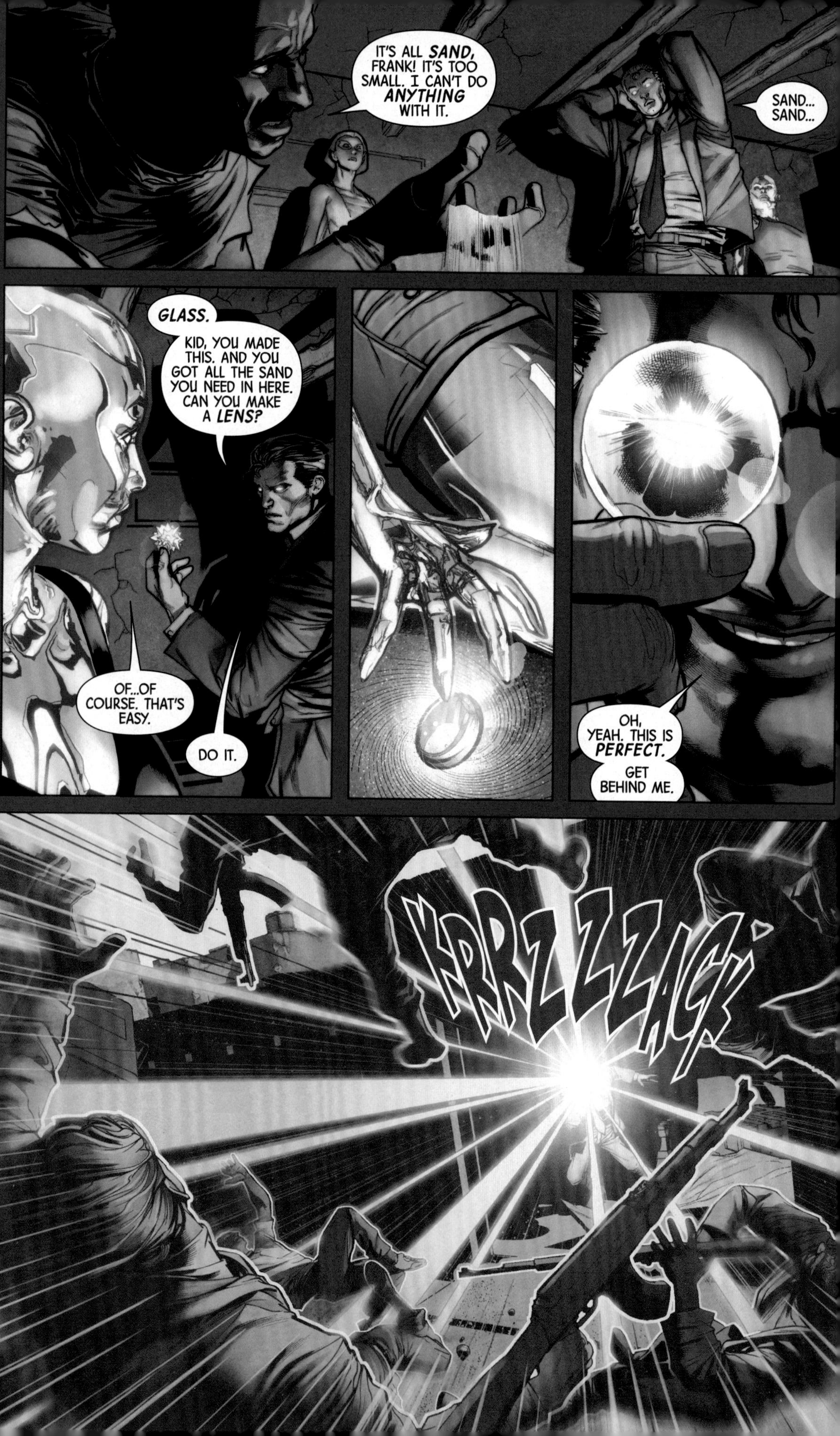
IT'S ALL SAND, FRANK! IT'S TOO SMALL. I CAN'T DO ANYTHING WITH IT.
SAND... SAND...
GLASS.
KID, YOU MADE THIS. AND YOU GOT ALL THE SAND YOU NEED IN HERE. CAN YOU MAKE A LENS?
OF...OF COURSE. THAT'S EASY.
DO IT.
OH, YEAH. THIS IS PERFECT.
GET BEHIND ME.
KRRZZZACK

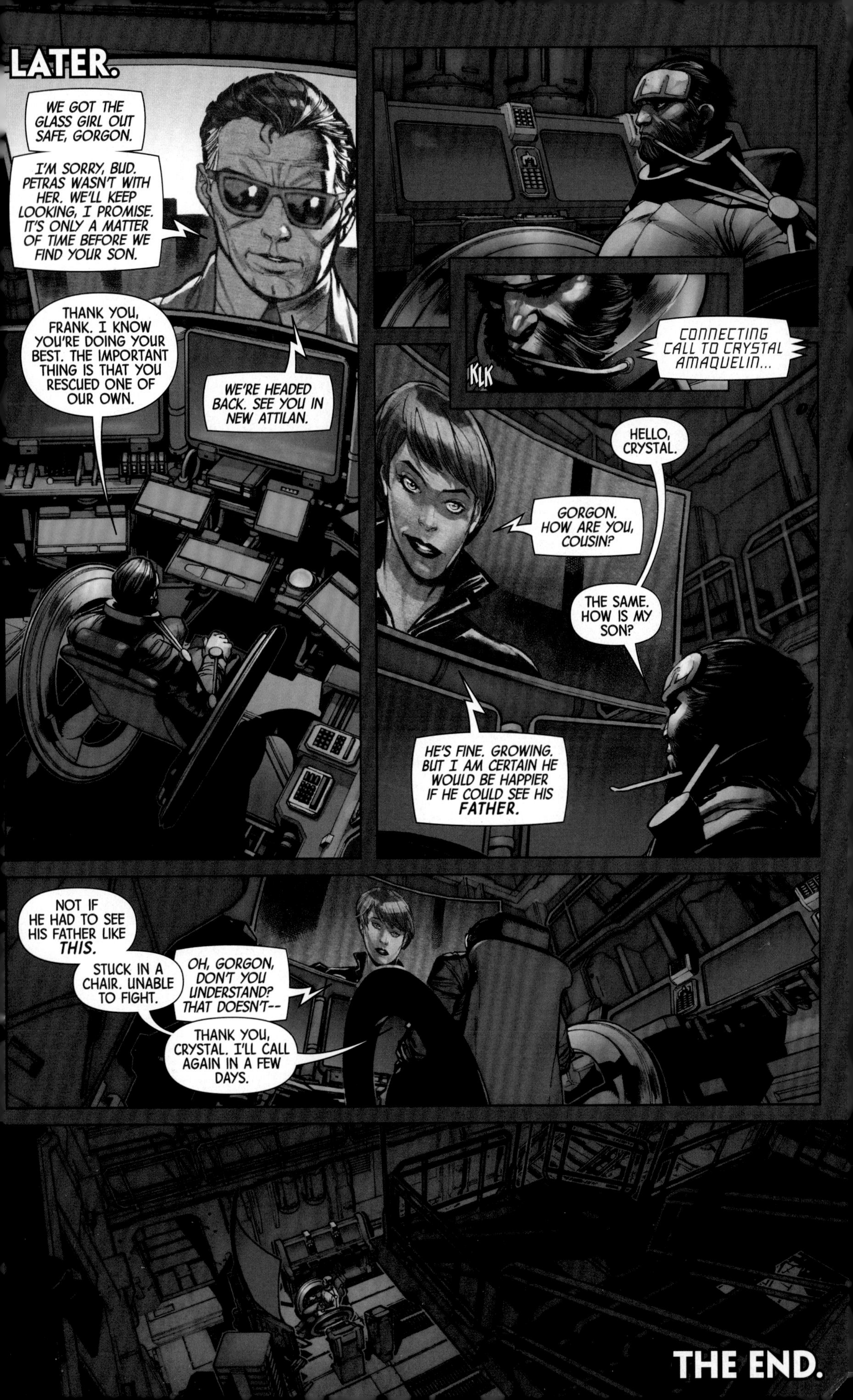
LATER.
WE GOT THE GLASS GIRL OUT SAFE, GORGON.
I'M SORRY, BUD. PETRAS WASN'T WITH HER. WE'LL KEEP LOOKING, I PROMISE. IT'S ONLY A MATTER OF TIME BEFORE WE FIND YOUR SON.
THANK YOU, FRANK. I KNOW YOU'RE DOING YOUR BEST. THE IMPORTANT THING IS THAT YOU RESCUED ONE OF OUR OWN.
WE'RE HEADED BACK. SEE YOU IN NEW ATTILAN.
KLK
CONNECTING CALL TO CRYSTAL AMAQUELIN...
HELLO, CRYSTAL.
GORGON. HOW ARE YOU, COUSIN?
THE SAME. HOW IS MY SON?
HE'S FINE. GROWING. BUT I AM CERTAIN HE WOULD BE HAPPIER IF HE COULD SEE HIS FATHER.
NOT IF HE HAD TO SEE HIS FATHER LIKE THIS.
STUCK IN A CHAIR. UNABLE TO FIGHT.
OH, GORGON, DON'T YOU UNDERSTAND? THAT DOESN'T--
THANK YOU, CRYSTAL. I'LL CALL AGAIN IN A FEW DAYS.
THE END.

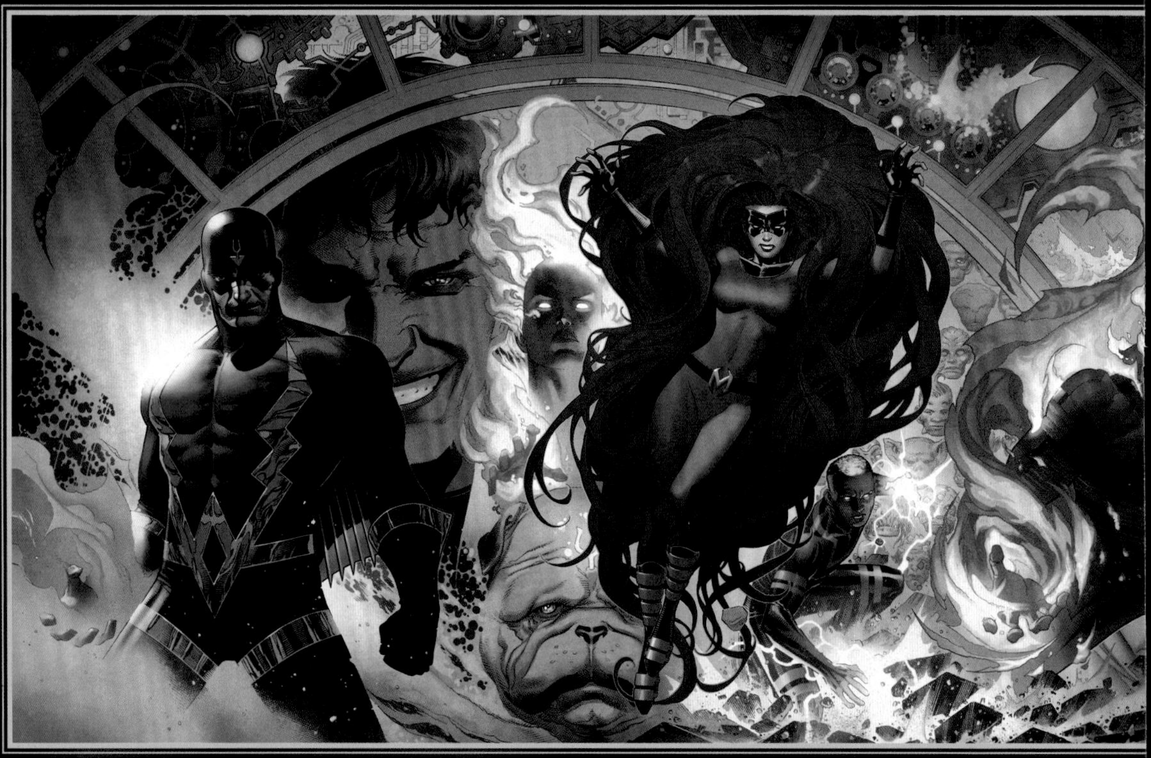

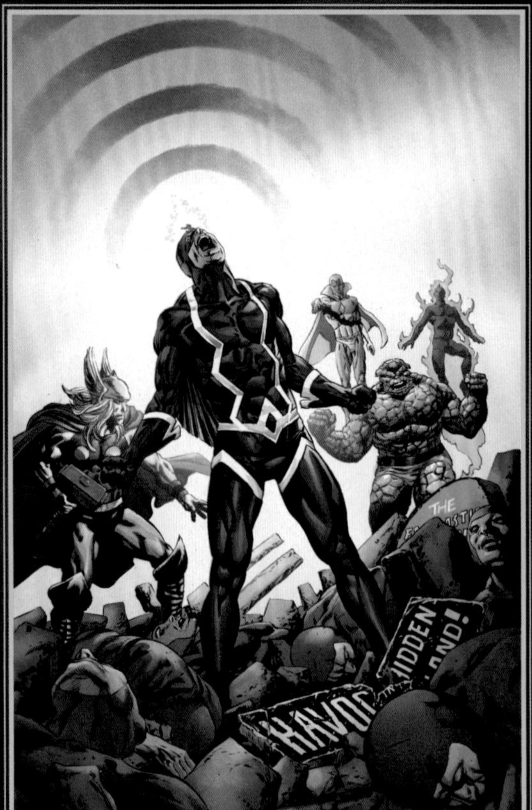

#0 AVENGERS VARIANT
BY MIKE PERKINS & ANDY TROY

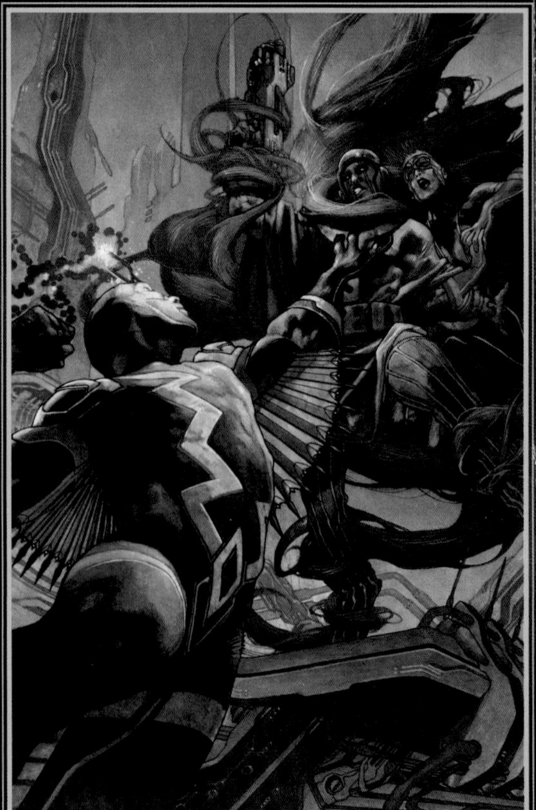

#0 VARIANT
BY SIMONE BIANCHI

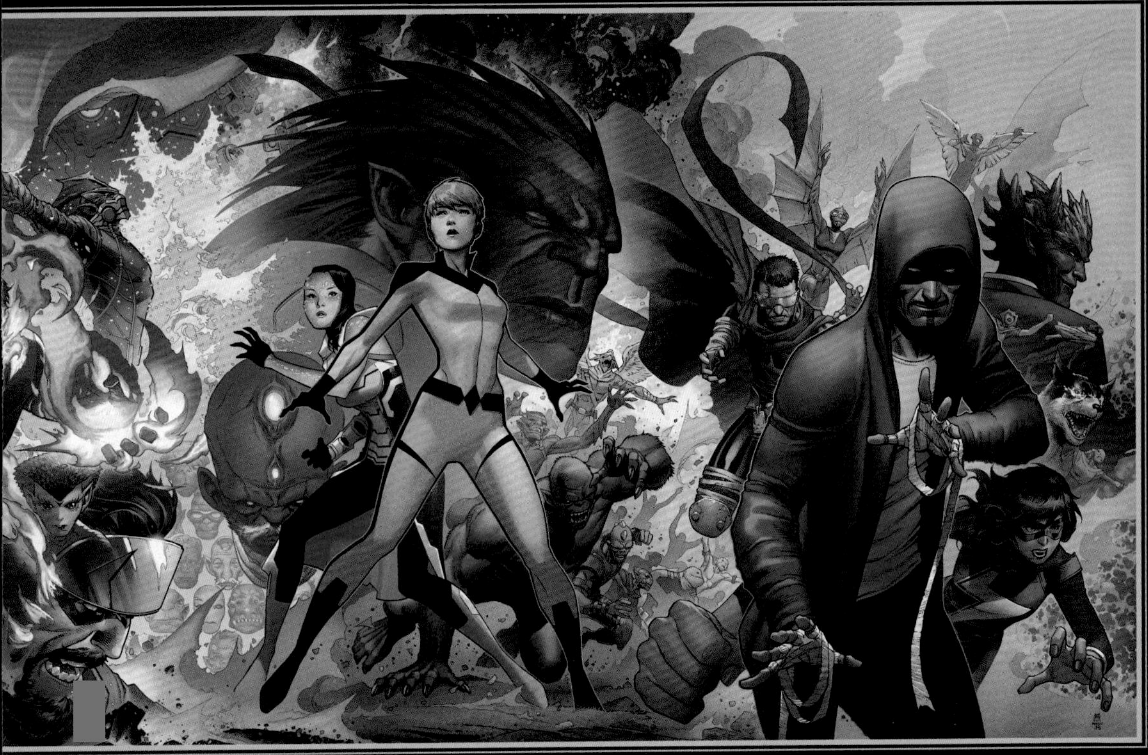

#0-4 CONNECTING VARIANTS
BY JIM CHEUNG & JUSTIN PONSOR

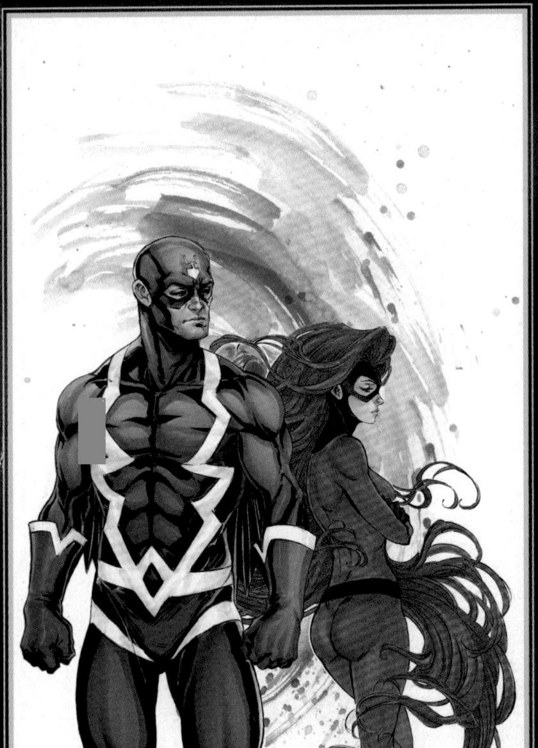

#0 VARIANT
BY SIYA OUM

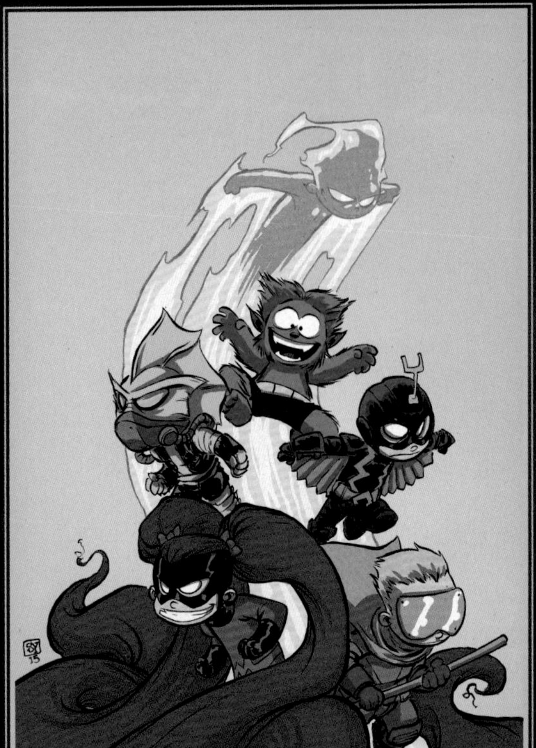

#1 VARIANT
BY SKOTTIE YOUNG

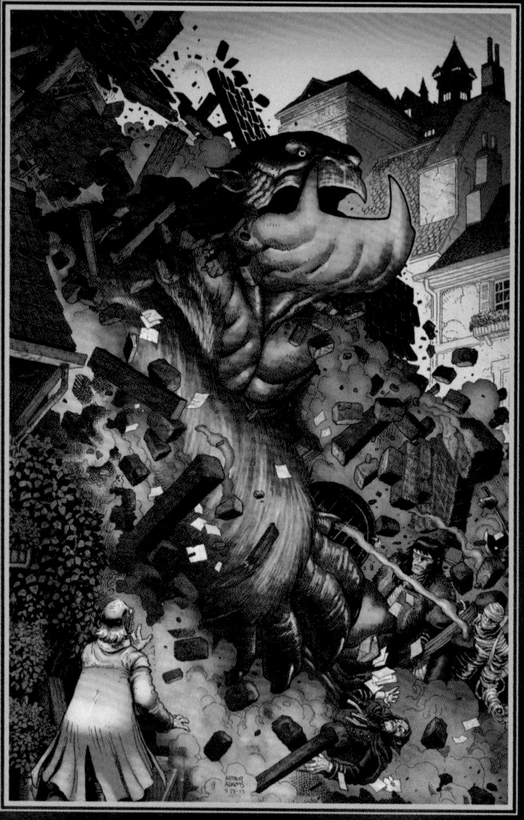

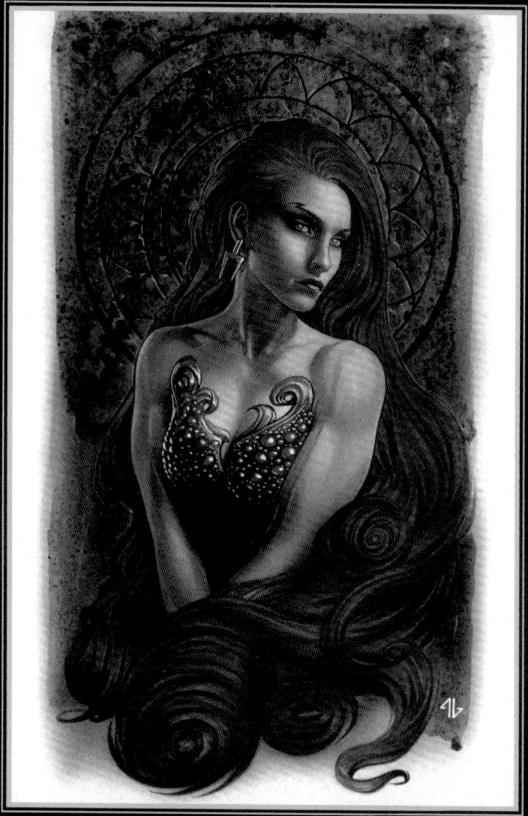

#1 KIRBY MONSTER VARIANT
BY ART ADAMS & CHRIS SOTOMAYOR

#1 VARIANT
BY ADI GRANOV

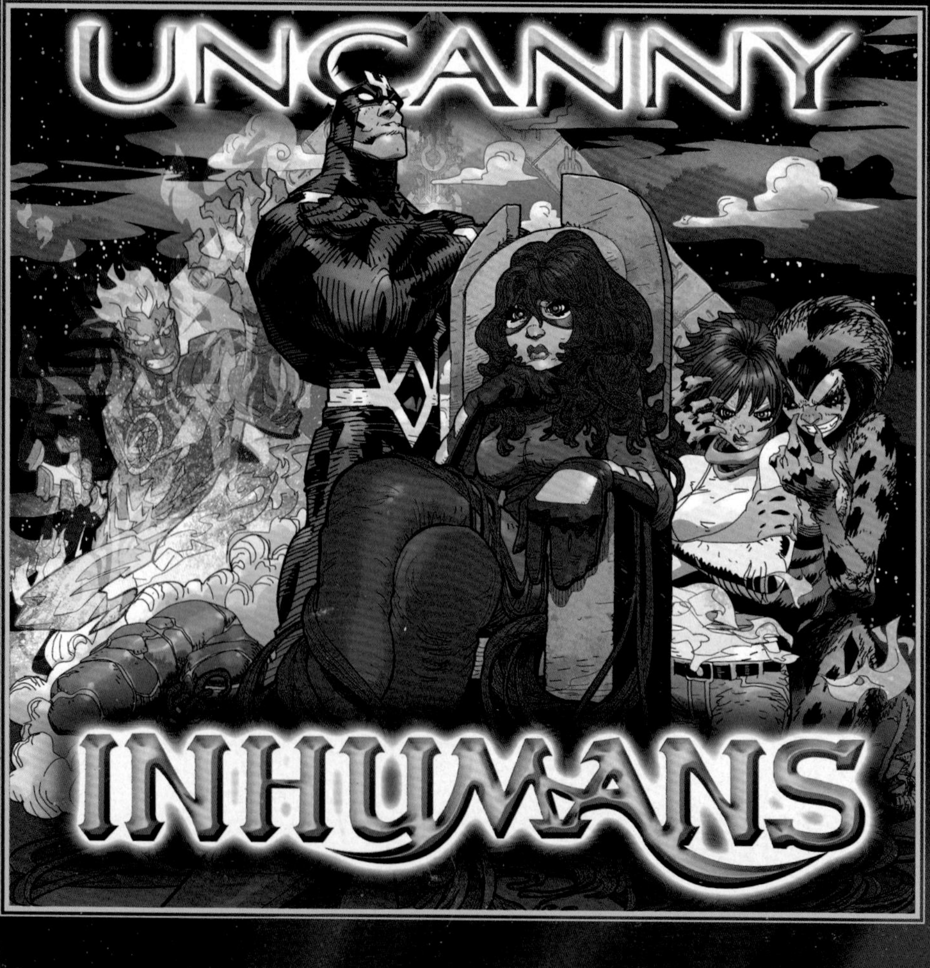
UNCANNY
INHUMANS

#1 HIP-HOP
VARIANT
BY DAMION SCOTT &
NELSON DANIEL